The Republic

Crofts Classics

PLATO

The Republic

TRANSLATED AND EDITED BY

Raymond Larson

SAINT JOHN'S UNIVERSITY
COLLEGEVILLE, MINNESOTA

WITH AN INTRODUCTION BY

Eva T. H. Brann

ST. JOHN'S COLLEGE
ANNAPOLIS, MARYLAND

HARLAN DAVIDSON, INC.
Arlington Heights, Illinois 60004

Library of Congress Cataloging-in-Publication Data

Plato.
The Republic.

(Crofts classics)
Bibliography: p.
1. Political science—Early works to 1700.
2. Utopias. I. Title.
[JC71.P35 1986] 321′.07 86-6247
ISBN 0-88295-118-1 (pbk.)
ISBN 0-88295-121-1 (hard)

MANUFACTURED IN THE UNITED STATES OF AMERICA
93 92 91 90 10 11 12 13 MG

*synoptic table of contents**

*The table of contents indicates the main logical division in the argument of the *Republic*. The traditional division into ten books does not always coincide with natural breaks in the argument.

preface and background to the Republic

Faced with the formidable task of reading the *Republic,* a person may well ask: Why bother? We surely have enough problems of our own to bemuse us, some of which concern the survival of our species. Why worry about obsolete issues raised by a man dead for over 2000 years?

This is a legitimate question, and the answer is that real problems do not go away but, like beauty, merely change their appearance. Science and technology have made great progress since Plato's day, but the central concerns of art and philosophy remain much the same. Plato was both an artist and a philosopher, and in spite of his outspoken hostility to poetry, he wrote poems, some of which have survived. One, an elegy on the death of his friend Dion, ends like this:

> Here in your broad-meadowed homeland you lie, honored by townsmen,
> O, you that maddened my soul with desire, Dion.

These lines, written by a man in his seventies, show that Plato was an emotional being and not just a detached intellectual wrapped up in navel-gazing and otherworldly speculation. And their poignant beauty still touches us. Beauty doesn't really change; she just changes her dress.

So also with the central issues of philosophy—they are still matters of life and death. Only their outward appearance has changed. The main question of the *Republic,* What is justice?, strikes us as odd; it is not one that we would be likely to ask, at least in this form. But when we penetrate the question's disguise and see that it means "How should a person live to be happy?" we perk up our ears. This could have something to do with us. As we read on, other gray, bewhiskered questions shuffle out and huddle around the first: What is the purpose of life? Is it pleasure, wisdom, happiness, or what? What is the good life? What form of government will allow us to live the good life and achieve its true purpose? Is there life after death? What does our answer to the last question mean for the way we live?

These are questions that people still ask, though perhaps not in Plato's words. Plato's answers to them deserve our attention, not only because he is a powerful, original thinker who may have thought of things that might escape us. Even his manner of expression, which strikes us as odd because of his remoteness from us in time and circumstance, can be valuable if it encourages us to view our problems in a different light. In reading Plato we come to recognize that though circumstances vary, human nature does not, and that his problems are really our own, seen from a different perspective. There is an old maxim in science: When you get stuck in a problem try to look at it from a different point of view. The same technique can be useful in philosophy, in questions of life and death. One could not find a better introduction to these than Plato's *Republic.*

Plato is not only a great philosopher; he is also a brilliant prose stylist. J. S. Mill nicely sums up the two sides of his genius: "[Plato's] dialogues . . . are the still unrivalled types of the dialectic process . . . and afford an example, once in all literature, of the union between an eminent genius for philosophy and the most consummate skill and feeling of the artist" (*Edinburgh Review,* April 1866, p. 332). Plato is master not of one, but of many different styles—from the elevated to the strikingly simple, from the pompously inflated to the colloquial—and he often juxtaposes them for incongruous or ironic effect. He also loves to parody the styles of other writers: philosophers, orators, and especially playwrights and poets. Irony, subtle as well as conspicuous, pervades his work. In the *Republic* (392c–398b), for example, he makes

Socrates ban from the ideal state literature of the type of Plato's own dialogues—including the *Republic*—as being morally subversive. Plato is as fond of absurdity as he is of relentless logic; he enjoys metaphors, jingles, and puns; and he delights in the music of language.

It will be obvious that no translation can match the style of such an original. Nevertheless, I have often strained for effects in English similar to those of the Greek, in the hope that behind these awkward attempts the reader may sense an author of great power, brilliance, and beauty.

The translation of Greek terms into English is notoriously difficult: words like justice, temperance, excellence, and wisdom are inadequate to express the meaning of their Greek counterparts. For want of better alternatives, however, I have retained most of the traditional Platonic vocabulary; significant departures are indicated in the footnotes.

One about to read the *Republic* for the first time may be curious about the historical and cultural situation in which its author lived. Plato was born into a time of political, moral, and intellectual upheaval. The Peloponnesian War (431–404 B.C.) had been raging for three years and was to drag on for another twenty-four before ending in Sparta's defeat of Athens. Almost all of Greece was embroiled in this civil war, which pitted city against city and divided cities and even families into bloodthirsty factions of "oligarchs" (pro-Spartans) and "democrats" (pro-Athenians). The political stage was awash with the blood of civil slaughter and poisoned with party strife, which drove its victims to place party loyalty above public safety and vengeance above self-preservation. Old governments fell overnight by treachery or force, disgruntled partisans of one side or the other betrayed their cities to the enemy and handed their fellow citizens over to be murdered and enslaved. Thucydides, an eyewitness, describes the poisoned atmosphere in chilling terms:

> If a man plotted and succeeded he was considered intelligent; if he suspected a plot he was more clever still. But the man who planned ahead in order to have no need of plots or suspicion was considered disloyal to his party. . . . It went so far that party affiliation

> bound men closer than family ties, because party members were more ready to commit open aggression. . . . It was more important to avenge an injury than to avoid being injured in the first place. . . . Thus every kind of wickedness arose in Greece because of civil war (*History of the Peloponnesian War,* 3.82–83).

The civil strife that rent the rest of Greece did not break out in Athens until late in the war. Despite two plagues that swept the city shortly before Plato's birth (one of which killed Pericles in 429 B.C.), and despite frequent reversals and heavy losses on the battlefield, life went on much as usual. Throughout most of the war, Athens kept the political and cultural supremacy she had acquired under Pericles with the founding of an empire and with the production of such masterpieces as the tragedies of Aeschylus, Sophocles and Euripides, the statues of Phidias, and buildings like the Parthenon—works that moved Plutarch, five centuries later, to declare: "Each possessed even then an instant archaic beauty, yet remains to our day in the prime of freshness and youth. A kind of eternal newness blooms upon them, preserving an aspect untouched by time, as though these works were endowed with a perennially blossoming spirit and an ageless vitality" (*Life of Pericles,* 13). These words describe Plato's dialogues as aptly as they do the works of the Periclean Age. By the beginning of the war Aeschylus was dead, but Sophocles and Euripides were still to produce some of their finest tragedies, and Aristophanes had not yet written his first comedy.

Philosophy flourished during the war as never before. Athens, long a center of intellectual activity, attracted learned men called "sophists," who lectured and taught to admiring crowds. Socrates roamed the streets looking for truth. Young men argued and discussed philosophical questions in the gymnasiums and wrestling schools. This was the intellectual heyday of Athens, the period in which most of Plato's dialogues are set. But the end of the war brought a drastic change. Athens lost her naval empire and with it much of her optimism and verve. Political and social life fell into disarray and only gradually recovered. Sophocles and Euripides were dead, political comedy was no longer performed, and the arts entered a period of decadence. From our point of view, Athens' greatest period of philosophy was yet to come, with the founding of Plato's and later of Aristotle's school. Athens would remain the cultural and intellectual leader of the West for many centuries. But to Plato the fall of Athens and the death of Socrates a few years later must have signified the end of the age of giants.

Such were the circumstances in which Plato grew up. He came from an old aristocratic family, rich, powerful, and respected; and his birth and upbringing marked him out for a career in politics. Perhaps the most momentous event in his life was meeting Socrates. This must have happened when Plato was quite young, because his older brothers Glaucon and Adeimantus (who play important roles in the *Republic*) and his uncles Charmides and Critias were all companions of Socrates.

From Socrates Plato picked up interests that remained with him for the rest of his life. Socrates wrote nothing; he carried on his relentless search for truth by cross examining people. This method of question and answer, the famous Socratic *dialectic,* determined both Plato's philosophical approach and the form of his writings, which are all *dialogues* between a questioner (usually Socrates) and one or more respondents. Socrates discussed moral issues rather than questions of natural science, which had been the main preoccupation of earlier philosophers. He looked for universal definitions. He would ask a person to define some common word that applied to a large number of disparate things or to a wide range of dissimilar acts. To a question such as "What is justice?," for instance, he was seeking not an example in the form of this or that just act, but the essence underlying all just acts, the universal "justness" whose presence in any particular act makes it just and allows us to recognize it and so designate it. His respondents, confident of their ability to define the terms they used every day, naturally became annoyed when they ended up looking like fools under Socrates' interrogation. The unpopularity he won by deflating the self-importance of important men was one of the things that eventually brought him to trial.

Toward the end of the war, civil strife also broke out within the walls of Athens. As the tide of war turned against the Athenians, more and more of the city's people began to criticize the democratic government, which had made a series of bad mistakes, had often acted arbitrarily, and had sometimes degenerated into mob rule. This dissatisfaction enabled the oligarchic party to seize power in 411 B.C., but the democracy was quickly restored. After their victory in 404 B.C., however, the Spartans replaced the Athenian democracy with a pro-Spartan regime of thirty rulers, called the "Thirty Tyrants." Two of the Thirty, Critias and Charmides, were Plato's relatives, and Plato had high hopes that they would put an end to the ineptitude of the discredited democracy and establish a just government founded on reason and order. His hopes were drowned in blood. The Thirty liquidated 1500 leading citizens (among them Polemarchus, who appears in Book 1 of the *Republic*), drove another 5000 into exile, and confiscated their property. This regime, says Plato (*Letter 7,* 324d), "made the former one look like gold." It did not last long. In the following year (403 B.C.) the exiles returned, overthrew the junta of thirty, and restored the democracy. Plato's uncles were executed. The restored democracy put an end to bloodshed and recrimination, and even critics of democracy, like Plato, praised its moderation. Yet four years later this government tried and executed Socrates, who had defied the Thirty and whom Plato calls "the justest man then living" (*Letter 7,* 324e).

These events had a shattering effect on the young Plato. He resolved to give up his plans for a political career and devote himself to philosophy. But he never ceased thinking about political problems. The events of his youth made a deep impression on him. The strife that had torn Greece convinced him that civil war was the greatest evil for a state and unanimity the greatest good. The greed and violence of the Thirty filled him with hatred for tyranny, while the unjust, arbitrary acts of the Athenian democracy, especially the execution of Socrates, confirmed his distrust of democracy. He came to the conclusion "that all existing states are governed badly and their laws are almost incurable without incredible resources and some luck" (*Letter 7,* 326a). All his life he worried about the problem of good government. His solution, that either philosophers must become kings or kings philosophers, is one of the theories presented in the *Republic* (473c, ff.).

He even tried to put his theory into practice. At forty he visited Syracuse and met Dion, then about twenty. The two formed a passionate, lifelong attachment, immortalized in the poem cited above. Plato introduced Dion to his philosophy, and Dion introduced Plato to his father-in-law Dionysius, the tyrant of Syracuse. Both learned quickly: Dion was attracted by the force and beauty of Plato's ideas, Plato was repelled by the viciousness and intrigue of Dionysius's court. Plato sailed home, but after the death of Dionysius some twenty years later, Dion and others urged him to return. The new ruler, Dionysius II, was young, teachable, interested in philosophy, and a king—the perfect candidate for philosophical kingship. Plato reluctantly went, but his attempt to educate Dionysius was a fiasco. Plato blamed the failure on Dionysius, but the truth was that political realities had refused to conform to philosophical schemes. Plato was induced to return and try again a few years later, with equally disastrous results. He went home in defeat. Shortly thereafter Dion took Syracuse by force. Bloodshed and confusion ensued, and Dion was assassinated. Thus ended the attempts to put a philosopher king on the throne of Syracuse.

These events occurred many years after the time of the Peloponnesian War, to which we must now return. Concurrent with the war, Greece had undergone a revolution in its moral and intellectual life. Central to this process were the *sophists,* traveling professional teachers, who began to arrive in Athens around the middle of the fifth century, B.C. They taught natural science and the new disciplines of logic and rhetoric. These studies caught on quickly at Athens. Their effect was to undermine belief in the traditional religious and moral values that had formed the basis of society. Natural science seemed to dispense with the gods, and logic seemed to reveal that truth was unattainable or even nonexistent. Rhetoric was an important subject in a democracy like Athens, where political power depended on one's ability to speak persuasively in the Assembly. But if truth is unknowable and if the gods do not exist or care about men, then the object of rhetoric is obviously not truth but persuasion, and telling lies is neither shameful nor immoral—provided you don't get caught.

By the end of the war, therefore, Athens—or at least a large part of her population—had developed an attitude that was both skeptical and relativistic in religion, morals, and thought. Natural laws, not the gods, govern the universe and society. Traditional moral standards, once considered absolute, were no longer seen as guides to right conduct, since they clearly had not been handed down by the gods but invented by men. It followed that laws and customs based on these standards are merely human inventions and so bound to be fallible, since a number of men are no more exempt from error than one. Society can hardly claim, therefore, that it knows what is right for the individual better than the individual himself. Once the rules of religion and society have lost their validity, right conduct—justice—becomes a matter of individual choice. But no two individuals choose the same way: Who is to decide between them? I may, for example, believe it right to murder my father to inherit his estate. If so, no one can persuade me that I am wrong, because I can always argue that it is right *for me.* Some external, universally recognized standard is needed to judge the act. Without it, right conduct for me consists in killing my father without getting caught.

Plato fought all his life against this vicious relativism, which infected not only ethics, but logic, science, politics, and religion. In his search for universal standards Plato continued and extended Socrates' search for universal definitions, and he did it by much the same method: dialectic. As a result of his studies he discovered the Forms, which provide absolute standards not only for ethics and logic, but for all areas of human life. To learn more about the Forms, the reader is referred to the Introduction, and to the text of the *Republic.*

The page and section references printed in the margins of the text are those of the Stephanus edition, which are used universally for citing passages from Plato. The division of the *Republic* into ten books is due not to Plato but to his early editors and probably to the length of the papyrus rolls ("books") on which the dialogues were written. The books have become traditional, even though the divisions are sometimes not very logical.

I should like to express my sincere thanks to those who

read this work in manuscript and made many helpful suggestions: first, to my wife Lucy, who struggled through each draft; then to Robert Spaeth of St. John's College in Annapolis, and to John Thavis and Donald Matsen of St. John's University in Collegeville, Minnesota; and finally to the readers of AHM Publishing Corporation. I would also like to thank Eva Brann for her fine introduction.

Raymond Larson

introduction

The *Republic* is a dialogue, that is to say, a conversation. Since it is a conversation recorded between the covers of a book we cannot help but begin by *reading* it, but I think the author wants us as soon as possible to *join* it, to be converted from passive perusal to active participation, to be drawn in among the other silent "interlocutors." As it happens, in a number of Platonic dialogues there are people present who say nothing or next to nothing out loud; in the *Republic* we are told of four (328 b). In fact one of these, Clitophon, who makes only a brief intrusion into the conversation here, is to be thought of as having a few things to say on his own about the topic at hand, which is justice. For there exists a brief but brisk dialogue between him and Socrates, a companion piece to the *Republic* which, if it is not by Plato, is at least by someone versed in the spirit of Platonic dialogues. The reader is, I think, invited to be present just as these people are, and with them to smile or snicker at witticisms and inside jokes, to groan in outrage at trick arguments, to nod approval at satisfying formulations, to recall contradictory passages of conversation, to appreciate the return of a theme and, in sum, to check and fill out the recorded conversation with an unwritten inner accompaniment—to be always just on the brink of breaking in. Indeed the vocal characters themselves make it clear that they are by no means Socrates' unwitting stooges, but wary and critical participants. For example, at one point Adeimantus somewhat pugnaciously breaks in:

> "Socrates, no one could dispute what you say—your listeners are in the same position as always. . . . They think that because of their inexperience at question and answer the argument leads them astray a little bit

> at a time until finally, when all the bits are collected, they find themselves lost in apparent contradiction to what they said at the start. . . ." (487 b).

—a rebuke to which Socrates yields quite gracefully.

Perhaps nothing in or about the Platonic dialogues is more worth dwelling on than their dialogue form, especially in the *Republic* which itself contains a discussion of its own literary type. In Book 2 (392 d ff.) Socrates divides all myth telling and poetry into two styles. One is the *narrative* style, in which a poet candidly and on his own account retells an event. The other is the *imitative* style in which he speaks as a dramatist with the voice of another and conceals his own authorship. The former style is honest, the latter deceptive. It is to this latter style that the *Republic* itself appears to belong (*see* Book 3, Note 15), since Plato is entirely hidden behind this imitation of a conversation between Socrates and others.

This distinction between narration and drama may not appear so very interesting until one becomes concerned with the truth-telling and thought-provoking powers of the written word, the word which has been abandoned by its speaker. For then it appears that narrative, from myth to treatise, is indeed an undisguised attempt by an author to talk *at* a reader, an attempt which leaves that reader the defense of well-directed resistance or bored disengagement, while drama and dialogue draw him helplessly into a fictive world of vivid but spuriously attributed speech. Now Plato will not talk *at* us, that is, write clear and convincing treatises, because he considers that knowledge cannot be simply conveyed into the soul by words (518 c), nor will he involve us in one of those exciting dramas which provide nothing but an artificially heightened appearance. The ingenious solution is the dialogue written, like the *Republic,* in the *first person.* For that form does retain some of the immediacy of drama, and yet at least one of the authors of the dialogue, namely Socrates, is very much present and responsible as the teller of the tale. Such a dialogue form overcomes the dangers of poetry while preserving its power to move the soul. And given a chance, that is what the "reading" of a Socratic dialogue will do.

Given a chance—there is the trouble. For through centuries the very assumption that readers needed to be introduced to these dialogues has well and truly obstructed access to them. Most works of advanced learning begin so abruptly, in a place and on a plane where we are not, that we need to be prepared for and led into them. Not so with a conversation guided by Socrates, which is carefully devised to begin where any human being already is and to go on by such steps as everyone can follow. Dialogues are themselves nothing if not patient preparations—for what they themselves best reveal.

Therefore anyone who undertakes, as I am about to do, to write yet another introduction should do so with some embarrassment and many warnings. One convincing way to issue such warnings is to enumerate—and illustrate—some of the sins against the text an introducer will perforce commit.

part I

on "backgrounds"

The first service we have come to expect from an introduction is to be provided with a "background" to the work, an intellectual, historical, politico-socio-economic, or biographical frame within which it will first become intelligible. Raymond Larson gives us a background statement (see p. xv), but he would be the first to caution us on the use of background frames of reference in interpreting the text.

One such frame is Plato's and Socrates' Greek origin, which presumably makes them "Greek thinkers." (There is, of course, a much larger origin whose impact is, however, so controversial that it is usually dismissed: These men happen to belong to the human race, a circumstance which may override the fact of their birth in an alien time and place.) Now as to the illumination supposedly provided by this Greek background, let us set aside a small quandary, namely that "what the Greeks thought" is not least of all culled from the Platonic writings themselves. There still remains a question: Is it possible for a writer to be so deep, so original in the strong sense, that he can be defined neither from, nor even against, his social setting? It is a question to be especially asked about a writer who gives this description of the way in which a philosopher might be received by his society upon his return from the realms of thought:

> ". . . They'd say he came back from above with ruined eyes. . . . And if they could get their hands on the man who was trying to release them and lead them upward, wouldn't they kill him?" (517 a).

—the very fate, of course, of Plato's older friend Socrates. Hence an introduction to a work in terms of the intellectual history of the time is apt to amount to an implicit denial of its originality.

But surely a sketch of the historical or political setting is needed to make a text accessible! For example, the "dramatic date" of the dialogue *Republic,* that is, the time at which it is taking place, is an interlude of peace during the Peloponnesian War (whose main parties were Athens and Sparta) in the latter part of the fifth century B.C. Athens is at this time still a democracy. The scene of the dialogue is the port of Athens, the Piraeus, a proletarian stronghold of democratic feeling, at the house of a rich merchant whose family will later be destroyed by the democratic party. A hilariously repellent description of democratic modes and morals, uncannily reminiscent of conservative accounts of the turmoils of our sixties, is put by the aristocrat Plato into the mouth of the craftsman Socrates (562 c ff.), who has already foretold his own execution, also by a later democratic regime. Hence students are usually introduced to the *Republic* as a deeply antidemocratic book. But let me cite a bit of text. Socrates has just been satirizing democracy:

> "And, you know, it's just the place to go shopping for a regime."
>
> "How come?"
>
> "Because it's permissive and has every kind, so that anyone who wants to construct a city, *as we just did,* ought to shop in a democracy as in a regime bazaar. . . ." (557 d).

I have italicized the telling phrase. It seems to me to indicate that the book is far from being uncompromisingly antidemocratic, for within it attention is being drawn to the fact that a dialogue concerning ideal cities is best carried on, and is indeed being carried on, in a democracy. In this point many introductions prejudice our reading of a text, whose judgment on our favored political form is justly complex, by making too coarse an application of historical circumstance. So also with economic conditions: The fact that the priviledged Plato, a slave-owner to boot, conceives through Socrates a communitarian society so radical as to leave modern communism, scientific or utopian, looking quite pale should warn the reader to use the author's local situation most cautiously in interpreting his work. For where real thinking is going on, external facts determine at most the the point of departure of the inquiry. Mere circumstance is precisely what thought penetrates and goes beyond.

Similarly inessential may be authors' biographies. Those facts that do have some significance, like Socrates' trial and condemnation for corrupting the youth of Athens, are usually written right into the text. One circumstance, which lends the *Republic* a certain special pathos, is not mentioned, namely the fact that Socrates' young interlocutors, Glaucon and Adeimantus, are Plato's brothers. Neither of them achieved any distinction in later life, and that too turns out to have a certain significance, as we shall see.

For the rest, a list of the chief dates in Plato's life is supplied us here by the translator (p. xlvii). Of special interest is the fact of Plato's middle trip to Sicily, subsequent to the composition of the *Republic* (see especially Mr. Larson's discussion, p. xix). He had gone rather reluctantly, yielding to the demand that he should have the courage to try in practice his alternative plan for the realization of the best regime: that "kings and regents become genuine philosophers." Long before the composition of the *Republic,* its first and preferred plan, namely that philosophers might themselves be accepted as kings, had been demonstratively dashed by the execution of Socrates. Now the philosophical education of the Sicilian tyrant Dionysius had proved to be a failure as well. We may cautiously conclude that before, during, and after the writing of the *Republic* (which he kept revising until his death), Plato knew that its central proposal was impractical. This understanding too can, as we will see, help to cast a certain light on the intention of the work.

The list also contains a rough ordering of Plato's works. Such chronologies are a scholarly preoccupation intended to determine the development of a writer's thought by establishing the date of his writings, but that sometimes serve the reverse cause. Such a list, however, can be useful; in inviting comparison, for instance, of Plato's last work, the *Laws,* with the *Republic.* The Greek title of the *Republic* is *Politeía,* which literally means "Political Regime" or "Constitution" and signifies a conception of thought, while the *Laws* naturally contains a multitude of practically applicable laws. The latter dialogue explicitly refers to itself in comparison with the *Republic* as a "second sailing," that is to say, a second best or even least worst way. Both the speaker Socrates and the very word philosophy are missing from the *Laws,* which takes place during a long day's walk under the Cretan sun, just as the *Republic* goes on well through the night at a house in the port of Athens. The differences between the two dialogues is, crudely, that between theory and practice.

retelling plato

A second standard introductory effort is to convey some appreciation of the context and style of a work, and perhaps to lighten the labor of study by telling what is in it. It is an almost irresistible, though rather graceless, exercise to pull out from a text certain favorite frisky ideas and to hold them up to view by the scruff of the neck. For example, I have already mentioned that notorious notion, proposed by Socrates as his most rousingly disreputable idea near the center of the dialogue, which is that

> "Until either philosophers become kings, or those now called kings and regents become genuine philosophers, so that political power and philosophy coincide, . . . there will be no end to evils." (473 c-d).

The limited legitimacy in citing this and its equally unheard-of complement, that only those can be trusted to govern who have an ardent desire not to do so (520 d), lies in displaying them as examples of the characteristic cast of all such Socratic "paradoxes": They strike one at first hearing as pretty bizarre, after some assimilation as fairly obvious, and in the long development as very deep. For example, in the case at hand, it seems at first absurd to draft rulers when there are so many eager volunteers; on reflection, reluctance to rule seems an increasingly attractive qualification; and finally we begin to appreciate the depth of a conception of human excellence which sees it as incompatible with a desire for political power.

A duller, yet more dangerously distorting, exercise is to retell "what Plato said" in straighter and more easily appreciable terms, perhaps introducing each recounting with some such phrase as "Plato believed that. . . ." For as it happens one of the most fundamental—no, *the* most fundamental—distinction of the dialogue, on which its central development rests, is that between mere "belief"—"opinion" is an equivalent Socratic term—and "knowledge." "Opinion" is that sort of half-thought, the predictable reflection of a "mentality," that is to say, a set of habitual mental reactions, which is often expressed through the prefatory phrase "I feel that. . . ." "Knowledge," however, is the deeply grounded, fully conscious result of long thought. Hence the presentation of a Platonic proposition as a belief is simply a prejudgment against it. A thinker in Socrates' sense does not have a "mentality."

Again, introductions often point readers toward the felicities of style and diction of a work. But any reader who has gotten a quarter of an hour into Raymond Larson's truly and faithfully colloquial translation, will have seen for himself that here indeed is a lively text, full of linguistic byplay and mimicry, from dreadful puns to sudden spoofing modulations into expert's jargon, which can on occasions rise through great elegance of expression to solemn grandeur. Much of the subtlety of the Greek is saved in the translation simply because Mr. Larson has employed a method oddly rare among translators: He puts into the most natural possible English no more and no less than is in the Greek, and preserves as much as possible the Greek order.

That this order is of consequence is confirmed by an ancient anecdote, which is probably invented, but significantly invented. It is said that after Plato's death a tablet was found on which were written the opening words of the *Republic* "variously transposed." The version Plato published begins with Socrates' words "I went down . . .", surely a significant beginning for a work whose central event is the descent of the philosopher into the political community. Similarly the final words, not always put in their proper place, are mentioned by Plato in his letters as having special significance for him. They mean at once "we shall bid adieu," "we shall fare well," "we shall do well," "we shall do right."

An introduction may also draw the reader's attention to the peculiar depths of Platonic diction and the consequent difficulties in choosing the right word to render characteristic "Socratic" terms. Indeed, it is almost quicker to learn Greek than to familiarize oneself with the objections attending each choice.

The choices incorporated in the present translation seem to me felicitous and in one case justifiably bold. For example, a central Socratic term is *areté.* It is traditionally and defensibly translated as "virtue;" a word which, however, having lost its original sense of "manliness" and retained an outmoded connotation of chastity, has a prissy ring to present-day ears. The Greek word has been supposed to share a root with Ares, the name of the Greek god of war, signifying power and vigor and preeminence, a sphere of meaning well caught by the word "excellence" which Mr. Larson has used. Another case is the frequent Socratic phrase exemplified by "the beautiful itself," which is sometimes rendered as "absolute beauty;" this latter version again has a repellent sound to modern ears—we are scared off by any reference to the absolute—and it is, in addition, a gratuitous elaboration of Socrates' simpler wording, which Mr. Larson preserves.

But the greatest Socratic term is *eídos* (plural *eíde*) and its equivalent *idéa.* The most common translation is "form," for the English word idea, has as Mr. Larson points out, no longer anything to do with the Platonic "Theory of Ideas." (Not that such a "theory" is to be found within the dialogues —the word *eidos,* I hope to show, is not a systematic term.) "Idea" to us means a mental object, something our mind contains or grasps or peels off from reality, a dim image or a concept or an *abstraction.* The *eide,* in contrast, are emphatically not abstractions. Although they are intelligible, that is to say, present to the intellect, they are not "in our mind." Nor are they meant to be thin or insubstantial; indeed, it is their very character to be substantial, to be rich. This stable, self-subsistent plenitude is precisely what Socrates calls "being."

Mr. Larson has chosen to break with convention and to render at least one of these scintillatingly paradoxical Socratic words, namely *idea,* as "shape," a word with a more visual connotation than "form." So also the literal meaning of *eidos* (a little too odd for adoption) is "looks," namely that which presents itself to sight, a "sight"; the *eidos* of a thing is what we see of it, its *aspect* for us. (*See* Book 5, Note 13.) For example, a boy can be said to be "beautiful in *eidos,*" that is, in face or looks. Derivatively the word comes to mean "kind" or "class." (The exact Latin equivalent of *eidos* is "species.") The explanation of this meaning is that in order for any perception to be classifiable and assignable to its kind it has to have a recognizable shape, an identifiable "look." It is because everything around us wears its own aspect that we recognize what it "looks like," as when we say: "That looks like a boy" or "that looks like a good thing."

Now Socrates' term is a witty misnomer for what he means, because the first thing to be said of a Socratic "shape" is that it is *invisible.* It is a hypothesis, a supposition—not, as I have said, a well-defined term in a systematic theory, but an assumption pursued, in public at least, with serious playfulness and relaxed persistency, an assumption to which and from which all roads of inquiry lead. And yet, once again, to say that the shapes are suppositions is not in the least to say that they are mere mental constructs. It is precisely because they are behind and beyond all our thinking and truth-telling, because they *are* the beings that collectively constitute being, that they are not amenable to argumentative proof, but only to serious conjecture and thoughtful conviction.

The reason why Socrates finds such suppositions to be necessary to intelligible speech—and thus to his life—is this: In his every effort to discern the truth and to delve into the nature of things (an effort called philosophy, without which human life is an elusive dream), he comes on infinitely various appearances, which are, as has been pointed out, surprisingly amenable to being gathered into classes by the looks they present. Each such collection is named by one word. For example, all deeds of a certain kind are called "just." Over and over Socrates feels compelled to suppose that behind this inconsistent welter of deeds called just there must stand one pure and potent being, the *eidos* Justice. This *eidos* gives the appearances their common shape (without itself coming forth to the sight of the eye) because it truly *is* what they only *appear* to be. Socrates calls this *eidos* (and every other *eidos* similarly) "Justice *Itself,*" because it is that which shines through the appearances as what is alone truly named and truly known.

A preparatory simile, suggesting how these beings can be the source of a world of appearances which reveals and yet screens them, is set out in the center of the dialogue, at the end of Book 6 and the beginning of Book 7. (Incidentally, there is no place for the term "reality," which literally means "thinghood," in Socrates' view of the world: The shapes have being, but by no means the hard tangibility attributed to things perceived here and now; neither are the appearances possessed of any thing-like solidity, being only a dry sparkle for the senses.)

Socrates, then, makes the supposition of the shapes as sources of the visible (and audible and tangible) world mainly because they are what we *know* and speak of in the world of appearances. Whenever we inquire, rather than merely sound off, what our words reach is not the shifting sensual sight but the stable invisible looks; beyond what we see is what we know. The Socratic shapes are therefore the condition which makes possible the distinction between opinion which is talk caught in mere appearances, and knowledge in which speech has reached beings. Or, to say the same thing another way: the central activity of the *Republic,* philosophy, whose literal meaning is "love of wisdom," would not be possible without the presupposition that there are indeed objects to which a faithful and longing search can lead. For to love wisdom means, at least for Socrates, precisely to desire to see through the illusory and confusing sights of sense to the firmly knowable invisible shapes—the *eide,* which are what they are truly and purely.

on interpreting

And finally there is the introducer's most precious (and most pernicious) prerogative, which is to offer an interpretation of the work.

The interpretation of the work of another's thought is always a curious business, for it is unavoidably an effort of *exposure.* Some interpretations merely explain, that is, lay out flat the bare bones hidden under the fancy flesh of the presentation. Others aim to expose deliberately or unconsciously concealed motives. For example, it has been claimed that what is behind the *Republic,* obscured by sham-rational verbiage, is Plato's hatred of egalitarianism, conditioned by his suffering under the political instability of the Athens in which he grew up. The implied prejudgments of the former sort of interpretation are that the manner of presentation is a mere embellishment on substance and can be expertly peeled away, and of the latter, that all authors are cunningly self-deceived or deceiving.

Another kind of interpretation looks for a meaning which is implicit in the text and is intended to be discovered there, but not without some attention and labor. For after all, beyond appearing as a lively and open-ended conversation for the reader to join, the dialogue is also a discussion carefully guided by Socrates and yet further, a work artfully composed and perfected by Plato. But that suggests that the conversation may be contained within a revealing structure and marked by significant turns and pregnant omissions, all designed as invitations to speculative interpretation. At certain crucial points Socrates is even quite willing to be explicit about the deliberate exclusion of those very teachings for which the dialogue is a preparation. For example, both a full-scale inquiry into the parts of the soul and a direct discussion of the Good are withheld (504 b, 506 e). The latter especially belongs among the so-called "unwritten doctrines" of Plato's school, unwritten because in the words of the seventh of his letters, "this knowledge is not something that can be put into words."

Anyone who has read a given Platonic dialogue fairly often is apt to be in possession of this kind of interpretation, and it surpasses ordinary powers of self-restraint to refrain from offering it, even to a beginning student. And yet that is a pedagogically naughty enterprise, and I can only hope that the first-time reader will stop looking at the introduction at this point and come back to Part II later. Not that plenty of interpretation has not already been committed, but the reader should decline to be persuaded into an opinion before being in a position to test its plausibility, and should refuse to be drawn under the textual surface before having seen the text. The reader, in short, should avoid being presented with a meaning except by Plato himself.

part II

the central dialogue: the philosopher's city

The observation of structures and patterns usually yields a clue to the author's intention. The *Republic* indeed has a rather large and obvious architecture, a symmetry which suggests too much to be a pattern for pattern's sake. Let me set it out roughly by books:

1 and 10:	The rewards of justice;
2–5 and 8–9:	The construction and corruption of the best city;
2 and 10:	The critique of poetry;
6 and 7:	The philosopher's function and education.

This arrangement may be imagined as a set of concentric circles with the themes lying on a diameter through them. The major themes are repeated going into the center and coming out, of course under a different light. For example, the critique of poetry in political communities in the second book is confined to its content, its misrepresentation of excellence and of the gods. However in the tenth book, in the light of the preceding philosophical discussion, the critique becomes a radical condemnation of poetry as a kind of perverse absorption in images and a deliberate distancing from being.

But what the concentric construction primarily effects is the clear definition of a dialogic center, namely Books 6 and 7, in which are contained the heights and the depths of the dialogue. What is presented there is "a way to be pursued" —this is the literal meaning of the Greek word "method" which as yet has no connotation of a mechanical procedure. It is an education which has scarcely any of the usual modern aims: It is intended neither to broaden or to sharpen the mind, nor to inform or indoctrinate it, and least of all to train people to "be creative" or to "develop their whole personality." Instead it is meant to employ the appropriate parts of the soul to lead the young learner in accordance with the nature of things to a view of the Whole. That is to say, it is an education intimately related to philosophy, even to "a" philosophy.

In the center of the Western tradition's first book on political theory, then, politics is replaced by philosophy. This is an observation backed by an acute although not disinterested reader, Rousseau. He says in his fictive pedagogical case history, *Émile,* which represents the individualistic modern replacement of Plato's work:

> To get a good idea of communal education read Plato's *Republic.* It is not a political treatise, as those who merely judge books by their titles think. It is the finest treatise on education ever written.

Perhaps then it is better to say that Socrates transforms a political question into an educational one. To mark this transformation, the dominating desire of the dialogue, namely that justice should be proved to be compatible with and even conducive to happiness, is for the moment thrust aside: To those who guide and those who undergo such an education the doing of justice is, on the whole, not a source of happiness but a simple sacrifice. For justice demands that they should leave the realm of being to act in the world of appearance (516 c ff.), and this is for them a mere harsh duty, a moral obligation without assured reward; indeed, they must rather expect loss of bliss, submission to distraction, risk of contumely, and even danger of death. That is the judgment of Socrates who himself "went down," among the populace.

This transformation of politics into pedagogy is necessitated by what might be termed the "founding paradox" of the ideal city. For suppose such a city has been constructed in argument, how is it to be realized? It is under the pressure of this question from Glaucon that Socrates gives the absurd, or at least not very commonsensical, answer already cited: Such a city can come about only if either philosophers become kings or kings philosophers. But for kings to become philosophers there must take place one of those wrenching conversions described in the Cave Image (515 c ff.), which has to be effected with the aid of someone who has, in turn, already somehow, perhaps by a miracle of birth, become a philosopher—yet nothing within the dialogues or in Socrates' and Plato's life supports the expectation that if such a philosopher were to occur, he could bring about such a conversion. If, on the other hand, philosophers are to be kings, the following circle of conditions must somehow be broken through: The likely candidates would have to grow up in a city which can give them a truly philosophical education such as will keep them from becoming like those smart injurious intellectuals now rightly rejected by the people. It would, further, have to be a city already so constituted as to be willing to accept philosophical rule, or there would scarcely be much incentive for educating them to it. In sum, the future philosophers must already be born into Socrates' ideal city. But that city can come about only if some true philosophers happened to be born into some existing city, happened to come to power there, and happened thus to be in a position to send all the adults into the wilds and to seize command of their children's education (540 d ff.)—the comic counsel of despair with which Socrates closes the discussion of the philosophical curriculum.

The resolution of this paradox is given in the passage which seems to reveal most directly the inner intention of the *Republic.* When the argument, now past the center, reverts to the original task of proving justice advantageous, Glaucon and Socrates have their last exchange concerning the philosopher city:

> ". . . You mean the city we've been founding in words; I don't think it exists on earth."
> "But perhaps it is laid up as a model in heaven for anyone to look at who wishes *to found himself.* It makes no difference whether it exists or ever will exist here. He'll practice the politics only of it and of no other." (592 b).

I have italicized Mr. Larson's faithful rendering of Socrates' oddly abrupt phrase "to found himself." It reveals in direct words that the point of the *Republic* is not a political but a personal founding, a self-constituting, which is accomplished both in and by the dialogue. Socrates resolves, or rather, bypasses, the founder's paradox by founding, through conversation, *right here and now* an educational community whose members are all the present and future participants in the dialogue. The very development of this community "in speech," that is, the course of the argument itself, educates his interlocutors "in deed." ("In speech and in deed" is a common Greek opposition which Socrates himself employs in this context, 473 a.) The establishment of this dialogic community and the conversion and reformation of its philosopher-citizens is itself *the* Socratic accomplishment—not the preparation of future philosopher kings, as the choice of the obscure Glaucon as chief interlocutor signifies.

The course of education which Socrates sets out for the sake of our education has what we no longer expect of such a course—an end. It is intended to effect not so much an advance into a subject matter as an ascent to this end, which is called with stupefying grandeur, "the shape of the Good," or simply, "the Good" (508 e). It is not some one good thing, nor a moral imperative or rule of right conduct, nor an excellence or a substance, nor, indeed, a being at all. Rather it is beyond the other shapes, "beyond being"—it is their governing source. In other contexts, we know, its name was "the One." Here it is referred to as "the source of the whole" (511 b), which might even possibly be rendered as "the source which is the whole," or, again, as "the ruling principle of everything." (The Greek word for source, rule, principle, even government, is *arché.*) As I have mentioned, Socrates refuses to explicate the Good directly because it is not to be attained and conveyed in speech, but he does provide a likeness, the Sun Simile (506 e). The Good is like the sun in two ways: it gives being and substance to the realm of invisible shapes, as the sun gives growth and sustenance to the whole visible world, and it gives intelligibility and articulation to the different beings within being, as the sun gives illumination and distinctness to the appearances within the world. The Good is "beyond being" because it is not yet another being in addition to the shapes, but rather the wholeness and oneness itself of all being.

the divided line

Under the presidency of the Good, then, there arises a cosmos of substance and shadows, of being and appearance, which Socrates sets out by means of a geometric diagram, the Divided Line (509 d ff.). The proportioned segments of this line represent the realms which arise as being is successively reflected: First it casts its rational shadows, the objects of mathematics; these are in turn imaged in the bodies of the natural world, and these, again, throw off surface reflections. (*See* Book 6, Note 10 for the actual diagram.)

Corresponding and appended to these four realms are four appropriate powers of the soul. Now if there is any mode of thinking which might be called characteristic of the dialogue it is this mode of correspondences or correlations: To the parts of the soul correspond the chief passions and their controlling excellences (435 c ff.); to different human types correspond different political regimes (544 e); and to different powers of the knowing part of the soul correspond different objects of knowledge. In most cases Socrates begins the correlation with what is closest to us, with ourselves and our powers:

> "Then we clearly agree that opinion is different from knowledge . . . and *being different powers each naturally pertains to a different thing:* knowledge pertains to what *is,* to know how it is, whereas opinion, we say, conjectures." (478 a, my italics).

This central section, however, is an exception, for there he is giving a preview, albeit an abbreviated and inadequate one, of the ascending realms of being, and therefore he presents the objects as primary over the powers by which they are known.

Reversing Socrates' order, in the following interpretative setting-out of these powers and their objects, I begin with those represented by the highest and presumably largest segment of the line. There intellection or thought *(nóesis)* moves, rising and falling among the things of thought, the beings or "shapes," by and through which it approaches and departs from the Good. This motion is called "dialectic," which here does not have the usual meaning of dialogic discussion, argument or refutation, but is the specific activity of the intellect among the shapes, the highest kind of thought. In the *Republic* Socrates is reluctant to say much about it.

The next segment below stands for thinking or understanding *(diánoia).* It is a more restless, technical and incomplete activity which works through pure images, such as mathematical shapes. Its business is the making of assumptions or hypotheses, such as are the axioms and objects of mathematics. In fact, the words with which we name the shapes of being without quite knowing them, words like "justice," for instance, are also hypotheses of the understanding—these are the very assumptions dialectic turns into knowledge. The movement of mathematical understanding is characteristically deductive, downward, as in Euclid's geometric proofs. It reaches conclusions but it does not ascend beyond its own suppositions. These two upper parts together represent the realm of knowledge *(epistéme)*.

Opinion *(dóxa)* is represented by the two lower lengths, which are cut in the same ratio as the upper two, both subsections reflecting the overall ratio, that between knowlege and opinion.

The third segment down stands for trust *(pístis)*. It is the way we have of dealing with all the apparently solid things in the world around us. By and large we take them for granted, believe in them and trust them to behave predictably: The sun will rise, the ground will support us. It can be proved that as this line is divided, the two middle segments are of equal length, which shows that the realm of mathematics and its phenomenal reflection, the realm of nature, are coextensive, that is to say, of equal standing in the scale of being. (In another dialogue, the *Timaeus,* which is a sequel to some occasion when Socrates retold his conversation on city building, some friends, to reciprocate, invite him to a feast of cosmos construction; among other things, they show him, in a most modern vein, that the physical world is literally constructed *out of* mathematics, which is to say that the two realms are more than coextensive—they are identical.)

Finally, at the bottom, is the shortest segment standing for the most peculiarly Socratic power, the most dubious and the most necessary, the lowest and the first. It is the power whose name *eikasía* is often, not very plausibly, translated as conjecture. Actually, Socrates has appropriated a rare word and used it in its literal sense, which is "imagizing." It can be rendered as "imagination," or as, in the present translation, "imaging." It is the wonderful power of dealing with an image *(eikón) as* an image, the power of recognizing likenesses. To recognize a likeness *as* a likeness is the first of philosophical feats, for it involves seeing that something (an image) has the look of something else (the original) which it *is not*—thus it is the first step in distinguishing appearance from being. Socrates signals the pervasive nature of this power when he performs the mathematical operation of "alternation" by which he transforms the proportion:

Intellection is to understanding as trust is to imaging

to:

Intellection is to trust as understanding to imaging, which means that understanding, the power of doing mathematics, is immediately related to image recognition (534a). This relation will be very plausible to anyone who has ever drawn a misshapen ovoid on a blackboard and said "Let this be circle C," meaning, "Recognize this as an image of a true, physically unachievable circle." That "imaging" should be *the* pervasive power is not surprising where the ascent of learning depends on recognizing the objects of each lower realm as shadow images cast by a higher.

In fact, an overwhelming interest in the nature of images and their seeming, in what makes it possible that a shape should at once *be* and *not be* that which it is, runs through a number of dialogues. Understandably so, for the image which is not what it seems to be is a kind of prime exemplar of that realm between being and nonbeing (477 ff.), that shifting shadow world of mutability, variousness and seeming, which Plato sometimes calls "becoming," that is, our world of appearances. Within the *Republic,* this interest shows itself in a way that must always have scandalized readers, namely in the thorough censoring of the products of the imagination. They are called "music," that is to say, the poetry, song, painting, and other works of the Muses, which, together with physical training, form the prephilosophical upbringing of children in the ideal city. His fierce attacks on the poets as irresponsible image-mongers stem from the fact that, unlike us, Socrates is dead serious about the potency of poetry, since he sees it as a seductively charming corruptor of the primary power of philosophical ascent, which is precisely the power of image recognition.

the cave image

In Book 7 Socrates turns to the human cost and effort of this ascent. He begins, cleverly, with an invitation to use this very power of image recognition: We are to recognize our world as a cave. (A schematic representation of this worldly underworld is given in Note 1.) He describes the wrenching, disorienting conversion undergone by the unchained prisoners when they are first forced to turn around to look at the opinion-making and image-manipulating that goes on behind their backs. This first turnabout enables them to recognize as mere images of images the shadow plays performed for them on the screen at the bottom of the cave before which they have been sitting enchained all their early lives. (The contemporary application to television is comically obvious.) Then they are dragged and hauled, still unwilling, up into the blinding light of the sun, the very sun of the Sun Simile. Just when they have begun to rejoice in this bright upper world, they must force themselves to descend again and to undertake the dangerous task of enlightening their fellow citizens in turn.

the philosopher's education

Then follows a detailed account of a curriculum which is the realization of that upward haul, the "winch to lift the soul from becoming to being" (521 d). It picks up where the training in gymnastics and music (which corresponds to the lower two parts of the Divided Line—those representing nature and images) had left off, putting habituation and training behind in favor of thinking and true education. It is the first detailed systematic exposition of the traditional liberal arts, particularly of those four skills of mathematics and physics called the "quadrivium" in medieval times. The mathematical "method" here is not a technical but a philosophical preparation, a road leading not to application but to reflection—that is precisely what makes it liberal.

The first and fundamental subject is nondimensional *mathematics,* that is, arithmetic, the study of collections of units, whose importance lies not in reckoning but in its function as a logical preparation for the approach to *the* One, that is, the Good. Thereafter the studies advance dimensionally through plane and solid geometry up to harmony, the study of solids in rational motion—pure *physics,* as we would say.

The crowning study, not to be undertaken until maturity,

is *dialectic,* the thoughtful motion of the intellect among the shapes (532 ff.), aided by internal and external dialogue, that is, by reflection and conversation, and culminating in a view of the Whole, namely the shape of the Good.

Now what is most remarkable in this curriculum ostensibly meant for philosopher statesmen is that it excludes completely all political theory and all science of government. I have already argued that this education is in fact meant more for philosophers than for statesmen. But it turns out that from the point of view of the curriculum that hardly matters. For were these philosophers destined actually to govern, they would do so not through law and a science of government—the constitutional and administrative features of the philosopher's city are minimal—but in the light of the Whole, by a contingently applied wisdom. That is the reason why the One is in this dialogue named the Good—because from its contemplation flows the possibility of action which is not rule-ridden but truly adjusted to each case. Only because it is not a mere neutral oneness which encompasses and unifies the world, but the *Good,* can the world be the scene of unifying, fitting, effective, human, personal action (517 c), in short, of *justice.*

the outer dialogue: the degenerate cities

The outer rings of the dialogue are concerned with the building up and the breakdown of the just "city," but, "in speech," as Socrates repeatedly says—that is, for the sake of argument. In fact, on the way into the center of the dialogue, a whole series of "cities" (the Greek word is *pólis,* which is best rendered as "political community") is described, each embodying justice with more complexity than the preceding one. Past the center their degeneration, as the citizens lose their moral tone, is pursued through similar stages: First the philosophers' knowledge fails, then the soldiers lose their spirit, then the traders become intemperate and finally the craftsmen throw off their justice. Each of these stages is a commonly recognized real regime. (It is to be noted that in the real cities individual character precedes and determines the political conditions, but in the ideal cities the reverse is the case.) A chart may be useful:

Ideal City	*Real Regime*
Philosopher City	———
Guardian City	Aristocracy (rule of the best)
Warrior City	Timocracy (rule of the honorable)
Trader City	Oligarchy (rule of the wealthy few)
Craftsman City	Democracy (rule of the people)
———	Tyranny

I leave it to the reader to determine whether there is not evidence enough to distinguish the five left-hand cities not as mere stages in the genesis of the philosopher city, but as essentially different polities. For the rest, I have already argued that the highest and happiest city is actually a dialogic community including Socrates, Glaucon, and the reader, a league of learning which, though not a merely private affair, is yet antecedent to a full-fledged political foundation. The lowest and worst and the most miserable regime, tyranny, however, is indeed truly private, for the tyrant is defined by the fact that he exploits the whole city as his private means for servicing his boundless desires. So both of these cities, the best and the worst, are really not true political communities.

It is the "guardian city" which has, as an apparently realizable political ideal, given most scandal and even brought on Plato the charge of totalitarianism. This is the city in which the older warriors of the Warrior City are separated off to become the guardians (414 b) of a new, radically communistic city, in which there is no private property, wives and children are held in common so that the family is abolished, men and women are equally trained for war, and a rigid caste system resting on the testing of human types is enforced.

Let me at least suggest certain mitigating factors. First, the city is not totalitarian but unitarian, for it is not so much under total control as completely unified—that, at least, is Aristotle's criticism, who thinks that such unity is contrary to nature. Second, the ruling group itself lives under the harsh communal discipline, in contrast to totalitarian regimes, while the members of the lower class are, as far as one can tell, allowed families, property and all the ordinary pleasures and private latitudes.

justice in socrates' city

But the argument which supersedes all others is the circumstance, so often repeated by Socrates, that this is a city only built for the sake of argument. It is quite literally a utopia (a Greek word coined by Thomas More, meaning "no-place"). It is, after all, only a device Socrates has introduced for the sake of answering the main question: What is justice? That device is a projection of justice on the largest possible screen, the political community, so that its nature may be easier to discern (368 d ff.). It should be noted that this projection becomes possible only by reason of another such principle of correspondence as was mentioned above: Each excellence is located analogously in the city and in the soul.

In their preliminary arguments about justice in Book 1, the participants had assumed, rather as a matter of course, that justice is a matter of relations among people, a matter of external conduct. But even then Socrates had already pointed out that if it is indeed an excellence, and if excellences are powers and functions of the soul, justice might rather have to be primarily a matter of internal soundness (353 d ff.).

Now, of course, it is impossible to construct a constitution which will display justice unless a hypothesis about its nature is built in from the beginning. This supposition about justice will, not surprisingly, be rediscovered at the end of the exercise as the sought-for feature of the construction. Socrates' presupposition is precisely that justice is not a condition like the fair distribution of goods or equal treatment under the law, but an excellence, an excellence concerned with self-relation. The definition of this justice, as it emerges in Socrates' city, seems at first disappointingly drab and uninspiring. It is quite literally, "to do one's own thing" (433 b), not of course in the current sense of expressing and pleasing oneself, but in the sense of having a competence and not overstepping its limits. (It is a definition made more immediately plausible by the fact that the Greek word for a vicious type is a *panurge,* or "do-all.")

In its political application this definition means that a just city is, first, an aristocracy, that is to say a government of those best fitted and most competent to govern, and second, a thoroughly articulated community in which no one is allowed or, indeed, even wishes, to step out of his properly assigned place. In such a city justice does belong to the whole community, but it is above all the peculiar excellence of that majority whose part it is to do their own specialized work, work which is vital in its place, but limited in scope. Socrates' justice belongs specifically to "the people."

In respect to the individual, this definition of justice means that that soul is just, each of whose parts performs its function well and submits to the direction of the part which is best and most fit for rule, the reasonable part. Hence a just soul is a potent yet controlled soul, happy in the vigor of its parts and the clarity of their relations, a well-disposed soul, whose just external relations are a mere reflection of its inner order.

What gives aptness and force to justice as "doing one's own business" is that so understood it becomes the excellence of excellences in a world under the rule of the Good. For that the Good rules can only mean that in its light each being is both good in itself and good as a part of the whole. But that is precisely what justice accomplishes in our working world, which is a reflection of the realm of being: To be just according to Socrates is to be both good on one's own and good for others.

the final myth

In the middle books of the *Republic* Socrates uses projections, similes, diagrams, and images to lift the discussion, as it were, above itself. In the introductory first book, however, only the notorious Socratic dialectic appears, dialectic, that is, in the usual understanding—a winding argument, full of quibbles, quandaries, and refutations. By contrast, the last book concludes with a very grand myth. In every great Platonic dialogue the logical argument is complemented by a mythical tableau. A Platonic myth is always a cosmic image which encompasses the world of heaven and the world of hell, the realm where the soul sees true being and the realm where it meets retribution—the world above and the world below, between which lies our earthly place. It provides that vision of the Whole which no argument can convey.

The strange and suggestive visual ambiguities of this word

image of the invisible shape of the Whole are pointed out by Mr. Larson in the Appendix. In the Myth of Er we are shown the cosmos as a setting for the judgment of former and the choice of future lives. The myth is meant to foster the conviction that the process of living has behind it a controlling shape, the pattern of our life taken as a whole, which we ourselves have already chosen, expressing in that choice the disposition of our soul. But the moment for another choice, the myth implies, cannot fail to come, and the best preparation for doing well then is to engage seriously in the inquiry concerning justice now.

Eva T. H. Brann

principal dates

(the order of dialogues is uncertain
and the list is not exhaustive)

428 B.C.	Birth of Plato at Athens. Fourth year of Pelponnesian War (between Athens and Sparta)
423	Aristophanes' comedy *Clouds* performed (parody of Socrates)
404	End of Peloponnesian War. Athens surrenders to Sparta. Reign of the "Thirty Tyrants" (among them Plato's relatives Critias and Charmides). Polemarchus (who appears in Book 1 of the *Republic*) murdered by the Thirty
403	Overthrow of the Thirty and restoration of the Athenian Democracy
399	Socrates' trial and execution for impiety and corrupting the youth (70 years old)
399–387	Early dialogues: *Apology, Euthyphro, Crito, Laches, Carmides, Ion, Lysis, Protagoras, Gorgias*
387	Plato's first trip to Syracuse (in Sicily); friendship with Dion, son-in-law and brother-in-law of Dionysius I, tyrant of Syracuse
386	Foundation of Plato's Academy at Athens

386–367	Middle dialogues: *Meno, Cratylus, Euthydemus, Phaedo, Symposium, Menexenus, Republic, Phaedrus, Parmenides, Theaetetus*
384	Birth of Aristotle at Stagirus, in Macedonia
367	Plato's second trip to Syracuse; attempt to educate Dionysius II into a philosopher-king. Aristotle joins the Academy at age 17
366–361	*Sophist, Statesman*
361	Plato's third trip to Syracuse
360–347	Late dialogues: *Philebus, Timaeus, Critias, Laws*
357	Dion captures Syracuse amid violence and bloodshed
356	Birth of Alexander the Great in Pella, Macedonia
354	Dion assassinated. Plato's *Seventh Letter*
347	Death of Plato at Athens

Book 1

SOCRATES: I went down to the Piraeus yesterday with Glau- 327
con, Ariston's son, to pray to the goddess and see how they'd manage her festival, which was being held for the first time.[1] I thought our local procession was beautiful, though it seemed no nicer than the Thracians' procession. When we had prayed and watched the processions we started back to
town. Polemarchus, son of Cephalus, spotted us hurrying b
home and ordered his slave to run up and tell us to wait for him. The boy pulled at my cloak from behind: "Polemarchus tells you to wait," he said. I turned around and asked where the master was. "There," he said, "right behind you. Just wait."

"We will," said Glaucon.

A little while later Polemarchus came up with Glaucon's c
brother Adeimantus, Niceratus, son of Nicias, and some others who must have come from the procession. Polemarchus said: "You seem in a rush to get back to town, Socrates."

"Not a bad guess," I replied.

"Do you see how many of us there are?"

"How can I help it?"

"Well," he said, "either overpower us or stay here."

"Isn't there another alternative?" I asked. "We could persuade you to let us go."

"Can you persuade someone who won't listen?"

"Hardly," Glaucon replied.

"Well," said Polemarchus, "you can be sure that we won't."

"Say," said Adeimantus, "did you know there's going to 328
be a torch race on horses for the goddess this evening?"

[1]The Piraeus is the main port of Athens, about five miles southwest of the city. The "goddess" is probably Bendis, whose festival was introduced into Athens from Thrace in 411 B.C. The characters of *The Republic* are all historical: Glaucon and Adeimantus were older brothers of Plato. Cephalus, in whose home the discussion takes place, was the father of Polemarchus, Euthydemus, and Lysias the orator. Thrasymachus was a well-known sophist and orator.

"On horses?" I said. "That's something new. You mean a relay race on horses, handing off torches?"

"Exactly," said Polemarchus. "They're having an all-night
carnival too, which should be something to see. We're going
out after supper to watch. There'll be lots of young men
there to talk to, so stay with us and don't try anything differ-
b ent."

"It looks like we'll have to," said Glaucon.

"If you think so," I said, "then that's what we'll do."

So we went home with Polemarchus and found his brothers, Lysias and Euthydemus. Thrasymachus of Chalcedon
was there, Charmantides from Paeania, and Clitophon, son
of Aristonymus. Polemarchus's father Cephalus was also at
home. I hadn't seen him for a long time and he seemed very
c old. He was sitting in a chair on a pillow and wearing a
wreath because he'd just come in from making a sacrifice in
the courtyard.

There was a circle of chairs in the room, so we went in and
sat down. As soon as he saw me, Cephalus greeted me and
said: "You really ought to come down to the Piraeus and see
us more often, Socrates. If I still had the strength to walk up
to town you wouldn't have to bother because we'd come and
d see you. As it is, you'll have to visit us more often. You know
I love a good talk—in fact, my desire for conversation increases as my bodily pleasures decline. So please don't say
no—you can get together with these young fellows and still
visit us. Think of us as friends and almost a part of your
family."

"Of course, Cephalus," I said. "I enjoy talking with old
e people anyway; they've gone before us down a path that we
too may have to walk. I think we should try to find out from
them what it's like—rocky and difficult or easy and smooth.
I'd especially like to hear from you, Cephalus, since you're
now on what the poets call 'the threshold of Death.' What's
your report? is it a hard time of life or what?"

329 "Well, I'll give you my opinion, Socrates. A few of us old
fellows get together now and then, like regular birds of a
feather. Most of us sit and cry about the good old days,
yearning for the pleasures of youth and reminiscing about
the joys of sex and parties and drinking and all that. They
fret as though they'd been deprived of something important,
saying that then they lived well and now they're not even

living. Some complain that their families abuse them, and b
make that an excuse to bewail old age, as though age were
the cause of all of their miseries.

"Now it seems to me that these people put the blame in
the wrong place, Socrates. If age were the cause, it would
have the same effect on me and everyone else who's old. But
I've met old people who aren't like that. Once I was with the
poet Sophocles when someone asked: 'How's your sex life,
Sophocles? Are you still able to enjoy a woman?' 'Hush!' c
said Sophocles. 'The greatest happiness of my life was es-
caping from that cruel and raging tyrant.' That seemed like
a good reply then, and now it seems even better. Old age
frees you from that sort of thing and gives you peace, and
when your desires relax and stop driving you it's exactly as
Sophocles said: release from bondage to a pack of raging d
tyrants. So, Socrates, the cause of a person's attitude toward
these desires is also the cause of his family's attitude toward
him: not age, but a man's character. If he's orderly and
cheerful, old age will be tolerable. If he's not, Socrates, even
youth will be a burden to him."

I was delighted to hear him speak like that and wanted to
hear more. So to stir him up I said: "Cephalus, I'll bet most e
people won't accept what you say. They probably think old
age is easy for you because of your money and not your
character. The rich have many consolations, they say."

"You're right, Socrates, they won't. There's some truth in
what they say, too, but not as much as they think. Themisto-
cles put it well when a man from Seriphus was insulting him 330
and accused him of not being honored for himself but for
his city: 'I wouldn't be famous if I were from Seriphus; nor
you if from Athens.'[2] The same for a man who's not rich and
finds old age difficult: age isn't easy for a good man if he's
poor, nor will a bad man ever be cheerful with himself even
if he's rich."

"Cephalus," I said, "did you inherit most of your money
or make it yourself?"

"What did I make?" he said. "Well, Socrates, at making b
money I come somewhere between my grandfather and my
father. My grandfather, whom I was named after, inherited

[2]Themistocles was a famous Athenian statesman during the Persian war. Seriphus was an insignificant little island.

a fortune about the size of mine and increased it many times over. My father Lysanias made it smaller than it is now. And I'll be satisfied if I leave my sons here as much as I inherited, or a little bit more."

"The reason I asked," I said, "is that you don't seem
c overly fond of money, and that's usually true of people who haven't made it themselves. Self-made men love it twice as much as others. They're like poets fond of their own poems or fathers fond of their children—they take money seriously not only because it's useful, as everyone does, but also because it's their own creation. So they generally make tiresome company because all they can do is rave about money."

"That's true, Socrates."

d "Indeed," I said. "But tell me, Cephalus, what do you think is the greatest good you've enjoyed from being rich?"

"One that I don't think many people would believe. But, Socrates, it's a fact that when a man faces the thought that he will die, fear comes upon him and he starts thinking about things that never occurred to him before. The old tales he used to laugh at—about Hades and how a man must suffer
e there for any injustice[3] he's committed here—now begin to torment his soul with the fear that they might be true. And so, whether because of the infirmity of age or perhaps because he's closer to the other world and sees it more clearly, he's filled with apprehension and begins to reckon up his life to see if he's done anyone any injustice. And the man who finds he has committed much injustice in his life often starts from sleep in terror, like a child, and lives with evil forebod-
331 ings. But the man who knows he has committed no injustice always has sweet hope as his nurse, as Pindar says. He puts it so gracefully, Socrates, when he says that a man who has lived a just and a holy life has a

> sweet, heart-tendering nurse
> assisting his tottering age:
> Hope, who chiefly directs
> our mortal, faltering purpose.

[3]First mention of justice/injustice, the central question of *The Republic.* The quotation from Pindar below is from a lost poem.

That puts it astonishingly well. And it shows what I think is
the greatest value of wealth—not for every man, perhaps,
but for one who is decent and orderly: it is a great help in b
avoiding even unintentional cheating and lying, and it keeps
him from having to leave life in the fear of owing debts to
men or sacrifices to the gods. Of course money has many
other uses, but taking them all in all, Socrates, I'd say for a
sensible man this is its most useful purpose."

"Beautifully put, Cephalus," I said. "But speaking of jus- c
tice, do you really think it's as simple as telling the truth and
returning what you receive, or are both these acts sometimes
just and sometimes unjust? Look at it this way: if you received a weapon from a friend in his right mind and he asked for it back when he was insane, no one would say you ought to return it. A just man wouldn't do that, or tell him the whole truth either."

"You're right," he said. d

"So telling the truth and returning what you receive isn't the definition of justice."

"If we're supposed to believe Simonides[4] it is," Polemarchus interjected.

"Well," Cephalus said, "I'll leave the discussion to you. I've got to go and take care of the sacrifice."

"You mean I inherit all that's yours?" asked Polemarchus.

Cephalus laughed. "Of course," he said, and went out to the sacrifice.

"As heir to the argument," I said, "what do you think e
Simonides correctly says about justice, Polemarchus?"

"That it's just to give 'each his due.' That seems well said to me."

"It isn't easy to disbelieve the wise and godlike Simonides," I said. "Undoubtedly you know what he means, Polemarchus, but I don't. He's obviously not referring to the
example we just used—that you ought to return something
to someone not in his right mind. Yet the thing held in trust 332
is somehow his due, isn't it?"

"Yes."

"But it shouldn't be returned if he's not in his right mind?"

[4]A lyric and elegaic poet who died about the time Socrates was born (ca. 470 B.C.).

"No."

"Then Simonides must have something else in mind when he calls it just to give each his due."

"Of course he does, by Zeus. By 'due' he means you owe it to your friends to do them good rather than evil."

"I see—you don't return money due to a friend if doing
b so would harm either of you. Is that what you think Simonides means?"

"Yes."

"But you do return what's due to an enemy?"

"Of course you do," he said, "—what's due to him. And what's due, I think, is something appropriate to an enemy—something bad."

"Simonides seems to speak like a poet," I said, "—in
c riddles. He apparently intends to say that justice consists in giving each man what's appropriate to him, but he calls it his 'due.' "

"Well, why not?"

"By Zeus, Polemarchus, what do you think Simonides would say if we asked him, 'What due and appropriate thing does the craft called medicine give, and to what?' "

"Obviously that it gives food, drink, and drugs to the body."

"And cooking?"

d "Flavor to food."

"Then what due and appropriate thing does the craft called justice give, and to what?"

"If we have to follow your examples, Socrates, then it must give help and harm to friends and enemies."

"So he means justice is helping your friends and harming your enemies?"[5]

"I think so."

"Who can best help his friends and harm his enemies in regard to health and illness when they're sick?"

"A doctor."

e "And in regard to dangers at sea when they're sailing?"

"A captain."

"What about a just man? In what activity and in what regard is he the best man to help his friends and harm his enemies?"

[5]The traditional view of Greek justice.

"I'd say in fighting against them and in being an ally."

"All right, Polemarchus. But a doctor is useless when people aren't sick."

"True."

"And a captain when people aren't sailing."

"Yes."

"Therefore a just man is useless when people aren't fighting."

"I don't think so, Socrates."

"Justice is useful even in peacetime?"

"Yes, it is." 333

"So is farming, isn't it?"

"Yes."

"Because it provides us with food."

"Yes."

"And shoemaking, because it provides us with shoes."

"Of course."

"Well, what need would you say justice provides for to make it useful in peacetime?"

"For contracts, Socrates."

"By contracts do you mean partnerships, or what?"

"Exactly—partnerships."

"Who would make a better partner for playing checkers b
—a just man or a skilled player?"

"A skilled player."

"What about laying bricks, Polemarchus? Would the just man be a more useful building partner than a bricklayer?"

"No."

"Well then, in what kind of partnership would a just man be better than a bricklayer or a lyre player?—the way the lyre player would be a better music partner than the just man."

"In one involving money, I think."

"Not for using it, I'll bet. If you had to buy or sell a horse
I think a trainer would be more useful; if a ship, a shipbuilder c
or a captain. Isn't that right?"

"It seems so."

"Then for what joint use of money is the just man the most useful partner?"

"For depositing it and keeping it safe, Socrates."

"You mean when you're not using it, but letting it lie idle?"

"Yes."

d “So justice is useful for money when money is useless.”

“It looks like it.”

“And justice is jointly and individually useful for storing a pruning knife, but to use it you need viniculture, and it’s useful for storing a shield or a lyre, but to use them you need military science and music. Is that right?”

“It seems to follow.”

“Generally speaking then, justice is useless when things are in use, useful when they are not.”

“I guess so.”

e “Justice can’t be very serious, my friend, if it’s only useful for useless things. But examine this: isn’t the fighter who’s the most skillful at throwing a punch also the best at guarding against one?”

“Of course.”

“And a doctor who can guard against a disease is also the
334 best at secretly causing it, just as the best man for guarding
an army is the one who can steal a march on the enemy and
also his plans.”

“Certainly.”

“So a good guard of something is also a good thief of it.”

“So it seems.”

“Then if a just man is good at guarding money he’s also good at stealing it.”

“According to the argument, at least.”

“Therefore, it seems, the just man is exposed as a kind of
thief. You must’ve learned that from Homer, Polemarchus.
b He admires Odysseus’s grandfather Autolycus, you know,
for excelling all men ‘in thievery and bearing false witness.’[6]
According to you and Simonides and Homer then, justice
seems to be a kind of stealing; done, to be sure, to help
friends and harm enemies. Is that what you meant?”

“No, by Zeus,” he said. “I don’t know any more what I meant. But this much still seems right to me: justice is helping your friends and harming your enemies.”

c “By friends do you mean men who *seem* honest or men who *are* honest even if they don’t seem so, and the opposite for enemies?”

[6] *Odyssey* 19.395–96.

"You'd expect a man to love people he thinks honest and hate those who seem bad."

"But don't people often make mistakes and think men honest when they're not, and vice versa?"

"Yes, they do."

"So for them good men are enemies and bad men are friends."

"Yes."

"And justice for them means helping bad men and harming good ones." d

"Apparently."

"Surely good men are just and do no wrong."

"True."

"According to your argument then, it's just to injure men who do no wrong."

"Never, Socrates. The argument must be wrong."

"Maybe it's just to harm the unjust and help the just."

"That sounds better."

"Then for the many bad judges of character, Polemarchus, it turns out to be just to harm friends, who are bad, and e
to help enemies, who are good. So we'll say justice is the
exact opposite of what we said Simonides said."

"It surely does turn out that way," he said. "But let's back up; I'll bet our definition of 'friend' and 'enemy' was false."

"Which definition was that?"

"When we said a friend is one who seems good."

"How would you put it now, Polemarchus?"

"A friend is one who not only seems good, but is good.
One who seems good but isn't is only a seeming friend. And 335
so for an enemy."

"By this definition, it seems, a good man is a friend and a bad one is an enemy."

"Yes."

"And you want to add that to our earlier definition and say justice is helping a friend if he's good and harming an enemy if he's bad. Is that correct?"

"Yes. I think that's very well said, Socrates." b

"Polemarchus," I said, "does a just man ever harm anyone?"

"Certainly," he said. "He ought to harm bad enemies."

"If you harm a horse do you make him better or worse?"

"Worse."

"By impairing his excellence[7] as a dog?"

"No, as a horse."

"But if you harm a dog you impair his excellence as a dog."

"Necessarily."

c "Then shouldn't we say that if you harm a man you impair his human excellence?"

"Of course."

"Is justice a human excellence, Polemarchus?"

"That's necessary too."

"So when you harm someone you necessarily make him less just."

"It seems so."

"Can musicians use music to make people unmusical, or trainers use horsemanship to make them poor riders?"

"Impossible."

"But the just can use justice to make people unjust and,
d in a word, the good can use excellence to make people bad. Is that correct?"

"No, that's impossible too."

"I don't think cooling is a function of heat, but of the opposite."

"Yes."

"And wetting isn't a function of dryness, but of the opposite."

"Of course."

"Then harming isn't a function of the good, but of the opposite."

"So it seems."

"Is a just man good?"

"Of course."

"Then, Polemarchus, harming someone, a friend or anyone else, isn't a function of the just man, but of his opposite, the unjust man."

"That seems perfectly true to me, Socrates."

[7] *Arete,* "excellence" or "virtue" is the quality that makes any thing distinctively that which it is, or allows it to function as it should, especially that which makes a man a man. It consists of several parts (justice, courage, wisdom, temperance, etc.), which themselves are called "excellences."

"So if someone says justice is giving each man his due and e
by 'due' means help to friends and harm to enemies, he's not a very wise man. Because it isn't true—we've proved that it's never just to harm anyone."

"I agree," he said.

"And if anyone claims that Simonides or Bias or Pittacus[8] or any other of the wise and blessed dead said that, we'll make common cause and fight him tooth and nail."

"I'll be your partner in that fight, Socrates."

"Do you know who I think is really the author of the saying 336
that it's just to help friends and harm enemies?"

"Who?"

"I think it was Periander or Perdiccas or Xerxes or Ismenias of Thebes or some other rich man who thought he had great power."[9]

"You're absolutely right," he said.

"Well," I said, "we've shown that this isn't justice either. Does someone else have another suggestion?"

Several times during our discussion Thrasymachus had b
been about to jump in, but the others had prevented him because they wanted to hear how it would end. But now, during the pause after my last words, he held his peace no longer. He bunched himself up like an animal and pounced on us as if to tear us apart.

Polemarchus and I shrank back in terror. Thrasymachus roared into the group: "Socrates, what kind of asinine foolishness is this? Why do you scrape and bow to each other like c
a couple of imbeciles? If you really want to know what justice is, don't ask questions to show off and make your answerer look like an ass. You know it's easier to ask than to answer. So answer: what do *you* say justice is? And make it clear and precise: none of this nonsense about benefit, profit, gain, d
duty, or advantage. I won't tolerate those barren vapidities!"

His words staggered me and his looks filled me with terror. I think I'd have been speechless if I hadn't seen him before he saw me,[10] but I had glanced at him first when the

[8]Bias and Pittacus (both sixth century B.C.) were two of the "seven wise men" of Greece.

[9]The first three were despots, Ismenias a traitor.

[10]A reference to an old superstition that if a wolf sees you first, you become speechless.

e discussion began to annoy him, so I could reply in a trem-
bling voice: "Don't be angry with us, Thrasymachus. If Polemarchus and I are making a mistake in our investigation it
isn't intentional. If we were searching for gold, you know
we'd never let politeness and deference keep us from finding
it. So don't think that when we're searching for justice, a
thing far more precious than gold, we'd be so silly as to defer
to each other and not look for it as hard as we can. We're
looking, my friend, but I guess we're just not up to it. So we
337 really deserve pity rather than anger from clever fellows like
you."

He laughed sarcastically and said: "Oh, exquisite—the
famous Socratic irony I warned these fellows about! I knew
if someone asked you a question you'd act ignorant or do
anything to get out of answering it."

"You're a wise one, Thrasymachus. You know if you asked
b someone how much twelve is and said: 'None of this nonsense about two times six or three times four or four times
three or six times two—I won't tolerate such foolishness!' —
I think you know that no one could answer a question like
that. So suppose he asked: 'How in the world do you want
me to answer? Do I have to avoid the forbidden answers
even if one of them is true? Shall I tell you a lie, or what?'
c —What would you say to that?"

"As though that were a fair analogy!"

"Well, it could be," I said. "And even if it isn't but seemed
so to him, don't you think he'd give what he thought was a
truthful answer even if we tried to forbid it?"

"Is that what you've got up your sleeve? Are you planning
to give an answer that I disallowed?"

"I wouldn't be surprised," I said, "—if I examined it and
thought it was true."

d "What punishment would you earn if I gave a different
answer to the question of justice, better than those?"

"Why, I'll earn the punishment that ignorance should
suffer: learning from someone who knows. I guess that
makes my earning 'learning.' "

"Very funny," he said. "But you'll have to 'learn through
suffering'—by paying me a fine."

"Fine," I said. "I'll pay you when I have some money."

"You have," said Glaucon. "Go ahead, Thrasymachus,
speak for money. We'll all contribute to cover Socrates'
costs."

"Oh sure," he said, "—so he can give his usual act. He e
won't answer himself, but when someone else does he takes what he says and refutes it."

"But Thrasymachus," I said, "how can I give an answer when I don't even pretend to know it and when an eminent man has forbidden me to tell anything I think I might know?
You really ought to respond, since you claim to know. So 338
humor me and don't begrudge teaching Glaucon and the rest."

Glaucon and the others also urged him to speak.

Now it was obvious that Thrasymachus thought he had a fine answer and was eager to tell it and be held in repute. But he pretended to be eager to win his point and have me
respond. Finally, however, he gave in. "Here you see Socra- b
tes' wisdom," he said. "He refuses to teach but runs around learning from others and doesn't even pay thanks."

"It's true that I learn from others," I said, "but you lie when you call me ungrateful. I pay what I can, but since I have no money all I can give is praise. As soon as you answer, you'll see how enthusiastically I praise someone when I think he speaks well—because I'm sure you'll speak very well."

"Here's my answer then: I say justice is nothing but the c
advantage of the stronger. —Well, where's your praise? You're holding out on me."

"You'll get it as soon as I understand what you mean by 'advantage of the stronger,' Thrasymachus. I suppose you don't mean that if Polydamas the boxer is stronger than us and it's to his body's advantage to eat beef, then it's also just
and advantageous for weaklings like us to do the same." d

"You're a rat, Socrates. You twist a statement so you can ruin it."

"No I don't, Thrasymachus. Just explain more clearly what you mean."

"Well, even you must know that cities are governed either as tyrannies,[11] democracies, or aristocracies."

"Of course," I said.

"And that the government in each has the power."

"Certainly."

"Well, each government frames laws for its own advan- e
tage, a democracy for democrats, a tyranny for tyrants, and

[11]"Tyranny" and "tyrant" are used throughout in the Greek sense of "dictatorship" and "dictator."

so on. In so legislating, the rulers represent this—their own advantage—as justice for their subjects, and anyone who breaks their laws is punished as a lawbreaker and a criminal. Therefore I contend that justice is the same thing in every
339 state: the advantage of the established ruling class. And since that presumably is the stronger class, anyone with a brain can calculate that justice is the same thing everywhere —the advantage of the stronger."

"Now I know what you mean, but I still have to see if it's true. I note that you too call justice an advantage, Thrasymachus—a word you had forbidden me—though, to be sure, you added 'of the stronger.'"

b "A trivial addition!"

"It may be important," I said, "I'm not sure. But I am sure we must examine its truth. I agree that justice is a kind of advantage, but whether of the stronger or not I don't know. We'll have to examine it."

"Examine it then."

"Oh, I will. Do you also say it's just to obey the rulers?"

"Yes."

c "Are the rulers of any city infallible or can they make mistakes?"

"Of course they make mistakes."

"So in attempting to frame laws they frame some properly, but others improperly."

"I imagine."

"And 'properly' means to their own advantage, 'improperly' to their disadvantage?"

"Yes."

"But their subjects must do whatever they legislate, and that is justice."

"What else?"

d "According to your argument then, it's just to act not only to the stronger's advantage, but also the opposite, to his disadvantage."

"What are you saying?"

"The same thing as you, I believe. But let's examine this more closely. Didn't you agree that in prescribing what their subjects must do the rulers sometimes mistake their own best interests, and that it's just for the ruled to do whatever their rulers prescribe?"

"I think I did."

"Then you'd also better think you agreed that it's just to e
act to the disadvantage of the stronger. When rulers inadvertently enjoin their subjects to do something evil to them,
and if it's just to do whatever the rulers prescribe—then,
wise Thrasymachus, justice necessarily turns out to be the
opposite of your definition."

"By Zeus, so it does," Polemarchus said. "It's as plain as 340
day."

"Oh sure," Clitophon rejoined, "—on *your* testimony."

"What need is there of testimony?" asked Polemarchus.
"Thrasymachus himself admits that rulers sometimes prescribe evil to themselves, and that it's just to do whatever
they say."

"Thrasymachus said justice consists in obeying the dictates of the rulers, Polemarchus."

"But he also called it the advantage of the stronger, Clitophon. Then he admitted that the stronger sometimes com- b
mand the weaker—their subjects—to do something
disadvantageous to them. From this it follows that justice is
as much the disadvantage as the advantage of the stronger."

"By advantage," said Clitophon, "he meant whatever the
stronger *thinks* is to his advantage. This is what the weaker
must do, and this is what he posited as justice."

"Well," said Polemarchus, "that's not what he said."

"It doesn't make any difference, Polemarchus," I said. "If c
that's what Thrasymachus says now, then that's how we'll
take it. So, Thrasymachus, did you mean justice is whatever
the stronger *thinks* is to his advantage, whether it really is or
not? Is that how we should take it?"

"No. Do you think I'd call a man stronger when he's
making a mistake?"

"I thought you did when you said rulers are fallible."

"You're a damned shyster, Socrates. Would you call a d
man a doctor precisely because he bungles a cure? does a
mistake in his figures make a man an accountant? No. I
believe we use words loosely when we say a doctor or an
accountant or a teacher makes a mistake, because insofar as
they are what we call them they never make mistakes. So e
strictly speaking—since you're such a stickler for words—no
craftsman ever makes a mistake. He makes a mistake when
his knowledge slips, and at that moment he's no longer a
craftsman. No craftsman or wise man or ruler ever errs while

he's a ruler, though everyone says it was the doctor or the ruler who made the mistake. You may assume that this was how I spoke just now. Strictly speaking, however, no ruler,
341 insofar as he is a ruler, ever errs, and therefore he never mistakes his own self-interest in framing laws which his subjects must obey. So I still say what I said at the beginning: justice is doing what's advantageous to the stronger."

"So, Thrasymachus," I said, "I seem like a shyster to you?"

"You sure do," he said.

"And you think I deliberately tried to dupe you by asking you trick questions?"

"I know you did," he said. "But it won't do you any good
b because you'll never crush me in open debate or dupe me with some sneaky, underhanded trick."

"I wouldn't even try, Thrasymachus. But we can avoid misunderstandings like this if you'll tell me how we should take this 'ruler' and this 'stronger' to whose advantage it will be just for the weaker to act—loosely, or in the strict sense you just said?"

"I mean ruler in the strictest sense of the word. So swindle away and dupe that if you can—I won't ask for mercy!"

c "Do you think I'm insane enough to beard a lion or try to swindle a Thrasymachus?"

"You just tried, bungler that you are."

"Enough of these pleasantries," I said. "Tell me, Thrasymachus, is a doctor in your strict sense a moneymaker or a healer of the sick?—I mean a real doctor."

"A healer of the sick."

"What about a captain? is he properly a sailor or a ruler of sailors?"

"A ruler of sailors."

d "That he sails on a ship is not a real consideration. He isn't called a captain because he sails, but because of his skill and his command of sailors."

"True."

"Do the patient and the sailor each have something advantageous for them?"

"Of course."

"And the appropriate skill naturally exists to search out and provide this advantage for each?"

"That's right."

"Does a skill seek any advantage beyond its own perfection?"

"What does that mean?" e

"This: if you asked me whether the body is self-sufficient or has needs, I'd say it certainly has needs. That's why medicine has been invented, because the body is defective and dependent. The skill was developed to provide what's advantageous for the body. Does that strike you as a proper answer?"

"Yes."

"Well, is medicine itself defective? Does it or any other 342
skill need some further excellence—the way eyes and ears
need sight and hearing, so that they require skills over them
to consider and provide for their advantage in perception?
Is there some lack in the skill itself? Does each need another
to consider its advantage, and does this overseeing skill need
another which needs another, and so on to infinity? Or does
each consider its own advantage? But perhaps a skill needs b
neither itself nor another to consider its advantage against
its own lack because it has no lack or flaw. As long as each
skill retains its strict integrity, it fittingly seeks no advantage
but that of its subject and remains itself untouched, disinterested, and pure. Consider that strictly and tell me if it's true."

"It seems true," he said.

"So medicine considers the advantage not of medicine but c
of the body."

"Yes."

"And horsemanship not of horsemanship but of horses—no skill considers its own advantage, since it has no needs, but the advantage of its subject."

"That seems true."

"But a skill rules its subject and so is the stronger."

He very reluctantly agreed, and I said: "Then no knowledge considers or prescribes for the advantage of the
stronger, but for that of the weaker, which it rules." d

He finally admitted that too, though not without a struggle. When I got his admission, I continued: "Doesn't it follow then that no doctor in his capacity as doctor considers or prescribes for his own advantage, but for the advantage of his patients?—We agreed that a doctor in the strict sense isn't a moneymaker but a ruler of bodies, didn't we?"

He admitted it.

"And that, strictly speaking, a captain isn't a sailor but a
e ruler of sailors, and so doesn't consider and prescribe for his
own advantage but for that of the sailors he rules?"

He reluctantly admitted that too.

"Therefore, Thrasymachus," I said, "no ruler of any kind, insofar as he is a ruler, considers and prescribes for his own advantage, but for that of the ruled, the subject of his skill. That's all he looks to: everything he says and does is done to promote the fitting advantage of this subject."

343 When we had reached this point in the argument and
everyone could see that the definition of justice had been reversed, Thrasymachus asked: "Socrates, do you have a nursemaid?"

"Why do you ask a question like that instead of answering mine?"

"Because she lets you run around driveling and doesn't wipe your runny nose: you can't even tell her the difference between a shepherd and a sheep."

"What is that supposed to mean?"

b "Just that you think a shepherd looks to the good of the
sheep when he fattens them, instead of to the good of the
owner and himself. It's the same in every state, though you
seem unaware of it: the intentions of a true ruler toward his
subjects are the same as a shepherd's toward his sheep, and
he never considers anything night or day except how to
c fleece them. Some expert! Why, you don't even know that
justice is really someone else's good—the advantage of the
ruler—and the personal injury of his subjects who serve and
obey him. Injustice is the opposite and rules men who are
truly good natured[12] and just, because in doing what's advantageous to their ruler, the stronger, their service makes
him happy and them wretched.

d "Consider this, my good-natured friend: how the unjust
man gets the better of the just man in every way. When the
two of them form a partnership and then dissolve it, you'll
always find the unjust man getting the better of the just. And
when the state makes an assessment the unjust man pays
much less on the same property, and when there's a refund

[12] A euphemism for "simple minded." Cf. d below; 348c, p.23 and 400e, p.70.

he gets more. In public office, even assuming there's no e
other penalty, the just man's private affairs will fall into
shambles through neglect (of course he's too honest to help
himself from public funds) and his friends and relatives will
hate him for refusing to grant them unjust favors. The exact
opposite happens to the unjust man. I mean the man I just
referred to: one capable of satisfying his greed in great 344
things. He's the one to consider if you want to judge how
much greater the personal advantage of injustice is. You'll
most easily learn by considering that perfect form of injustice which brings bliss to its possessor but abject misery to
its victims and to those unwilling to do wrong. Its name is
tyranny. Tyranny doesn't steal other people's property by
force and by stealth a little bit at a time; it takes everything
—public and private, sacred and profane—all at once. A b
person caught committing individual crimes earns punishment and disgrace, and they call him temple robber, slaver,
housebreaker, embezzler, or thief after his partial offenses;
but when a man steals not only the citizens' property, but
also the citizens themselves and makes them his slaves, then
instead of those disgraceful names he is called blessed and
happy, not only by his countrymen but by all who hear that c
he has committed total injustice. Men condemn injustice
through fear of suffering it, not through fear of committing
it. So, Socrates, injustice—if carried far enough—is
stronger, freer, and more despotic than justice, and what I
said at the start is still true: justice is the advantage of the
stronger, and injustice profits and advantages oneself."

With that Thrasymachus intended to leave, like a bathboy d
who had dumped a bucket of words on our heads. Not that
the others would let him go—they demanded he stay and
explain himself, and I was especially insistent: "Thrasymachus, do you think you can throw out an argument like that
and then run off before you've taught us or learned yourself
whether it's true or not? Do you think it's a trivial thing to e
try to define a whole way of life that could be the most
profitable life for us all?"

"So that's what I think!"

"You seem to," I said. "Or else you don't care about us
—whether our lives will be better or worse because of ignorance of what you claim to know. Come on, Thrasymachus,
show us your knowledge—it won't be a bad investment to do 345

a good turn to so many people. I'll tell you what I think: I'm
unconvinced. I don't believe that injustice—even if
unimpeded and allowed to do whatever it wants—is more
profitable than justice. Let's assume that there is a perfectly
unjust man, capable of getting away with anything by
fighting or stealth: he still doesn't persuade me that injustice
pays better than justice. And I may not be the only one here
b who feels that way. So be a good fellow and persuade us
we're wrong to value justice higher than injustice, blissful
Thrasymachus."

"How am I supposed to do that? If what I just said didn't
convince you, what else can I do? Shall I spoonfeed my
explanation into your souls?"

"Please, Thrasymachus, not you. As a start though, you
might be consistent, or if you change something, do it
openly and don't try to deceive us. If you look back a little
c you'll see that after defining a doctor you didn't stick to your
strict method in defining a shepherd. You think that in his
capacity as shepherd he fattens sheep not for their own good
but for a banquet, like a guest getting ready for dinner, or
d to sell them, like a businessman instead of a shepherd. But
surely shepherding cares for nothing except providing the
best for what it's in charge of, since insofar as the skill itself
is perfect its own best interests have already been sufficiently
provided for. In the same way, I thought we were just now
forced to agree that in itself all rule, in politics or private life,
e considers what's best for its subject, that which it rules and
serves. But tell me, do you think rulers of cities—I mean true
rulers—rule freely?"

"My god," he said, "I know they do."

"But haven't you noticed that no one rules freely in any
of the other skills? They demand pay, as though they expected all the benefit of their rule to go to their subjects
346 rather than to themselves. Now tell me this, Thrasymachus:
don't we normally say that one skill differs from another in
having a different function? Answer what you really believe,
so we can finish this up."

"Yes, that's how they differ."

"And each skill provides a distinct benefit rather than a common one—medicine health, navigation safety at sea, and so on."

"Certainly."

"And wage-earning provides wages; that's its function. If b
you want strict definitions, as you said, then you can hardly call medicine and navigation the same. Even if sailing should improve a navigator's health, we still can't call navigation medicine."

"No."

"Or wage-earning medicine, if someone stays healthy by earning a living."

"No."

"Then if a man earns his living by curing the sick, that
doesn't make medicine wage-earning." c

"No."

"Didn't we agree that each skill provides a distinct benefit?"

"If you say so."

"Then if all craftsmen receive the same benefit from their different skills, this benefit must come from some one thing common to all skills."

"Presumably."

"So we can say that in benefitting themselves by earning a living, craftsmen practice the skill of wage-earning."

He reluctantly agreed.

"If we examine it strictly then," I said, "a craftsman d
doesn't get the benefit of wages from his skill, but from the associated skill of wage-earning. Medicine provides health and wage-earning wages, carpentry accompanied by wage-earning provides homes and salaries, and so on. Each skill does its own work and benefits what it's in charge of. If there were no wages, would a craftsman get any benefit from his skill?"

"Apparently not," he said.

"But he still *provides* a benefit even if he works for noth- e
ing?"

"I think so."

"Then, Thrasymachus, it should be clear that no skill—
not even a ruler's—benefits itself. It's just as we've been
saying all along: it benefits and provides for its subject, by
considering the advantage of it—of the weaker, not of the
stronger. That, my friend, is why I said no one rules freely
or undertakes to straighten out somebody else's troubles for
free. He demands payment, because a man who uses his skill 347
well never acts or prescribes for his own good but—as long
as he prescribes by his skill—for the good of the subject.

Hence, it seems, you must pay a man to make him willing to rule: either money or honor, or a penalty if he declines."

"Wait a minute, Socrates," said Glaucon. "I recognize two of your payments, but I don't understand what you mean by a penalty or how you can call it a payment."

"Then," I said, "you don't understand the payment that
b makes the best men rule, when they do. But you do understand that love of money and honor are both condemned for
being the unworthy motives they actually are."

"Yes."

"Therefore, Glaucon, good men don't rule for money or
honor. Not for money, because if they make it openly in
office they're called hirelings; if secretly, crooks. Not for
honor, because they're not ambitious. So there has to be
c some necessity or penalty to force them to do it. I imagine
that's why accepting power voluntarily instead of waiting for
it to be thrust on you is held to be shameful. And the greatest
penalty for one who declines is to be ruled by an inferior.
It's fear of this, I think, that makes decent men rule when
they do, and they accept rule not as a good to be enjoyed
d but as a necessity to be endured because they have no one
better or as good to hand it over to. If there were a city of
good men, I suspect nonrule would be as hotly contested as
rule is now, and it would be manifest that a true ruler naturally considers not his own advantage but that of the ruled.
Knowing that, who would choose to have the trouble of
helping others when he could benefit from somebody else?
No, I can't agree with Thrasymachus that justice is the ad-
e vantage of the stronger. But let's leave that for now. Far
more serious, I think, is his other contention, that the unjust
life is superior to the just. How do you vote, Glaucon? Which
view seems truer?"

"I think the just life is more profitable, Socrates."

348 "Did you hear the good things Thrasymachus just attributed to the unjust life?"

"Yes, but I'm not convinced."

"Would you like to find a way to convince him that he's wrong?"

"I certainly would."

"Well," I said, "if the advocates give speeches and take
b turns at listing the goods on each side, we'll need judges to
count them and decide the case. But if we keep on as we

have, examining and getting each other's agreement, then we can be both advocates and judges at the same time. How should we do it?"

"The way we have been," said Glaucon.

"All right," I said, "let's take it from the beginning, Thrasymachus. You say perfect injustice is more profitable
than perfect justice." c

"Yes, and I've explained why."

"I suppose you call one an excellence and the other an evil?"

"Of course."

"Justice an excellence and injustice an evil?"

"When I say injustice pays and justice doesn't? Don't be silly."

"What then?"

"The other way around."

"Justice is an evil?"

"No, a noble good nature."

"Then injustice is bad nature?" d

"No, more like good judgment."

"So you think that unjust men are sensible and good?"

"Yes, if they're capable of perfect injustice and can get whole countries and peoples under their control. You seem to think I mean purse snatchers or something. Crimes like that are nothing compared to true injustice, though even snatching purses pays if you don't get caught."

"I understand that," I said. "What surprises me is that you e
put injustice with excellence and wisdom, and justice with their opposites."

"Well, I do."

"That's a tougher one, my friend. It's hard to know what to say. If you conceded, as some do, that injustice is a shameful evil even though it pays, one could argue from traditional views. But since you had the nerve to put it with excellence and wisdom, I suppose you're going to call it strong and
beautiful and give it all the attributes we used to give to 349
justice."

"You've got the right idea, friend."

"Well, I can't give up," I said. "I have to examine this as long as I think you're saying what you really believe. And I don't think you're joking now, Thrasymachus. This seems to be your actual opinion about the truth."

"Refute the argument, not me. What difference does it make to you what I believe?"

b "None. So tell me if you think one just man would want
to do better than another just man."[13]

"Of course not. If he did, he wouldn't be the urbane, good-natured simpleton that he is."

"Better than a just act, then?"

"No."

"Will he expect to get the better of an unjust man and consider it just to do so?"

"He might, but he won't succeed."

"That's not my question. I want to know whether a just
c man will expect to do better than an unjust man but not
better than another just man."

"Yes, he will."

"What about an unjust man? Will *he* expect to get the better of a just man and a just act?"

"Obviously. He'll expect to do better than everyone and everything."

"Then he'll try to get the better of unjust men and unjust acts and compete to get the most of everything for himself."

"That's correct."

"Let's sum up then: A just man tries to get the better of
his unlike but not of his like; an unjust man tries to get the
d better of both."

"Excellently put, Socrates."

"And the unjust man is sensible and good, the just man isn't."

"Exactly."

"So the unjust man is like the sensible and the good, but the just man isn't."

"Obviously a man must be like what he is and unlike what he isn't."

"Good. Then each *is* what he's like."

"Well, obviously."

[13]"Do better than" or "get the better of" has two senses in Greek: a) get more than (one's share), and so be better off; b) outdo, or do more than. The idea is that overdoing an excellence is itself an evil.

"All right, Thrasymachus. You know there are musicians and laymen. Which is sensible and which is senseless?"[14] e

"The musician presumably is sensible, the layman is senseless."

"And he's good at things about which he is sensible, bad at things about which he is senseless?"

"Yes."

"The same for a doctor?"

"Yes."

"Now when a musician tunes a lyre, do you think he wants to get the better of other musicians and expects to outdo them in tightening and loosening the strings?"

"No, [he tries to get the right pitch]."[15]

"But he expects to do better than a layman?"

"Necessarily."

"When a doctor prescribes a diet does he want to do 350
better than other doctors and the science of medicine?"

"No, [he tries to get the right diet]."

"But he does expect to do better than a layman?"

"Yes."

"Does this seem to be true of all knowledge and ignorance then?—an expert doesn't want to do better in speaking or practice than other experts like himself, but tries to get the same results as they do, whereas a layman tries to get the better of both the ignorant and those who know." b

"That seems necessarily true."

"Isn't one who knows wise?"[16]

"Yes."

"And if he's wise he's also good?"

"Yes."

[14]I.e. "which is sensible *about the art?*" The argument is intentionally fallacious. In Greek, words like good, sensible, and wise imply an object: "sensible *about,* wise *in,* good *at* something." Thrasymachus is led to take them in this limited sense ("a musician is sensible *about* and good *at music*"), and Socrates takes them in their absolute sense ("a musician is sensible and good").

[15]Bracketed words are translator's additions, intended to make the argument clearer.

[16]The natural implication of this is "wise *in his field.*" So in the next question, "good *at it.*"

"So a good, wise man doesn't want to do better than his like, but better than his unlike and opposite."

"So it seems."

"But a bad, ignorant man wants to do better than both."

"Apparently."

"Didn't you say that an unjust man wants to do better than both his like and his unlike, Thrasymachus?"

"I did," he said.

c "But a just man only wants to do better than his unlike."

"Yes."

"So a just man is like the wise and the good, an unjust man like the ignorant and bad."

"I guess so."

"Didn't we agree that each *is* what he's like?"

"Yes."

"Therefore the just man turns out to be wise and good, the unjust man ignorant and bad."

Thrasymachus didn't make these admissions easily, as I've
d presented it. They had to be dragged from him with incredible struggle and sweat (since it's summer). And then I saw
something I'd never seen before: Thrasymachus blushing.

After he'd admitted that justice is excellence and wisdom, and injustice ignorance and evil, I continued: "Well, that's been established. But we also said injustice was strong. Do you remember, Thrasymachus?"

"Yes," he said, "but I'm not satisfied with your argument.
I've got a reply to it too, but if I give it I know you'll accuse
e me of making a speech. So either let me speak as long as I
want, or if you prefer, keep asking questions and I'll nod my
head and say 'oh' and 'ah' the way we do when old women
tell stories."

"Don't say anything against your opinion, Thrasymachus."

"Whatever you say. If you don't want me to make a speech, I won't. Will there be anything else?"

"No, that'll be fine. I'll ask and you answer."

"Go ahead."

"Then I'll ask the same question I asked before so we can
351 examine the argument in an orderly way: what sort of a thing
is justice compared with injustice? You said injustice is
stronger and more effective than justice. But if justice is
excellence and wisdom, and injustice is ignorance and evil,

I think it'll be easy to show that justice is stronger. Anyone
could see that. But that's too simple, Thrasymachus. Let's
look at it this way: could there be an unjust city that would b
try to enslave other cities and perhaps even succeed in getting many of them under its control?"

"What else?" he said. "That's exactly what a good, perfectly unjust city would do."

"Yes," I said, "I understand that that was your argument.
But can one state get stronger than another without justice,
or must it necessarily have justice to have this power?"

"If it's as you say—that justice is wisdom—then it would c
need justice. If it's as I say, it would need only injustice."

"I'm very impressed, Thrasymachus. You're answering
beautifully and not just wagging your head."

"Anything to please," he said.

"Good boy. Now you can please me by telling me whether
a state or an army or a band of cutthroats for that matter can
carry out a joint criminal act if its members commit crimes
against one another."

"Certainly not." d

"They have a better chance if they don't?"

"Of course."

"I suppose injustice breeds conflict, hatred, and strife,
Thrasymachus, while justice brings harmony and friendship."

"As you say. I won't disagree with you."

"Very good, my friend. Then if the function of injustice
is to cause hatred wherever it appears, won't it produce strife
in any group of free men or slaves and make them unable
to act in common?" e

"Of course."

"What about in a group of two? Won't it cause hatred and
disagreement and make them enemies of each other and of
the just?"

"Yes."

"Will it lose its potency if found in only one?"

"Let it rage if you like."

"So in a city or an army or wherever it appears," I said,
"the function of injustice seems to be this: It makes joint 352
action impossible because of disagreement and strife, and it
makes the group an enemy of itself and of its opponents and
of the just. Isn't that right?"

"Of course."

"And I imagine it stays true to its nature in an individual. It makes him unable to act because of strife and internal discord, and it also makes him an enemy both of himself and of the just. Is that so?"

"Indeed."

"Are the gods just too, my friend?"

"If you wish."

b "Then the unjust man will also be an enemy of the gods,
Thrasymachus, and the just man a friend."

"I won't risk the enmity of these others by contradicting you," he said, "so enjoy your feast of words."

"Then serve me my dessert by answering as you have," I
said. "We've shown that just men are better, wiser, and more
capable of acting, and that unjust men can't work together
c at all—when we call them 'partners in crime' we're not telling the literal truth. If they were completely unjust they
wouldn't keep their hands off each other. They clearly have
some justice in them that prevents them from wronging each
other along with their victims and enables them to do what
they do. They rush into crime as demivillains, since an absolute scoundrel, perfectly unjust, would also be perfectly un-
d able to act. I know that this and not your first proposition
is true. But we still have another proposition to examine,
that just men are happier and live better lives. I think that's
been pretty well proved already, but let's examine it more
closely. This is no haphazard subject, you know: it concerns
the way we ought to live."

"Examine it then."

"Oh, I will. Would you say a horse has a function?"

e "Yes."

"Would you define the function of it or of anything else as what you can do best or only with it?"

"I don't understand."

"Well, can you see with anything but your eyes or hear with anything but your ears?"

"No."

"Then can't we justly call seeing and hearing their functions?"

"Of course."

353 "What about pruning vines? Can't you use a paring knife,
a butcher knife, or anything sharp?"

"Why not?"

"But nothing will work as well as a pruning knife designed for the job."

"No."

"So we can define pruning as its function."

"Yes."

"Now I think you see what I mean: isn't the function of a thing that which can be done either only by it or better by it than by anything else?"

"Yes, now I understand you," he said, "and I think that's what the function of anything is." b

"Well," I said, "do you think everything that's assigned a function also has an excellence? Can we run through the same list and say that eyes and ears and everything else have an excellence as well as a function?"

"We can."

"Now look: will eyes or ears or anything else ever perform their functions well if they lack their proper excellence and c
have the corresponding evil?"

"How could they? I presume you mean blindness and deafness in place of sight and hearing."

"Whatever it may be—I'm not interested in the names right now, but only in whether the function is performed well with the proper excellence and badly with the evil."

"Yes," he said, "that much is true."

"Therefore ears will perform their own function badly if deprived of their own excellence."

"Of course."

"Does the same reasoning apply to all the other things?" d

"I think so."

"Now examine this," I said: "'The soul has a function that no other existing thing can perform.' Can we justly attribute things like management, deliberation, and rule to anything else and call them proper to it?"

"No."

"What about life?"

"That's the soul's most important function."

"Do we say the soul also has an excellence?"

"Yes."

"Will it ever perform its own functions well if deprived of e
its proper excellence? Or is that impossible, Thrasymachus?"

"That's impossible."

"So a person with a bad soul will necessarily rule and manage badly; one with a good soul will do well[17] in all of these things."

"Necessarily."

"Didn't we agree that justice is an excellence of the soul and injustice an evil?"[18]

"Yes."

"Therefore a just soul and a just man will live well, an unjust one will live badly."

"So it appears from your argument."

354 "Surely," I said, "a man who lives well is blessed and happy, and one who does not is miserable."

"Surely," he said.

"Then the just man is happy and the unjust man is miserable."

"As you say."

"Surely it pays to be happy, not to be miserable."

"Surely."

"Then, happy Thrasymachus, injustice is never more profitable than justice."

"Well, Socrates," he said, "I hope you've dined well on this festival of Bendis."[19]

"The service was excellent after you calmed down and quit being angry, Thrasymachus. But I really didn't dine
b very well. It wasn't your fault but mine. I acted like a glutton who snatches food from every platter and is so busy tasting new things he doesn't have time to enjoy what he already has. Before I found what we were searching for first—what justice is—I dropped it and rushed to examine something about it: whether it's ignorance and evil or excellence and wisdom. Then another question turned up—whether injustice is more profitable than justice—and I couldn't resist charging into that one too. The result of our discussion is
c that I don't know a thing. As long as I don't know what

[17]"Do well" has two senses in Greek: "do something well," and "fare well." Socrates picks up the second for his conclusion below, "live well."

[18]Thrasymachus agreed in 350d (p. 26) that justice was an excellence, though not specifically an excellence "of the soul."

[19]Cf. the opening sentence.

justice is," I said, "I can hardly know whether it's an excellence or not and whether its possessor will be happy or unhappy."

Book 2

I thought that was the end of our talk, but it seems it was 357
only the prelude. Glaucon, who is always bold in everything,
wouldn't accept Thrasymachus's surrender. "Socrates," he
said, "do you want to *seem* like you've persuaded us that it's
in every way better to be just than unjust, or do you really b
want to persuade us?"

"Really," I said, "—if it's up to me."

"Well, you aren't succeeding," he said. "Look, does there seem to you to be a kind of good that we choose to have for its own sake and not for its consequences—joy, for instance, and harmless pleasures that bring nothing beyond their immediate enjoyment?"

"Yes, Glaucon, it seems so to me."

"And a kind we cherish both for itself and for its conse- c
quences—like thinking, seeing, and health?"

"Yes," I said.

"Do you see a third form of good that includes exercise,
being cured, and earning a living? We call these things arduous but beneficial, and we choose to have them not for
themselves but only for their consequences—for the profit d
and other benefits they bring."

"Yes," I said, "but what is this all leading up to?"

"In which class do you place justice?"

"In the most beautiful one, I think—among the things a 358
man must cherish both for themselves and for their consequences if he's going to be truly happy."

"That's not what most people think; they put it with the arduous things that ought to be shunned for themselves but pursued for profit and a reputation based on appearance."

"I know. Thrasymachus has been disparaging justice as being like that for some time now, Glaucon, while extolling injustice. But I seem to be a slow learner."

b "Listen," he said, "it seems to me that Thrasymachus was
tamed too easily. It was like charming a snake. But the presentation wasn't up to my expectations on either side: I want
to hear what justice and injustice each *are* and what power
each of them has by itself when in the soul. Leave profits and
consequences out of it. So if it seems all right to you, here's
c what I'll do: I'll revive Thrasymachus's argument and first
present the popular view of the nature and origin of justice.
Then I'll maintain that all who practice it do so unwillingly,
not as a good but as a necessity. Finally, I'll argue that this
attitude is reasonable, because people actually believe the
unjust life is the better. That's not how it seems to me,
Socrates; it's an opinion that Thrasymachus and hordes of
others have drummed into me until I'm thoroughly baffled.
But I've never heard the argument for the superiority of
d justice presented as I'd like—I mean justice extolled for its
own sake—and I think I can hear it from you. So I'll praise
the unjust life as forcefully as I can and in the process show
you how I want you to do the opposite. Do you approve of
my plan?"

"Oh yes, Glaucon. That's a topic an intelligent man can
enjoy discussing again and again."

e "Fine," he said. "I'll begin with my first subject then: the
nature and origin of justice.

"People say that injustice is by nature good to inflict but
evil to suffer. Men taste both of its sides and learn that the
evil of suffering it exceeds the good of inflicting it. Those
unable to flee the one and take the other therefore decide
359 it pays to make a pact neither to commit nor to suffer injustice. It was here that men began to make laws and covenants,
and to call whatever the laws decreed 'legal' and 'just.' This,
they say, is both the origin and the essence of justice, a thing
midway between the best condition—committing injustice
without being punished—and the worst—suffering injustice
without getting revenge. Justice is therefore a compromise;
it isn't cherished as a good, but honored out of inability to
b do wrong. A real 'man,' capable of injustice, would never
make a pact with anyone. He'd be insane if he did. That,
Socrates, is the popular view of the nature of justice and of
the conditions under which it develops.[1]

[1] The first presentation in literature of the "social contract" theory of justice.

"That men practice justice unwillingly out of inability to
do wrong may be seen by considering a hypothetical situation: Give two men, one just and the other unjust, the oppor- c
tunity to do anything they want and then observe where
their desires take them. We'll catch the just man ending up
in the same place as the unjust. This is because human
nature always wants more, and pursues that as a natural
good. But nature has been diverted by convention and
forced to honor equality.

"Our two men would have the opportunity I mentioned
if we gave them the power once given to the ancestor of
Gyges, the famous king of Lydia. They say he was once a d
shepherd serving the man who was then king. One day a
great earthquake opened a chasm in the place where he was
pasturing sheep. Astonished, he climbed down into the
fissure and saw, among other fabulous things, a hollow
bronze horse with windows in it. He peeped inside and saw
the body of a man, seemingly larger than life and wearing
only a golden ring. He took the ring and left. Later he wore e
it to the monthly meeting of shepherds, at which they made
their reports to the king. As he was sitting there with the
others he happened to turn the setting of the ring toward
him. Suddenly he became invisible, and the others began to 360
speak of him as though he were gone. Amazed, he turned the
setting away from him again and reappeared. After further
experiments had convinced him that the ring indeed had the
power to make him visible and invisible at will, he contrived
to become a messenger to the king. He seduced the queen, b
with her help murdered the king, and usurped the throne of
Lydia.

"Now if there were two such rings and we gave one to our
just man and one to the unjust, no one, they say, would have
the iron will to restrain himself when he could with impunity
take what he liked from the market, slip into houses and
sleep with anyone he wanted or kill whomever he wished, c
free people from jail, and like a god among mortals, do
whatever he pleased. In that situation there'd be no difference between our two men; both would act alike. So a person may use this as evidence that no one is willingly just,
since whenever a man thinks he can get away with injustice
he does it. Justice is practiced only under compulsion, as
someone else's good—not our own. Everyone really believes that injustice pays better than justice; rightly, accord- d

ing to this argument. Because if a man had the power to do
wrong and yet refused to touch other people's property,
discerning men would consider him a contemptible dolt,
though they'd openly praise him and deceive one another
for fear of being harmed.

e "We'll be able to make a proper judgment on these two
ways of life only if we contrast the perfectly just man with the
perfectly unjust. Make each a perfect specimen of his kind.
The unjust man should act like a skilled craftsman. An accomplished doctor or navigator distinguishes between
what's possible and impossible in his field and attempts the
361 one but ignores the other. And if he botches something he
knows how to straighten it out. So with our accomplished
criminal: he should discriminate nicely and get away with his
crimes. If caught he's a bungler. And injustice's highest perfection is to *seem* just without *being* so. Deprive our perfectly
unjust man of nothing, therefore, but lend him utter perfection: Let him contrive the greatest reputation for justice
b while committing the most heinous crimes, and if he should
bungle something, grant him the ability to straighten it out;
give him the persuasion to sway juries when informers denounce him, and the wealth, influence, courage, and vigor
to use force when force must be used.

"Alongside this paragon of perfidy let us place our perfectly just man—a man noble and simple, desiring, in Aeschylus's words, 'not to *seem,* but to *be* good.'[2] All right, let's
take away seeming. A reputation for justice will bring him
c honor and rewards and make it uncertain whether he practices justice for its own sake or for the rewards. So strip him
of everything but justice and make him the exact opposite
of our other specimen. Let him win the worst reputation for
injustice while leading the justest of lives, to test him and see
if his justice holds up against ill repute and its evil effects.
And let him persevere until death, seeming unjust while
d being just, so we may examine the extremes of justice and
injustice and decide which makes the happier life."

"Uncanny, Glaucon!" I cried. "You've scoured these two
types for our judgment as though they were bronzes."

"I do my best, Socrates. Now with these two men before
e us it shouldn't be hard to tell what sort of life awaits each.

[2] *Seven against Thebes* 592.

And if it sounds uncouth, Socrates, don't blame me, but the champions of injustice. They say our just man will be whipped, racked, chained, and after having his eyes burnt out and suffering every torment, be run up on a stake and 362
impaled, and so learn that one ought 'not to *be*, but to *seem* just.' Aeschylus's words rightly apply to the unjust man who, since he doesn't live by opinion but pursues what clings to the truth, desires 'not to *seem*, but to *be un*just:'

> out of the deep furrow of his mind
> reaping a crop of faultless designs.[3] b

Because he *seems* just, they say he'll rule in his city, marry into the family of his choice, form partnerships with anyone he wants, match his daughters with whomever he wishes, and from his lack of aversion to committing injustice reap advantage and gain. He'll get the better of his enemies by defeating them in lawsuits, public and private, and so grow rich and able to help his friends and harm his enemies. With c
ostentatious sacrifices, dedications, and gifts, he'll serve the gods and the men of his choosing far better than the just man, and one can reasonably expect he'll be more loved by the gods. Thus, Socrates, both gods and men, they say, see to it that the unjust man enjoys a better life than the just."

I was about to reply to Glaucon's speech when his brother d
Adeimantus said: "You don't think that's the whole story, do you?"

"Isn't it?" I asked.

"He didn't even mention the main point."

"Well, 'brother with brother,' they say, so help yours if he left anything out. What he said, though, was enough to pin down and disable this defender of justice."

"Nonsense, Socrates. Listen to this. In order to clarify e
what Glaucon, I think, wants to say, we should go through the opposite arguments that praise justice and denounce injustice. Fathers and others in charge of someone give them advice and exhort them to justice. They recommend it not 363
for itself but for the reputation it brings, so you'll *seem* just and get the offices and marriages and everything Glaucon just said, which come to a just man from his good reputation. The emphasis is all on the rewards of appearance and a good

[3]Aeschylus, *Seven against Thebes* 593–94.

reputation. When they come to the rewards of a good repute
with the gods they really wax eloquent, expounding the
blessings the gods bestow on the pious. They sound like our
noble Hesiod and Homer. Hesiod says:

> b The oaks of the just man the gods make to bear
> acorns on top and bees in the middle. His sheep
> they make heavy with wool.[4]

And so on. Homer says much the same:

> Gifts to a good king who upholds just laws:
> the earth yields him harvests of barley and wheat,
> c his trees teem with fruit, his ewes drop him lambs,
> and the seas grant abundance of fishes.

Musaeus[5] and his son make the gods bestow even headier
gifts on the just. They transport them to Hades, put
wreathes on their heads, and set them down to a party where
d they spend all eternity drunk on wine, as though virtue's
highest reward were to be perpetually drunk. Others extend
the divine rewards even further, saying that the descendants
of pious, trustworthy men will continue to flourish. So much
for their praise of justice. The unjust and impious are buried
in mud or forced to carry water in sieves after death, and
while still alive they get bad reputations and the kind of
e punishments that Glaucon attributed to just men who seem
bad. And that's all they have to say. So much for the praise
and blame on each side.

"Now consider another form of argument, Socrates, given
364 by laymen and poets alike. With one voice they celebrate
temperance and justice as good but tiresome things. Injustice and intemperance, they say, are sweet and easy to reach,
shameful only by opinion and law. For the most part, they
say, injustice pays better than justice; they blithely acclaim
b rich and powerful rascals, and though they admit they are
better, despise men who are weak and poor. Their most
astonishing arguments have to do with excellence and the
gods. The gods, they say, often grant misfortune and evil

[4] *Works and Days* 233–34. The following quotation is from *Odyssey* 19.109–113.

[5] A legendary poet and mystic.

lives to good men while scoundrels wallow in bliss. Mendicant priests and soothsayers come to the doors of the rich and dupe them with their 'divine powers,' which they claim to unleash by incantations and rites. They offer to expiate
crimes in the family, new or inherited, with revels and fun, c
and for a trifling fee they'll torment an enemy—just or unjust—with spells and enchantments which, they claim, bind the gods to their service.

"As witnesses they drag in the poets. Some chant Hesiod's lines on the ease of vice: 'Evil is easy to get in abundance;/
the road is short, she dwells nearby;/before excellence the d
gods have placed sweat.'[6] And he speaks of a long, rugged, and uphill path. Others quote Homer to show that the gods can be manipulated:

> The gods themselves may be bent; with sacrificial
> feasts, libations, and the smoke of burnt offerings e
> men propitiate them for transgressions and sins.

With baskets of instruction books by Musaeus and Orpheus,[7] 'descendants of the Moon and the Muses,' as they call them, they gull individuals and whole cities into believing that sacrifices and games can purify and absolve us from 365
crimes in this life, while mysterious rites, called 'initiations,' will free us from the dread punishments that await the uninitiated beyond.

"With stories like that floating around, Socrates, what do you think will be the reaction of a naturally good and discerning young man who flits from argument to argument gathering information on what he should do and be to lead
the best life? He may well quote Pindar and ask: ' "Whether b
by justice or crooked deceit to climb higher," and dig in on the top of the heap? If I *am* just without *seeming* so, they say my reward will be dead loss and hard labor. No, thanks. But the crook who finagles a just reputation lives like a god, they
say. All right, since appearance is the key to happiness that c
"forces even reality," as the men in the know have revealed, then I'll ply it with a vengeance, by god. I'll draw a shadow-sketch of excellence around me like a cloak, but behind me

[6] *Works and Days* 287–89. The following quotation is from *Iliad* 9.497–501.

[7] A legendary singer and miracle worker.

the fox of Archilochus, rapacious and wily.'[8]—'Fine,' a
friend might remark, 'but it's a hard role to play.'—'Nothing
d worth doing is easy,' he'll say, 'but this is the happiness trail
that the arguments have blazed for us. We can form gangs
and political societies for cover, there are rhetoric profes-
sors to teach us mob oratory and techniques for swaying a
jury, so that between force and persuasion we'll take all we
can get but our punishment.'—'But you can't force or fool
the gods.'—'So what? If they don't exist or care about us,
e why should we care about them? If they do, we only know
it from hearsay and poets—the very ones who tell us that the
gods may be "bent" by feasts and offerings. We must accept
both statements or neither. If both, we take, and appease the
366 gods from the takings. Honest, we only escape divine punishment; we're cut off from the profits of crime. As crooks
we use part of our profits to buy off the gods and end up
ahead both in this world and in the next.'—'But they'll get
us in Hades for the crimes we do here—us, our children, or
our children's children!'—'My friend,' he replies with cool
calculation, 'initiations and savior gods are very good for
b that sort of thing, according to our greatest cities and poets
—sons and spokesmen of gods—who all assure us it is so.'

"Against such talk from both the many and the elite what
reason can you give for preferring justice to the foulest
injustice which, if we assume a counterfeit grace, will permit
us to do as we like with gods and men both here and in the
c world to come? What stratagem can you devise, Socrates, to
persuade a man with birth, wealth, or strength of body or
soul that he ought to respect justice and not snicker at the
very word? Even if a man knew that justice is best and could
expose all that we've said as a lie, he still wouldn't be angry
with the unjust but forgive them, knowing that men abstain
from injustice only through knowledge or god-given natural
d aversion. The rest are unwillingly just and condemn injustice out of cowardice or old age or some other weakness that
prevents them from doing it. The first to get power is the
first to do wrong, and as much as he can.

"The cause of all this is the same one that inspired these

[8]The metaphor is also mixed in Greek. Archilochus (seventh century B.C.) was an elegaic and iambic poet. His fable of the fox has been lost.

harangues that my brother and I have been making at you,
Socrates. Here's what we've been trying to say: 'Strange,
how all you self-proclaimed champions of justice, from the e
earliest heroes whose words have survived down to the men
of the present day, have declined to praise justice and denounce injustice except for the reputations and honors and
gifts they may bring. Not one of you, in verse or in conversation, has ever adequately explained what each of them does
by its own power when in the soul, even if hidden from gods
and men: how injustice is the soul's greatest evil and justice
its greatest good. If you had done that from the beginning 367
and so taught us from childhood, we would not now be on
our guard against one another; we'd each be our own best
guardian, for fear that by committing injustice we invite
catastrophe into our souls.'

"That, Socrates, and perhaps even more, is what
Thrasymachus or another might say about justice and injustice. Frankly, I think it's a crude misrepresentation of their
powers, but I've presented it as strongly as I can in order to b
get you to present the opposite view. And don't give us some
merely theoretical proof of the superiority of justice over
injustice. Show what each in itself does to its possessor to
make justice good and injustice evil. And exchange their
reputations, as Glaucon said. Otherwise we'll accuse you of
praising not justice but its seeming, of condemning not injustice but its seeming, of inciting us to be unjust covertly, c
and of agreeing with Thrasymachus that justice is someone
else's good—the advantage of the stronger—and that injustice profits and advantages oneself, to the disadvantage of
the weaker. Since you said justice is one of those great goods
worth possessing for their consequences but still more for
themselves—like seeing, hearing, thinking, and health, d
which produce their effects not by appearance but by their
own nature—then treat it that way: as something good in
itself, which helps its possessor as injustice harms. Leave
rewards and reputations for others to praise. I might take
that kind of thing from someone else, Socrates, but not from
you, because you've spent your whole life doing nothing but
examining this very question. And remember: no theoretical e
proof. Show what each in itself does to its possessor—
whether or not he's noticed by gods and men—to make
justice good and injustice evil."

I've always admired the natures of Glaucon and Adeimantus, but never more than then. I was filled with joy and said:
368 "Sons of that man, Glaucon's lover didn't do badly when he
opened his poem with you, for having distinguished yourselves at the battle of Megara, calling you 'Sons of Ariston,[9]
divine race of a glorious sire.' Well put, I'd say. There must
be something divine in you if you can defend injustice so
vigorously and still believe justice is better. I'm convinced
b that you do, because I judge you by your characters. If I only
had your speeches to go by I'd never believe it. But my faith
in your honesty only increases my perplexity. I don't know
what to do—I can't defend justice if you won't accept my
proof to Thrasymachus, and I can't not defend it either,
because I'm afraid it would be impious to stand by while
c justice is being attacked and not defend it to my last gasp.
So that's what I'd better do, as well as I'm able."

Glaucon and the others urged me by all means to take up
the defense and track down the truth about what justice and
injustice are and the benefits of each. So I told them my plan:
"I don't think this will be an easy investigation—it'll take
d sharp eyes. Now since we're not very bright, here's how I
suggest we go about it: if you told a man with poor eyes to
read something small at a distance and he noticed that the
same thing was written elsewhere in large letters on a larger
background, he'd probably jump for joy because he could
read the big writing first and then examine the small to see
if both were really the same."

"True," said Adeimantus, "but where do you see some-
e thing like that in our search?"

"I think I've got an idea," I said. "Isn't justice found in a state as well as in an individual?"

"Certainly," he said.

"And a state is larger than an individual?"

"Of course."

"Then maybe justice is also larger in a state and easier to
observe. So let's first inquire what justice is like in states.
369 Then we can examine it in the individual and see if the
smaller resembles the larger."

"Good idea, Socrates."

[9]Also Plato's father. There is a word-play on the name, which means "the best."

"If we watch a city coming into being in words, we may
also see its justice and injustice come into being, and when
it's finished we should have a better chance of seeing what
we're after. Shall we try it that way? Consider this carefully b
—I think it'll be a lot of work."

"We have," said Adeimantus. "Let's try it."

"Well," I said, "I think a city begins because the individual is not self-sufficient but has many needs. Can you suggest some other origin?"

"No, that's the one."

"So when a number of people have gathered together in c
one place as common partners and helpers, each inviting
others to provide different services (for they have many
needs), can we call that settlement a city?"

"Yes," he said.

"And if each person shares with the others he does so because he thinks it's for his own good?"

"Certainly."

"Well, then," I said, "let's build a city of words from the
beginning. It seems it will be created by our needs, of which
the most important is providing food for existence and life, d
next shelter, then clothing, and so on."

"Correct."

"Then we'll need a farmer, a carpenter, and a weaver. Will that do, or shall we add a shoemaker or some other craftsman to help provide for the needs of the body?"

"Let's."

"So our absolutely necessary city will consist of four or five men."

"Apparently." e

"What about the work? Should each make the fruits of his
own work common to all, so that the farmer spends all his
time and labor providing food for four, or should he spend
only a fourth of his time producing his own food, a fourth 370
working on his house, a fourth making clothes, a fourth
making shoes, and tend his own business all by himself without bothering to share with the others?"

"Perhaps the other way would be easier, Socrates," said Adeimantus.

"That's hardly a strange observation," I said. "Now that you mention it, it occurs to me that people are quite differ-b ent by nature and each is naturally fitted for a different job. Do you agree?"

"Yes."

"Then will one man naturally do better at only one trade or many?"

"Only one," he said.

"I think it's also clear that if you miss the right time for a job you'll botch the whole thing. The work won't wait for
c the worker; he must devote full time to it and not make it a sideline."

"Necessarily."

"So when each one is freed from other work to do the one thing he's naturally fit for at the right time, more work gets done easier and better."

"Absolutely."

"But if we have specialization we'll need more than four citizens. If our farmer's going to have a good plow he won't make it himself, and the same for the others. And each needs
d many things. So it looks like blacksmiths and toolmakers and all sorts of craftsmen will have to be partners in our community. Our little city is beginning to grow."

"It certainly is, Socrates."

"But it still won't be very big if we add shepherds and cowherds and other kinds of herdsmen. Our farmers need
e oxen for fieldwork, and the builders need them for hauling building materials. The weavers and shoemakers need wool and hides."

"It's going to take quite a town to hold all that."

"Yes," I said. "And it'll be almost impossible to found it in a place that doesn't require imports, so we'll need people to import goods from other cities."

"True."

"But if our servant goes out empty-handed he'll come
371 back the same way. Our city will have to produce a surplus for trade. That means extra farmers and craftsmen."

"It certainly does."

"And we'll need other servants to bring goods in and out of the city. They're called traders, aren't they?"

"Yes."

"If we have sea trade we'll need another group skilled in
b the sea-faring trades."

"Yes—a large one too."

"What about the sharing of products within the city? That was the reason we established the principle of partnership and community and founded a city."

"It'll have to be done by buying and selling, Socrates."

"So the result will be a marketplace, and currency as a token of exchange."

"Of course."

"If a farmer or workman brings his produce to the market c
at the wrong time and misses the people who need it, he'll loaf around the marketplace neglecting his work."

"Not at all—there are people who see this as an opportunity to provide a service. In a well-regulated city they're mostly weaklings no good for any other job, so they sit
around the marketplace exchanging money for goods with d
those who need to sell, and goods for money with the ones who need to buy."

"So this need is the origin of retail trade in our city," I said. "Don't we call people who serve by buying and selling in the marketplace retail merchants, and those who travel from city to city traders?"

"Of course."

"I believe there are still other menials, not worth accept- e
ing as partners in our community on mental grounds, but strong enough for hard labor. They sell their strength for profit, called a wage, and are called wage-earners. Do they complete our city, Adeimantus? Has it reached its full extent?"

"Probably."

"Then where are justice and injustice?" I asked. "Which group did they come in with?"

"I don't know, Socrates, unless they're found in some of 372
the dealings between groups."

"You could be right. Adeimantus—we'll have to keep looking. But first let's see how people will live in our city. They'll produce only grain, wine, shoes, clothing, and houses. Summers they'll work mostly naked and barefoot,
but in winter they'll be bundled and warm. For nourishment b
they'll grind barley and wheat, kneading from the former noble patties, baking fine loaves of the latter, upon which, served up on reeds or fresh leaves, the rustic diners, wreathed and reclining on bunches of myrtles and vines, will feast, hymning the gods and washing it down with wine, and

so delight in one another's company, both themselves and
their children, which they'll not produce beyond their
c means, being cautious of the twin dangers of poverty and
war."

"No meat?" cried Glaucon. "It sounds like your diners
will feast only on bread."

"Oh, I forgot—they need something with it. They'll have
salt, of course, and olives and cheese, and greens and stuff
they boil up in the country. For dessert we could give them
figs, nuts, and berries, and acorns and chestnuts to roast on
d the fire and munch as they soberly sip their wine. Thus they
can expect to live in peace and good health, passing on at
a ripe old age and bequeathing the same life to their descendants."

"Socrates, that's the kind of feed you'd provide if you
were founding a city for pigs."

"Why, what else do they need, Glaucon?"

"The comforts of civilization: couches to lie on, tables to
e eat from, and snacks and delicacies like we have."

"I see—you don't want to examine the origin of a city, but
of a spoiled city. Not a bad idea, because then we may see
how justice and injustice grow up in a state. I think the city
we just described was true and healthy. Now we can look at
373 one with indigestion. No reason why we can't. It seems our
way of life won't satisfy some folks: they'll want couches and
tables and furniture, delicacies, perfume, incense, harlots,
pastries—and a great variety of everything. The list of necessities will grow—houses, clothing, and shoes won't be
enough. They'll have to meddle in painting and embroidery,
and they'll need ivory and gold and all that. Is that right?"

b "Yes."

"Then we'll have to enlarge the city again; our healthy one
won't be big enough any more. It'll be stuffed and crammed
beyond what's necessary for a city—with mobs of hunters
and packs of imitators, some concerned with figures and
colors, others with music: poets, playwrights, recitors, actors, dancers, and producers. There'll be craftsmen of all
kinds of articles, most especially for ladies' adornment.
c We'll need more servants: teachers, nurses, nursemaids,
hair-dressers, cooks, barbers, and bakers. There'll be hog
farmers too. They weren't needed in our other town, but
they'll be needed in this one. If people want other meat, I
suppose we'll need other kinds of livestock too."

"Yes, we will."

"Won't there also be a much greater need for doctors?" d

"People who live like that surely will need them."

"And the land, once enough to support everyone, will suddenly become scarce, I suppose."

"Yes."

"So we'll have to cut into our neighbors' land to get enough for plow and pasture, and they'll do the same to us if they've also overstepped the bounds of mere necessities and let themselves go after the unlimited possession of wealth."

"It's a necessary step, Socrates." e

"So we'll soon be at war, Glaucon, don't you think?"

"Yes," he said.

"Then," I said, "we've also discovered the origin of war. War, whether it does good or evil (we'll leave that question open for now), arises from the same cause that brings such great evils, public and private, to states: the desire for possessions."

"That's correct."

"So the population will jump by a whole army, which will
have to march out when someone attacks and fight for all the 374
property and luxuries we've mentioned."

"What? Can't they fight for themselves?"[10]

"Not if we were right when we began molding our city," I said. "Don't you remember, Glaucon?—We agreed that one man can't do well at several trades."

"That's true," he said, "we did."

"Well, isn't warfare a trade?" b

"Absolutely."

"Doesn't it need as much attention as shoemaking?"

"More."

"We prohibited our shoemaker from trying to do other
jobs while he's cobbling; to make good shoes he has to stick
to shoemaking. The same for the others: one job for each
man. A worker must be freed from other tasks to spend his c
life doing what he's naturally fit for, well and on time. Now,
doesn't warfare have to be done extremely well? Or is it so
easy that a man can pursue it as a sideline, even though he'll
never become a good checkers or dice player unless he's

[10]Armies in early Greece were made up of citizens; mercenaries became common in the fourth century B.C.

d practiced the game since childhood? Can you pick up a shield or a sword or any other tool of war and instantly become a skilled soldier? The tools of every other trade are useless unless you pick up practice and knowledge along with the tool."

"If that weren't so, tools would surely be precious."

"Since the guardian[11] has the most important job, doesn't
e he need the greatest freedom from other tasks and the most
skill and training in his own?"

"I think so."

"Doesn't his nature also have to suit his pursuit?"

"Naturally."

"Then our job is cut out for us, Glaucon: we have to try to determine what kind of nature is suited for guarding the city."

"We certainly do."

"It won't be child's play, by Zeus. Still, we can't give up
375 as long as our strength holds out. So tell me if you think the
nature of a well-born youth is as suited to guarding as a
noble pup's."

"How do you mean?"

"Well," I said, "I think both need sharp senses, speed to pursue what they spot, and strength to outfight what they catch. To fight well they must also be brave."

"Yes, they need all that."

"Can any animal be brave without spirit?—Have you ever
b noticed how invincible spirit is, Glaucon? It makes the whole
soul fearless and undaunted, ready to stand up to anything."

"Yes, I've noticed that."

"So it's clear what kind of a body a guardian must have."

"Yes."

"And also a spirited soul."

"That's clear too."

"How can we keep men with natures like that from being savage to each other and to the rest of the citizens?"

"It won't be easy, by Zeus."

c "They have to be gentle to the citizens and harsh to the
enemy, Glaucon. Otherwise they won't need enemies to destroy them—they'll do it themselves. Where can we find a
disposition like that? Gentleness and spirit are contrary na-

[11]First mention of the city's guardian.

tures, yet a good guardian needs both. It seems impossible to reconcile contraries, so it seems impossible to have a good guardian. What can we do?" d

"I don't know."

I was baffled and mulled over what we had said. Then I said: "It serves us right, Glaucon—we missed our own comparison."

"How do you mean?"

"We didn't notice that there are natures with exactly these contraries in them."

"Where?"

"In all sorts of creatures, probably, but surely in those puppies we just compared to a guardian. I suppose you e
know that a well-bred dog is naturally gentle to his family and to people he knows, but savage to strangers."

"Yes, I know that."

"So it's possible—what we're looking for in our guardians isn't something contrary to nature."

"It doesn't seem to be."

"But don't you think a guardian's soul must be naturally philosophical as well as spirited?"

"How come? What are you driving at?" 376

"At another trait of the dog; a remarkable one at that."

"But what is it?"

"Why, he rages at strangers even if they've done him no harm, but fawns on people he knows even if they've never been kind to him. Isn't that amazing, Glaucon?"

"I've never really paid much attention. It's true, of course."

"This subtle property of his nature shows that the dog is a philosopher, a true 'lover of wisdom.' " b

"How?"

"He judges a sight as hostile or friendly only by knowledge and ignorance. How can anything that defines the alien and the akin by knowledge and ignorance help but love knowledge?"

"There's no way at all."

"Love of knowledge is the same as philosophy, isn't it?"

"Yes."

"Then can we cheerfully assert the same for a man as for a dog?—to be gentle with acquaintances and kin he must c
naturally love knowledge and be a philosopher."

"Yes, we can."

"Therefore to become a good guardian, a man must be by nature a fast, strong, and spirited philosopher."

"Absolutely," he said.

"That," I said, "must be the guardians' basic character.
Now how should they be raised and educated? Is that a
pertinent question? Will it help us in our main task of discov-
d ering how justice and injustice come about in a state? We
don't want to overlook anything important or get bogged
down in a long digression."

Glaucon's brother replied: "I suspect it will help."

"Then we'll have to look into it even if it takes a long time,
Adeimantus. Let's educate the men in our discussion as
e though we were telling old tales at our leisure. What's our
education? Can we improve on the timetested formula: gymnastics for the body and poetry[12] for the soul?"

"I doubt it."

"Shall we begin teaching them poetry before gymnastics?"

"Of course."

"Doesn't poetry include stories, which have two forms: the true and the false?"

"Yes."

377 "Don't we have to teach both but begin with the false?"

"I don't understand," he said.

"But you do understand that we begin by telling children stories, Adeimantus. These are mostly false, I imagine, but they contain some truth. So we use stories with children before gymnastics."

"True," he said.

"That's what I meant when I said we must start with poetry before gymnastics."

"Yes, and you were right."

"And you know that the beginning of any task is always critical, especially with someone young and impressionable.

[12]"Gymnastics" means physical training in general. The word translated as "poetry," when referring to education, is literally "music," which had a wide range of meaning in Greek. It signified both music and poetry (inseparable in ancient Greece), as well as literature and art, for which there were no specific words. Since music and poetry formed the basis of education, "music" was also a synonym for "education." The adjective has been usually translated as "musical."

That's when he's most easily formed, ready to take any im- b
pression you want to stamp on him."

"Absolutely."

"So shall we permit the children to hear just any old story and receive impressions contrary to the opinions we think they should have when they grow up?"

"Not at all."

"Then it seems that our first task is to supervise the story-
tellers and separate those who make good stories from those c
who make bad. We'll persuade mothers and nurses to tell
the good stories to their children, to shape their souls with
them even more than their bodies with their hands. Most of
the stories they tell now will have to go."

"Which ones are they?"

"Many, but in the great we can also see the small. Both
have the same patterns and effects, don't you think?" d

"I suppose, but I don't even know what you mean by the great."

"Well," I said, "the stories told by Hesiod and Homer and the other great poets. Aren't they the ones who concocted those lying stories that they told and still tell?"

"Which stories? What do you condemn in them?"

"A terrible fault that must be condemned in anyone, especially if he doesn't lie properly."

"But what is it?"

"Misrepresenting the nature of gods and heroes, like a e
painter who paints a poor likeness."

"You're right to condemn that sort of thing, but how do they do it? what kind of stories do you mean?"

"Well, it isn't just fiction but a downright lie when a poet
makes his greatest characters do what Hesiod[13] makes
Uranus, Zeus, and Cronus do—chaining and castrating each
other and swallowing their children. Even if such stories 378
were true, I don't think they should be told lightly to the
young and thoughtless. The best thing is to suppress them,
but if they must be told, then only to as few as possible on
an oath of secrecy. And the initiates shouldn't have to sacrifice a pig, but something big and unattainable, so as few as
possible will hear."

"You're right, Socrates, they are crude stories."

"They won't be told in our city, Adeimantus. Nor will a b

[13]In the *Theogony*.

child ever hear that perpetrating some monstrous injustice, like cruelly punishing his father for a crime he committed, is nothing unusual but only what the first and greatest of the gods have done."

"No, by Zeus. That sort of thing isn't fit to be told."

"And if we want our future guardians to disdain quarrel-
c ing, they must never be told that gods war with gods or plot
against one another, which isn't true. The battles of the gods
and the giants, or any other family quarrels of gods and
heroes won't be told to them or embroidered on sacred
robes. We should try to convince them that no citizen has
ever fought with another and that such a thing is an affront
to the gods; this is what old people must tell them as chil-
d dren, and when they grow up we must force the poets to tell
them much the same thing. Those tales of Hera enchained
by her son and Hephaestus hurled by his father from Olym-
pus[14] for trying to defend his mother, and the battles of the
gods that Homer tells—none of these will be allowed in our
city, not even as allegories. A child can't distinguish allegory
e from fact, and early impressions are hard to wash out. For
this reason, perhaps, we must make sure that the first stories
he hears are well composed for the purpose of teaching
excellence."

"That makes sense. But what will we say if someone asks us exactly what the stories should be?"

"Adeimantus, for now we're not poets, but founders of a
379 city. You don't expect founders to write poems—they just
have to know what patterns the poets must compose their
stories in and not let them deviate from them."

"True," he said, "but what should the patterns be for stories about the gods?"

"Well," I said, "god[15] must always be represented as he
b is, I suppose, whether in epic, lyric, or tragedy. Isn't god
truly good, and mustn't we speak of him as being so?"

"Yes."

"Can anything good be harmful?"

[14]*Iliad* 1.586–94. The battles of the gods are recounted in *Iliad* 20 and 21.

[15]Plato uses "god" and "the gods" interchangeably. There is nothing monotheistic about the singular; the use is generic, like "man" for "mankind."

"I don't see how."

"Then it does no harm, and what does no harm can do no evil. Isn't that so?"

"Yes."

"What does no evil can hardly be the cause of any evil."

"Hardly."

"Is the good beneficial and the cause of well-being?"

"Yes."

"So the good isn't the cause of everything," I said, "but only of things that are good. It's not responsible for things that are evil."

"That's perfectly true," he said. c

"Then god, being good, isn't the cause of everything, as the many say, but of only a few things for man. There's far more evil in life than good, and god must be held responsible for all of the good but none of the evil. We have to find some other cause for evil."

"That seems as true as anything can be."

"So we won't tolerate any poetic error about the gods,"
I said, "especially Homer's mindless absurdity: 'two jars of d
lots stand in Zeus's hall:/one of good, another of ill./'[16] A
man to whom Zeus gives a mixed portion, he says, 'falls now
into good, now into evil,' but one who receives unmixed ill
is 'driven by a cursèd plague about the hallowed earth.' Nor
can we allow him to call Zeus 'dispenser of good and evil.' e
And we won't approve anyone who presents Pandarus vio-
lating the sworn treaties[17] if he makes Athena or Zeus the
cause, or who shows the quarrel of the goddesses and the
judgment of Paris as prompted by Themis and Zeus. And we 380
can't let the young listen to Aeschylus rant about how 'a god
breeds guilt into mortals/ when he wants to destroy their
line.'

"If anyone writes about the sufferings of Niobe (the subject of the play from which those last lines were taken), the
woes of the house of Pelops, the Trojan War, or a similar
topic, he must either say it wasn't the work of a god, or if it
was, find the kind of explanation we're looking for and show
that the god's acts were just and good and that the people b

[16] *Iliad* 24.527–32.

[17] *Iliad* 4.86, ff. The quotation from Aeschylus below is from a lost tragedy.

were helped by being punished. A poet must not say that in
punishing people a god makes them miserable, but he may
say that evil men are miserable because they need punishment and a god helps them by giving it. If our city is to be
ruled by good laws, we must take every precaution to pre-
c vent our citizens from saying or hearing, in prose or in verse,
that a god, being good, causes evil. That's pernicious, impious, and a self-contradiction."

"I'll vote for that law, Socrates."

"Then this," I said, "is our first law and pattern for religious speech and writing: god is the cause only of good."

"A good and sufficient law it is too," he said.

d "What about the second? Do you think god is a sorcerer
who treacherously appears in different shapes, sometimes
changing his form to appear to us in person and sometimes
deluding us into thinking he does, or is he simple and of all
things the least likely to depart from his own form?"

"Offhand I can't say, Socrates."

"Look at it this way: if a thing abandons its own form it
e must be changed either by itself or by something else."

"Necessarily."

"Aren't things in the best condition the least changed or
moved by something else—strong, healthy bodies least by
diet and exercise, healthy plants by sun, wind, and similar
381 forces?"

"Of course."

"And external influences least disturb or alter the courageous, intelligent soul?"

"Yes."

"By the same reasoning, I suppose, all composite things—houses, furniture, or clothes—that are well made and in good condition are changed least by time and other influences."

"That's a fact," he said.

b "So in every case a thing well formed by nature, art, or
both accepts the least change from something else."

"It seems so."

"Surely god and the divine are in every way perfect."

"Of course."

"Then god would be the least likely to take different shapes in that way. But would he change or transform himself?"

"Obviously, if he changes."

"Does he alter himself for the better or worse and become more or less beautiful?"

"Necessarily for the worse, if he changes. We can hardly c
say god lacks beauty or excellence."

"Right, Adeimantus. And since that is so, do you think anyone, god or man, would deliberately make himself in any way worse?"

"Impossible," he said.

"Then it's impossible even for a god to want to change himself. Being as good and as beautiful as he can possibly be, each god remains simply and always in his own form."

"An absolute necessity," he said.

"Let no poet, therefore, tell us that 'the changeable gods d
take on shapes of strangers/ and travel from town to
town.'[18] No lies about the transformations of Proteus and
Thetis, no Hera dragged into a poem or a play disguised as
a priestess and begging alms for 'the lifegiving sons of the
Argive river Inachus,' or any other lies of the kind. We can't e
let poets dupe mothers into frightening their children with
perverse stories about the gods spooking around at night in
outlandish shapes. Stories like that not only blaspheme the
gods; they also make the children fearful."

"No, we can't permit it," he said.

"So it's not the gods' nature to change," I said, "but maybe they use sorcery to delude us into thinking they do."

"Perhaps."

"Would a god want to lie by projecting a false appearance 382
in word or deed?"

"I don't know."

"Do you know that both gods and men detest a true lie, if I may use the expression?"

"What do you mean?"

"Just that no one would willingly accept a lie in the most vital place about the most vital things. To have that there terrifies us more than anything."

"What where?" he said. "I still don't understand."

"That's because you think I mean something highfalutin. b
All I mean is that no one wants to be deceived and ignorant

[18] *Odyssey* 17.485–86.

about reality in his soul; to have a lie there instead of the truth. Everyone would hate that."

"They certainly would."

"I think I was right in calling that a true lie: ignorance in
the soul of the deceived. A spoken lie is a kind of imitation
of this state of the soul. It arises as an image of it after the
c fact and so is not an unadulterated lie. Isn't that so?"

"Yes," he said.

"And both gods and men hate a true lie?"

"I think they do."

"But spoken lies seem more useful than hateful, don't you
think? They're like preventive medicine to use against enemies or to dissuade so-called friends from doing evil when
madness or folly drives them to it. Lying is also useful for
d the storytelling we've been talking about, because we don't
know the truth about ancient events. So we fabricate fictions
as close to the truth as possible to make useful stories."

"Those are the uses of lying, all right."

"Well, how is it useful to god? Does he have to use fiction because he doesn't know the past?"

"The idea is absurd."

e "Then there's no lying poet in a god," I said. "But maybe
he fears an enemy or needs lies to cure madness or folly in
a friend."

"Never. The gods have no fear, nor do they love the foolish or mad."

"Then a god has no motive for lying at all."

"None whatsoever."

"So the spiritual and divine is in every way truthful."

"Absolutely."

"God, therefore, is absolutely simple and true in both word and deed. He doesn't change or deceive others, asleep or awake, with visions, words, or signs."

383 "That's my opinion too, now that you've said it."

"Then do you agree that this is our second religious law and pattern?—the gods shall not be represented as sorcerers who change their shapes or as liars who mislead us in word or deed."

"Yes."

"Then, Adeimantus," I said, "we'll admire Homer for many things, but not for making Zeus send a false dream to

Agamemnon.[19] Nor will we admire Aeschylus when his Thetis tells how Apollo sang at her wedding and celebrated her happy progeny: b

> their long and happy lives, of illness free.
> He sang them and extolled my blessed fate,
> gratifying me. For I believed him,
> believed his deathless mouth could mouth no lie,
> the deep prophetic honey of his tongue.
> Yet he who sang that bridal song, he who
> spoke and feasted—he it is who now
> has killed my only child.[20]

When a poet writes things like that we'll indignantly prevent c
him from producing his play and forbid teachers to use it with children, so our guardians may grow up reverent and as nearly divine as humans can be."

"I fully agree with these patterns," he said, "and I would treat them as laws."

Book 3

"Such then, it seems, are the stories about gods that men 386
must hear or be prevented from hearing from childhood to make them honor the gods and their parents and value their love for each other. But how about making them brave? Mustn't they also be told stories that lessen their fear of
death? Or do you think a man who fears death can ever be b
brave?"

"No, by Zeus, I certainly don't."

"Adeimantus, do you think a man who believes there are terrors in Hades will be fearless and choose to die in battle rather than be defeated and enslaved?"

"No."

[19] *Iliad* 2.1–34.
[20] The lines are from a lost play. Thetis's only child was Achilles.

"Then it seems we'll have to supervise those who write about the afterlife too," I said, "and ask them to commend Hades rather than rashly disparage it, because what they say
c is both untrue and harmful to our future fighters."

"Absolutely," he said.

"Then let's censor them," I said, "beginning with verses like these:

> I'd rather follow a plow as the serf
> of a land-hungry, indigent peasant
> than be king over all these exhausted dead.[1]

d
> Lest . . . the horrible house of Hades stand open,
> putrid and wide, abhorrent even to gods.

> Alas! So something remains even in Hades:
> a soul and a wraith deprived of its senses.

> He alone had sense; the others flitted as shades.

> His soul left his limbs and flitted to Hades,
> mourning its fate, abandoning manhood and youth.

387
> Into Earth his soul retreated like smoke,
> gibbering as it descended.

> As bats in the depths of an awesome cave
> flutter and squeak when one falls from the clump,
> so came the souls, squeaking and gibbering.

b "We'll have to ask Homer and the other poets to pardon
us for scratching all such lines; not that they're unpoetic or lack popular appeal—in fact, the more poetic they are the more dangerous they become to men and boys who must be free and fear slavery worse than death."

"Absolutely, Socrates."

"We'll also have to throw out those terrible, terrifying underworld names: Cocytuses and Styxes—rivers of lamentation and hate—Underground Men, Withering Dead, and
c other bloodcurdling names designed to make people shud-
der. They may be good for something, but they make us

[1]The shade of Achilles to Odysseus in the underworld, *Odyssey* 11.489–91. The following quotations are also from Homer: *Iliad* 20.64–65, *Iliad* 23.103–04, *Odyssey* 10.495, *Iliad* 16.856–57, *Iliad* 23.100, and *Odyssey* 24.6–9.

shudder for our guardians, for fear that fear-induced fevers will melt them and make them soft."

"A well-placed fear too," he said.

"Should we reject them?"

"Yes."

"Should poetry and speech use the opposite type?"

"Clearly."

"What about pitiful laments of illustrious men?" d

"We'll have to reject them along with the others," he said.

"Let's see if we're right to do so," I said. "Don't we say that a good man doesn't regard death as something terrible to another good man who's a friend, and so won't mourn for his friend's sake as though he had suffered something terrible?"

"Yes."

"We also say that such a man is self-sufficient for a good life, distinguished from others in having the least need of others. If deprived of a son or a brother or money or any- e
thing else, therefore, he'll take the loss calmly and be the last to regard it as terrible."

"Correct."

"Then we'll rightly take these dirges away from notable men and give them to female characters—disreputable ones
—and to inferior males, so that those we claim to be rais- 388
ing as their country's guardians will disdain to act like them."

"Right," he said.

"So again we'll ask a favor of Homer and the rest: Please don't make Achilles, a goddess's son, toss in sorrow for his friend, lying 'now on his side, now on his back, now on his stomach,' then getting up and staggering 'along the beach
of the barren sea,'[2] or 'pouring black ashes on top of his b
head,' or executing any of the numerous variations on weeping and wailing that Homer presents. Kindly refrain from portraying Priam, descended from gods, as a suppliant, 'rolling in dung, calling each man by name,' and especially from presenting Thetis or any other god as weeping and mourn-
ing her fate: 'Alas for my sorrow, most blest and accursèd c

[2]*Iliad* 24.10–12. The following quotations are also from the *Iliad*: 18.23–24, 22.414–15, 18.54, 22.168–69 (Zeus speaking of Hector pursued by Achilles), and 16.433–34.

of mothers!' At least he should have the decency not to represent the greatest god so preposterously:

> Oh woe, to see with my eyes a beloved man
> pursued around the town. It tears my heart.

And again:

> Oh, oh, that fate should decree my beloved
> d Sarpedon to fall by the hand of Patroclus!

"If our young men take such nonsense seriously instead of deriding it as unworthy of the gods, they'll hardly consider it beneath their own dignity as mere mortals: they won't be ashamed and control themselves if they feel like speaking or acting that way themselves, and the slightest provocation will make them sing dirges and laments. Our argument just indicated that good men must refuse to carry on like that. Don't we have to stay with that conclusion till a better comes along?"

e "Absolutely," said Adeimantus.

"Nor must they be fond of laughter. When someone gives way to violent laughter, it usually provokes an equally violent reaction."

"It seems so to me," he said.

"Then we'll reject scenes that show worthy people, much
389 less gods, overcome with laughter."

"Certainly."

"Your argument condemns more lines from Homer: 'Unquenchable laughter rose from the gods/ as they watched Hephaestus bustle about.' "[3]

"Call it my argument if you like," he said, "but throw them
b out."

"Again, truth must be highly esteemed. If we were right in saying that lying is useless to gods and only useful to men as a form of medicine, then clearly it should be allowed only to doctors."

"Clearly."

"Then it's fitting for the rulers, if anyone, to lie on account of enemies or citizens for the benefit of the state. The rest mustn't touch it. We'll say that for a citizen to lie to such
c rulers is as grave or an even graver offense than for a patient

[3] *Iliad* 1.599–600.

to lie about his bodily condition to his doctor or an athlete to his trainer, or for a sailor to lie to his captain about the condition of the ship and her crew."

"Absolutely," he said.

"Any citizen, therefore, caught telling a lie in our city, 'of d
those who are craftsmen, whether prophet or healer/ or joiner of planks,'[4] will be punished for introducing a deadly practice that can sink a city as fast as a ship."

"I agree," he said, "if act follows word."[5]

"Mustn't our young also be temperate?"

"Certainly."

"And doesn't the popular definition of temperance stress
obedience to rulers and being ruler yourself over the plea- e
sures of food, drink, and sex?"

"I think so."

"So I think we'll approve the statement Homer puts in Diomedes' mouth: 'sit quietly, friend, and attend to my words,' and others like the one that follows it:[6] 'the Achaeans advanced breathing valor,/ silent, in fear of their leaders.' "

"Good."

"What about 'wine sack! dog-eyed and chicken-hearted!'
and the lines that follow? Is it good to present such imperti- 390
nence toward rulers in prose or in verse?"

"Certainly not."

"It wouldn't be surprising if scenes like this arouse a certain pleasure, but they're hardly suitable for filling the young with self-control. Homer doesn't really promote temperance when he makes his wisest hero say that the best things in life
are 'tables groaning with food, cups brimming with wine,'[7] b
and another call 'death by starvation' the worst. His Zeus is no model of restraint either, when lust for Hera makes him
forget all about the plans he's devised through sleepless c
nights, 'while other gods and mortals slept.' He's so smitten

[4]*Odyssey* 17.383–84.

[5]Equally cryptic in Greek. It may mean "if our city becomes a reality," or simply "if he puts his lie into practice."

[6]It doesn't follow in our text of Homer. The previous line is *Iliad* 4.412; this one is made up of *Iliad* 3.8 and 4.431. The following quotation is *Iliad* 1.225 (Achilles to Agememnon).

[7]Odysseus in *Odyssey* 9.8–10. The following quotation is *Odyssey* 12.342.

at the sight of her that he wants to sleep with her right there on the ground. Never before, he says, has he felt such desire, not even before they were married, when they used to get together 'behind their parents' backs.'[8] There are also scenes like the one where Hephaestus catches his wife in bed with Ares. What do you think, Adeimantus?"

"By Zeus," he said, "they seem most unsuitable to me."

d "What about famous men speaking and acting with endurance against all odds? should they be seen and heard? As when Odysseus 'struck his chest and rebuked his heart:/ bear up, old heart, you've endured fouler than this.' "[9]

"They certainly should," he said.

"If we want our men to be above bribery and greed," I
e said, "they mustn't sing that 'gifts move gods, move awesome kings.' And Phoenix, Achilles' old tutor, must not be admired for giving moderate advice when he tells his pupil to defend the Achaeans for gifts, but otherwise cling to his wrath.[10] We won't believe that Achilles could be so unworthy and avaricious as to accept gifts from Agamemnon
391 and refuse to return Hector's body without ransom."

"No, it's not right to admire that sort of thing."

"For Homer's sake I'm reluctant to say it," I said, "but telling and believing such things against Achilles is impious. We mustn't believe that he said to Apollo, 'you injured me, most pernicious of gods,/ and I'd fain pay you back if I
b could,'[11] that he disobeyed the river, a god, and was ready to fight him, or that he cut off his locks, consecrated to the other river Spercheius, saying 'these to Patroclus, to carry in death,' and then gave them to the corpse. We must denounce as lies his dragging of Hector's body around Patroclus's tomb and his slaughter of captives on the funeral pyre,

[8]This scene is from *Iliad* 14.294, ff.; the following one is from *Odyssey* 8.266–366.

[9]*Odyssey* 20.17–18.

[10]*Iliad* 9.515–23. For the gifts below, see *Iliad* 19.278–81. The release of Hector's body is the main episode of *Iliad* 24. But Achilles is not greedy, as Plato alleges, and has little interest in the gifts.

[11]*Iliad* 22.15, 20. The fight with the river occurs in *Iliad* 21.232, ff., the dedication of the hair in 23.141–52, the dragging of Hector's corpse in 24.15–18, and the slaughter of the prisoners in 23.175–76.

and keep our citizens from believing that Achilles, born of c
a goddess to Peleus—the most temperate of men and a grandson of Zeus—raised by Chiron, the wisest of Centaurs, was so filled with confusion that he harbored two conflicting diseases: slavish greed and overbearing arrogance toward gods and men."

"You're right, Socrates."

"We must also," I said, "reject stories of Theseus, Poseidon's son, and Perithous, son of Zeus, intent on foully ab-
ducting Helen and Persephone, and any other tales of divine d
sons daring the shocking, impious deeds falsely attributed to them now. Let's force the poets to deny the origin of either the deeds or the doers. They can't have both, or try to persuade our young that gods beget evil and that heroes are no better than men. Such stories are both impious and false,
because I think we proved that no evil can ever come from e
the gods."

"We certainly did," he said.

"They're also harmful to the listeners, because everyone will excuse his own evils if he's convinced that such things were and are done by

> those sprung from the gods and nearest to Zeus,
> their ancestral altars high upon Ida,
> whose veins still surge with the blood of gods.[12]

Stories like that must cease: they'll breed an easy openness
to depravity in our young. Now what kind is left? We've 392
considered stories about gods, spirits, heroes, and the dead. I suppose stories about people are the only kind left."

"Obviously," he said.

"But we can't deal with those yet," I said.

"Why not?"

"Because I think we'd say that poets and writers are wrong
about men in the most important things: they say that many b
unjust men are happy while just ones are miserable, that crime undetected pays, and that justice is a personal injury, good for somebody else. We'd prohibit all that and prescribe the opposite, don't you think?"

"I know we would," he said.

"But if you agree with me in that, I'll say you've conceded

[12]From a lost play of Aeschylus.

c the whole point of our search. We can't decide the human
stories until we discover what justice is like and show that it
naturally profits its possessor whether he appears just or
not."

"True."

"So much for subject matter then, Adeimantus. Now, to make our examination complete, I suppose we have to consider style, so we'll not only know *what* should be told, but *how.*"

"I don't understand that," he said.

d "Ah, but you must," I said. "Maybe this will make it easier:
isn't everything that a poet or a storyteller says a narration
of things in the past, the present, or the future?"

"What else could it be?"

"And it can be narrated by simple narration, imitation,[13] or both?"

"You'll have to make that clearer too," he said.

"I seem to be a ridiculously unclear teacher. I'll have to
e go at this like a poor speaker who can't explain the whole
and so takes a part to illustrate what he means. Do you know
the opening of the *Iliad,* where the poet says that Chryses
asked Agamemnon to release his daughter and then, when
Agamemnon got angry and refused, prayed to Apollo to
393 send a plague to the Greeks?"

"Yes."

"Then you know that up to the words, 'he beseeched all
the Achaeans,/ the two sons of Atreus most,'[14] the poet
himself speaks; he doesn't try to bamboozle us into thinking
that someone else is the speaker. But in what follows he
speaks as though he himself were Chryses and tries to make
b us believe that the speaker is not Homer but an old priest.
Almost the whole *Iliad* and *Odyssey* are narrated like that.
Isn't this narration, both in the speeches and in the parts in
between?"

[13]Plato regards all art as imitation, but uses the term here in the narrower sense of "impersonation," or "direct speech" in poetry. "Narration" or "narrative" is used in two senses: reported speech and action without direct speech ("simple narration"); and all literary representation, whether or not it includes (or consists entirely of) direct speech.

[14]*Iliad* 1.15–16.

"Yes."

"But when he presents a speech as though he were some- c
body else he'll make his own style as much like the speaker's
as he can."

"So?"

"Well," I said, "making yourself like another person in voice or manner is an imitation of that person. So can't we say that in speeches Homer and other poets narrate by imitation?"

"Yes."

"But when a poet avoids concealment his poetry and narrative come out free of imitation. I'll show you how it works d
so you can't say again you don't understand. If Homer had
said that Chryses came with ransom for his daughter and
implored all the Achaeans, especially the two kings, and then
continued as Homer and not as if he were Chryses, you know
it wouldn't be imitation but simple narration. Here's what it
would be like—without meter, because I'm not much of a
poet: 'The priest came and prayed that the gods might give e
them safety and the destruction of Troy, and begged them
to reverence the god by releasing his daughter and accepting the ransom. The others consented in reverence, but
Agamemnon grew angry and told him to leave and not to
return, or else the ribbons and staff of the god would not
help him a bit. His daughter would not be released, he said,
but would grow old with him back in Argos. He ordered him
to leave and not to provoke him, if he wished to get home 394
unharmed. In fear and silence the old man withdrew, called
on Apollo by his names, and reminded him of past favors—
sacrifices and temples he had built. In return for which he
prayed to the god to avenge his tears on the Achaeans with
his arrows.' That, my friend," I said, "is simple narrative
without imitation." b

"I understand," he said.

"Then understand that the opposite style occurs when you take out the parts in between and leave only the speeches."

"I understand that that's how tragedy works."

"Right, Adeimantus, and now I think I can make clear what I couldn't before: poetry and storytelling may consist entirely of imitation—in tragedy and comedy, as you say; of direct recitation by the poet—as in most lyric poetry; or of both, as in epic and many other genres, if you understand what I mean."

"Yes, now I get what you wanted to say."

"Now remember," I said: "we said we'd decided *what* the poets should write and must now examine *how.*"

"I remember."

d "Well, this is what I was trying to say: we must decide whether to allow our poets to narrate with pure imitation, with mixed imitation (and if so, which parts should be which), or with no imitation at all."[15]

"I've got a feeling that you're going to see whether we should allow tragedy and comedy in our city, Socrates."

"Could be," I said. "And it could be more than that too, I don't know yet myself. We'll just let the argument carry us along like a breeze."

"Well said," he replied.

e "Now, Adeimantus, consider whether our guardians should be imitators. Or does this follow what we said earlier, that one man can pursue only one pursuit well and if he attempts many he'll bungle them all and be outstanding at none?"

"Of course it does."

"Isn't it the same with imitation—one person can imitate one thing well, but not several?"

"Yes."

395 "If one man can't even do well in two types of imitation as closely related as the writing of tragedy and comedy seems to be, he'll hardly be able to imitate many things and at the same time do well in some worthwhile pursuit. Didn't you just call both tragedy and comedy imitations?"

"Yes, and you're right; the same man can't write both."

"An actor can't be a recitor too, or perform in both
b tragedy and comedy.[16] Isn't that all imitation?"

"Yes."

[15]I.e. with only direct speech (drama), direct speech connected by narration (epic; the modern novel), or straight narrative with no direct speech. Plato's dialogues belong either to the mixed class *(The Republic)* or to the pure, the two classes that Socrates (and Plato) bans from the city.

[16]Greek dramatists wrote either tragedies or comedies, but not both, and the actors acted in one or the other, but not both.

"Human nature appears even more splintered than that, Adeimantus. One man can't imitate several different things well, or even *do* the things that he represents in imitation."

"True."

"If we want to keep to our original idea, that our guardians must be freed from all other crafts to be painstaking
craftsmen of their city's freedom, pursuing nothing that c
doesn't contribute to this end, then they mustn't do or imitate anything else. If they imitate anything, it must from
childhood on be men with qualities befitting a guardian:
courage, temperance, liberality, reverence, and so on. They
must shun the clever imitation of slavish or shameful acts as
they would the acts themselves, to avoid reaping reality from
imitation. Or haven't you noticed how imitation, if practiced d
from childhood , settles into natural habits in speech, body,
and mind?"

"I certainly have."

"Then," I said, "we mustn't let our charges, if we want
them to grow into good men, imitate a woman[17] —nagging
her husband, boasting and challenging the gods, wallowing e
in seeming happiness or noisy grief—much less one who's
sick, in love, or in labor."

"Absolutely not," he said.

"Nor slaves, male or female, doing the work of slaves."

"No."

"Nor evil, cowardly men doing the opposite of what we
just said: ridiculing and abusing each other, drunk or sober,
with disgusting words, and debasing themselves and others 396
with the kind of speech and acts used by that sort of person.
Nor should they get in the habit of imitating maniacs. They
must recognize baseness and insanity in both men and
women, but never practice or imitate them."

"Very true," he said.

"Should they imitate blacksmiths and other craftsmen, or b
people like rowers and coxswains?"

"They can't very well imitate occupations they're supposed to ignore."

[17]Perhaps by watching her on stage. "Imitation" in Plato has three meanings: 1) a poet's representation of something, 2) a performer's presentation of it, and 3) the audience's participation in it.

"What about horses snorting and bulls roaring and rivers dashing and seas splashing and thunder crashing?"

"We've already forbidden them to act like maniacs."

"If I understand you correctly, Adeimantus, there's one
c form of narrative style used by a truly good man, and another, opposite form used by a man of opposite nature and breeding."

"What are they?" he asked.

"It seems to me," I replied, "that a moderate gentleman, when he comes in his narration to an act or a speech of a good man, doesn't hesitate to present it as though he himself were that man; he's not ashamed of that kind of imitation, which he makes close when the character acts sensibly
d and reliably, less close if he's tripped up by illness, love, drink, or some other misfortune. But when he comes to a man unworthy of him he's ashamed to liken himself seriously to someone inferior—except briefly, perhaps, when the man does something good—because he's had no practice in imitating such people and because he finds it repul-
e sive to efface his own character and mold it to the patterns of people he despises. If he does, then only for play."

"That seems likely," he said.

"Then he'll use the mixed style we just described in Homer, but with relatively little imitation and much narrative—or is this all nonsense?"

"No, it's the necessary pattern of such a speaker."

397 "But a worthless fellow will use more imitation in proportion to his own worthlessness: he'll consider nothing beneath him and stoop to imitating anything seriously even in public—thunder, howling winds, hail, squeaky wheels and pulleys, blaring trumpets, flutes, bugles, and every other instrument, as well as barking dogs, mooing cows, and
b chirping birds. His style will be almost all imitation of sounds and gestures with little or no narration."

"That's necessary too," he said.

"So those are the two forms of style I meant."

"Indeed."

"The first has little variation, so that if you give the words a suitable melody and rhythm, a proper speaker can recite nearly the whole thing to this one melody in almost the same
c rhythm. But the other form has multifarious variations, and

all melodies, modes, and rhythms are needed to recite it properly.[18] Isn't that right?"

"Absolutely," he said.

"Doesn't every poet or speaker hit upon one or the other of these styles or upon some blend of the two?"

"Necessarily."

"Well, what shall we do? allow them all, one of the pure d
styles, or the blend?"

"If I have my way, we'll take the pure one that imitates a decent man."

"But the mixed one's more pleasant, Adeimantus, and the opposite style from yours is absolutely delightful to children, teachers, and the masses."

"I know."

"But," I said, "you might point out that it's out of tune
with our regime because our men aren't variable: each does e
only one thing. Only in a city like ours will you find the shoemaker simply making shoes and not navigating on the side, the farmer not a part-time juror or the soldier a businessman."

"True, so it's not in tune at all."

"Then if cleverness has given some man the ability to 398
become anything and imitate everything, and if he should show up in our city to make a display of himself and his poetry, we'll bow down to him for being a delightful, supernatural wonder and tell him there's no one in our city like him and that it's unlawful for a man like him to be there. Then we'll annoint his head with oil, wreathe him with wool, and send him off to some other city.[19] We'll stick to our own
austere and cheerless storyteller because he's beneficial: he b
imitates the speech of a decent man and frames his stories on those patterns we set down in the beginning, when we undertook our soldiers' education."

"If it's up to us," he said, "that's what we'll do."

"Well, Adeimantus," I said, "I'd say we've completely covered the words and plots of poetry; we've said what
should be told and how. Now I suppose we should look at c
songs and lyric poetry."

[18]Greek lyric poetry was always sung to music, and often accompanied by dance.

[19]The poet here is probably meant to be Homer.

"Clearly."

"By now I think anyone could figure out what we must say about that to make it harmonize with the rest."

Glaucon laughed: "Then I'm not anyone, Socrates. I still couldn't guess what we should say, though I have an inkling."

"Well," I said, "at least you can say that lyric consists of
d three things: words, melody (set in a certain mode),[20] and rhythm."

"Yes," he said, "I can say that much."

"I should think the words must be set in the styles and patterns we've already established, and melody and rhythm have to follow the words, don't they?"

"Of course."

"Well, we said we didn't want dirges and laments, so tell
e me which modes are used in them. You should know, Glaucon—you're a musician."

"Modes like the mixed and the sharp Lydian."

"Throw them out," I said. "They're not good for decent women, much less men. Now drunkenness, idleness, and softness are unsuited to guardians, so what are the soft, convivial modes?"

"Certain Ionian and Lydian modes called 'loose.' "

399 "Are they of any use to warriors, my friend?"

"No, so I guess that leaves you the Dorian and the Phrygian."

"I don't know the names," I said, "—just leave one mode to imitate the voice of a brave man engaged in warfare or any enforced activity, who if he fails—coming on wounds, death,
b or some other misfortune—sustains his fate with unflinching endurance. And leave another for a man engaged in peaceful, voluntary activities: trying to move a god by prayer or a man by instruction and advice, or contrariwise, submitting himself to persuasion, instruction, or advice and acting on it with success; not arrogantly, but reasonably and temper-
c ately and accepting the outcome. These two modes—one enforced, the other voluntary—suited for imitating brave, temperate men in fortune and misfortune, are all we need."

[20]Greek music had more than a dozen modes, analogous to our major and minor keys. Each was strongly associated with a different emotional effect, and all had distinctive names (Dorian, Lydian, etc.) which were passed on to medieval Church music.

"You're asking for the two I just mentioned," he said.

"Then we don't need many-stringed instruments that have a wide range, like harps and lutes. We won't have to d
support people who make instruments like that."

"It doesn't look like it."

"Shall we admit flutists and flute makers? Or is the flute the stringiest[21] instrument of all, which instruments of wide range actually imitate?"

"Obviously."

"That leaves the lyre and the zither as instruments useful in town. Shepherds in the pastures will whistle on some pipes."

"That's what the argument would seem to indicate."

"We're not doing anything exactly new in preferring e
Apollo and his instruments to Marsyas and his."[22]

"By Zeus," he said, "I guess we're not."

"By the dog, Glaucon, we didn't even notice—we've been curing our city's indigestion."

"How temperate of us."

"Come on, let's finish the purge. As with melody, we'll reject intricate rhythms and multifarious steps. We'll have to
observe the rhythms that correspond to a brave and orderly 400
life and make the metrical feet and the music follow the words suited to such a life, rather than the words follow the feet and the music. What the rhythms should be, Glaucon, is for you to say."

"I'm sorry, Socrates, I can't. I've observed that the [metrical feet and their corresponding dance][23] steps are woven from three forms, just as in the notes there are four from which all the modes are made. But which imitates what sort of life I can't say."

"We'll have to confer with Damon," I said, "and find out b
which rhythms are suited to slavishness, insolence, madness, and other evils, and which to their opposites. I seem to remember him talking obscurely about 'composite military,'

[21]I.e. it has a wide range. The effect is intentionally ludicrous.

[22]Apollo's instruments were the lyre and the zither; Marsyas's the pipe and the flute. Marsyas was a satyr who challenged Apollo to a flute-playing contest, lost, and was skinned alive.

[23]Translator's addition. These technical details are as obscure to us as to Socrates. Damon, below, was a contemporary writer on music.

'dactylic,' and 'heroic' feet, arranging them I don't know how and making them end long or short and be equal up and down. And I think he called something an 'iamb' and something else a 'trochee,' giving them each longs and shorts.
c And in some I believe he praised and blamed tempo no less than rhythm, or maybe both together, I'm not sure. But this is a terrible snarl; let's let Damon untangle it."

"Yes, he can have it."

"But this much you can untangle," I said: "gracefulness attends good rhythm and awkwardness bad."

"Of course."

d "If rhythm and melody follow the words, as we said, then good ones follow and assimilate themselves to beautiful diction, bad ones to ugly."

"Yes, and they must follow the words."

"Do speech and manner of diction follow the nature of the soul?"

"Of course."

"And everything else follows diction?"

"Yes."

"So good speech, good grace, good harmony, and good
e rhythm all attend good nature. 'Good natured' is used as a euphemism for 'foolish,' but it literally refers to the good disposition of the mind."

"Positively," he said.

"If our young are to tend their own business, mustn't they pursue these qualities everywhere?"

"Certainly."

401 "Painting and similar crafts abound in them, as do weaving, embroidery, architecture, the making of all articles as well as the nature of the body and of other growing things —all are inherently graceful or awkward. Awkwardness, disharmony, and bad rhythm are kindred to bad speech and disposition; their opposites are kin and imitations of good, temperate disposition."

"Absolutely."

b "Then not only poets," I said, "but all craftsmen must be supervised and compelled to craft into their works the image of good disposition; we must forbid them to put awkwardness, slavishness, intemperance, or bad disposition into their buildings or other crafted objects or into the images of living things, and we must prohibit anyone who does so from

practicing his craft, so that our guardians may not grow up
among images of evil, as in a rank meadow where day by day c
they graze on weeds until they unwittingly fill their souls
with one massive evil. Instead we must seek out those craftsmen whose natural talent allows them to track down the
nature of grace and beauty, so that our young, inhabiting a
healthy region, may benefit from beautiful works all around
them, whose sight and sound will everywhere impinge on
them and whose influence, like a breeze wafting health from
agreeable places, will—from childhood on—insensibly lead d
them to likeness, friendship, and harmony with beautiful
reason."

"To nurture them so would be the most beautiful way."

"For this reason, Glaucon, the most sovereign nurture lies
in poetry,[24] because its rhythms and melodies enter the in-
nermost part of the soul and powerfully seize it, bringing
grace to make graceful one who is properly nurtured, graceless one who is not. A man properly nurtured in poetry will e
quickly spot shoddy, poorly made works and ill-grown
things, and his joy and aversion will be properly placed; he'll
approve beautiful things, joyfully take them into his soul,
and from their nurture grow beautiful and good; ugly ones 402
he'll hate and properly condemn even as a child before he
can grasp the reason, and when reason comes he'll know her
and embrace her as one of his own."

"For such reasons, I think, we educate men in poetry."

"It's like learning to read," I said. "We weren't satisfied
till we could recognize those few letters in whatever combination they occurred. We didn't disregard them or think
them beneath our notice in large writing or small—we were b
eager to distinguish them everywhere, because we knew we
wouldn't be good readers until we—"

"True," he said.

"Nor will we ever recognize their images reflected in water or a mirror until we know the letters themselves—it's all
part of the same skill and discipline. In the same way, I
maintain that we and the guardians we have to educate will c
never be musical[25] until we recognize the forms of temper-

[24] Also "music." See footnote 12, p. 48.

[25] I.e. "liberally educated," since "music" meant "education," as well as "poetry," etc.

ance, courage, liberality, grandeur, and their relatives and opposites in any combination, and notice both them and their images wherever they occur, not slighting them in anything, large or small, because we consider it all part of the same skill and discipline."

"Absolutely necessary," he said.

d "When beautiful characteristics occur in the soul and harmonize in agreement with those in the body, and both participate in the same pattern, isn't that the most beautiful sight for one who can see it?"

"By far."

"And the most beautiful is the most lovable?"

"Of course."

"Then the musical man will love men who are most like that. He'll never love someone discordant."

"Only if the lack is in the soul. If it's merely a physical
e blemish he'll put up with it and cherish him anyway."

"I see—you have or have had sweethearts like that, Glaucon, and I concede your point. Now, what does excessive pleasure have in common with temperance?"

"Nothing. It can be as maddening as pain."

"With any other excellence?"

403 "Nothing."

"With insolence and self-indulgence then?"

"Very much."

"Can you think of a stronger, sharper pleasure than sex?"

"No, or one more insane."

"Is it the nature of proper love to love order and beauty temperately and harmoniously?"

"Absolutely."

"Then should any madness or anything akin to self-indulgence beset proper love?"

"No, not at all."

b "Then neither must that strong pleasure beset proper love; a proper lover and his loved one should have nothing to do with it."

"No, by Zeus, it mustn't beset it at all, Socrates."

"Then, Glaucon, it seems you'll make a law in this city you're founding, permitting a lover to consort with his sweetheart and to touch and kiss him for beauty's sake, if he

consents, like a son.[26] No serious friendship should give
even the appearance of going beyond that, to avoid re- c
proaches of lack of education and taste."

"Indeed," he said.

"Well," I said, "does that bring our discussion of poetry to an end? It ended where it ought to have ended: the end of poetry is the love of beauty."

"I agree," he said.

"After poetry the young must be trained in gymnastics."[27]

"Certainly."

"Here too they must be carefully trained all through life
from childhood up. It's like this, I think: the excellence of a d
good body doesn't make the soul good, but the other way
around: the excellence of a good soul makes the body as
good as it can be. How do you feel about it?"

"The same," he said.

"So if we've adequately ministered to the mind, we can
turn the details of fussing with the body over to it and just
outline the patterns. That will keep our discussion from e
getting too long."

"All right."

"We said they must avoid drunkenness. We can't let a guardian, of all people, get drunk and not know where on earth he is."

"It would be absurd for a guardian to need someone to guard him."

"What about diet? Our men will be athletes in the greatest
competition—will the condition of ordinary athletes suit 404
them?"

"Probably."

"But it's a pretty sleepy condition and precarious for the health. Haven't you noticed how these athletes sleep their lives away and get violently ill at the slightest departure from their appointed routine?"

"Yes."

[26]As usual in Plato, "love" refers to the love of a man for a younger man. In Athenian aristocratic circles heterosexual love was considered rather vulgar, though the common people took the opposite view.

[27]I.e. "physical training" in general.

"Our military athletes," I said, "need a more sophisticated training program; they must be alert as watchdogs,
b sharp of eye and ear, and insensitive on campaigns to
changes of food and water, heat and cold. So won't the best
gymnastic training for them be a sister to the simple poetry
we just described?"

"How?"

"Good gymnastics, especially for soldiers, is probably simple and adaptable."

"In what way?"

"You could learn that even from Homer," I said. "In camp
he doesn't regale his heroes with fish, even though they're
c by the sea on the Hellespont, or boiled meat; only with roast
meat, the easiest thing for soldiers to prepare. It's almost
always easier to use a plain fire than to drag pots around."

"It certainly is."

"And I don't think he ever mentions sweets. But then every athlete knows you have to stay away from that sort of thing if you want to keep in shape."

"They've got the right idea there," he said.

"With that attitude, my friend, you probably won't recom-
d mend Syracusan cuisine, the infinite variety of Sicilian sea-
sonings, or the seeming delights of Attic pastry."

"I don't think so."

"Would you criticize a man for having a Corinthian mistress[28] if he wanted to keep fit?"

"I certainly would."

"If you compared that kind of food and that whole way of
life to a poem composed in every mode and rhythm, you
e wouldn't have a bad comparison. Variety in poetry breeds
self-indulgence; in gymnastics, disease: simplicity there puts
temperance in the soul; here it puts health in the body."

"Very true," he said.

405 "When a city gets bloated with self-indulgence and disease, courtrooms and doctors' offices burst open; and litigation and medicine take on airs when free men take them
seriously."

"How could it be otherwise?"

"Can you imagine greater evidence of depraved education

[28]Corinth was the pleasure-city of ancient Greece, and therefore notorious for its girls.

than when eminent doctors and judges are in demand not
only among workmen and rabble, but even among men with
pretensions to a liberal upbringing? Or don't you think be- b
ing forced through lack of personal resources to import
justice from others, as though they were one's masters and
judges, is shameful proof of bad education?"

"Yes. It's the most shameful thing there is."

"Don't you think it even more shameful, Glaucon, for a
man to waste his life on litigation in a courtroom and then
display his lack of taste by preening himself on his talent for
injustice and on his ingenuity at evading justice by twisting c
and turning and dodging until he finally wiggles out of it, all
for little or nothing, ignorant of how much better and more
beautiful it is to so arrange one's life as to have no need of
a drowsy judge?"

"Yes," he said, "that's even more shameful."

"And don't you think it shameful to need a doctor—not
to cure a wound or some common illness, but for gas and
runs (brought on by indolence and the kind of life we've d
described), which flood the body like a marshy bog and force
our elegant physicians to give them names like 'blasts' and
'downpours'?"

"Those new names surely are strange."

"They didn't have such things in Asclepius's[29] day," I
said. "I infer this from his sons at Troy: they didn't scold the e
girl when Euripylus had been wounded for the Pramnian
wine sprinkled with grated cheese and barley meal, which 406
she gave him to drink,[30] or criticize Patroclus either, who
was doctoring him. Yet this is just what we think of as an
inflammatory drink."

"It is a strange drink for a man in that condition."

"Not if you consider that the Asclepiads didn't use this catering to disease called modern medicine until, they say, Herodicus came along. He was a sickly trainer who com-

[29]The legendary inventor of medicine; doctors were often called "Asclepiads."

[30]I.e. they didn't scold her for giving him the drink after he had been wounded in battle. Also ludicrously stated in Greek—Plato has tongue in cheek and intentionally garbles the story (he relates it accurately in *Ion* 538d). In the *Iliad* (11.611, ff.), not Euripylus, but Machaon, himself a son of Asclepius, is wounded.

b bined gymnastics with medicine and fretted first himself to death and then many others after him."

"How did he do that?"

"By dragging out his death, Glaucon. He had a fatal disease he couldn't cure and spent his whole life, I believe, with leisure for nothing but treating himself and fretting whenever he strayed from his routine. So because of his cleverness he died slowly and finally reached old age."

"From his skill a noble wage!"

c "Appropriate," I said, "for one who didn't know why Asclepius kept that kind of healing from his descendants: not because of inexperience or ignorance, but because he knew that for men who obey good laws each has an assigned job in his city that he must do, and no one has leisure to be sick and lie around being treated all his life. It's ridiculous that we recognize this in a workman, but not in someone rich and
d seemingly happy. When a carpenter, for instance, gets sick he expects the doctor to bring the disease up with an emetic or down with a laxative, or to cut it out with the knife or fire. If someone prescribes a long treatment with bandages on his head and all that, he snaps back that he hasn't got time to be sick and that it doesn't pay to live like that—minding your illness while neglecting your work. He'll tell such a doctor
e to go to Hades; then he'll return to his routine, get well and tend his own business. If his body can't hold up, he'll die and be rid of his troubles."

"That's the right attitude for a man like that."

407 "Because he had a job to do and it didn't pay for him to live if he couldn't get it done."

"Obviously."

"But a rich man, we say, doesn't have a prescribed job like that to make his life worthless if he can't get it done."

"So they say."

"I guess you don't hear Phocylides[31] saying that when a man has enough to live on he should practice excellence."

"Even before then, I think."

"Let's not argue with him about that," I said. "Let's try to learn if that's the proper concern for a rich man, without
b which his life will be worthless, and if coddling a disease hinders the attention in a skill like carpentry, but is no hindrance to following Phocylides' advice."

[31]An elegaic poet (sixth century B.C.).

"By Zeus," he said, "there's hardly a greater hindrance than this excessive preoccupation with the body that goes beyond gymnastics. It upsets household management, military life, and even holding sedentary offices in the state. Worst of all, it makes it hard to study, think, or concentrate,
by constantly suspecting headaches and dizziness and blam- c
ing it on philosophy, so that wherever excellence gets practiced and put to the test in that way, it's hindered by this coddling of disease which always makes you think you're sick and never stops tormenting you about your body."

"Very likely," I said. "So let's say that Asclepius knew that and revealed the art of medicine for people who were
healthy by nature and habit but had some localized disease, d
which he removed by drugs and surgery, prescribing that they continue their normal routines so they wouldn't harm the political life of their city. He didn't try to make life long and miserable for a man diseased to the core by gradually flooding and draining him and permitting him, most likely, to spawn offspring like himself, or think he ought to treat a
man who couldn't share in the settled round of daily life and e
was useless to both himself and his city."

"You're presenting a civic-minded Asclepius," he said.

"Absolutely, and his sons were too. See what fighters they
turned out to be at Troy, and they practiced the medicine 408
I just described. Do you remember how they treated Menelaus when Pandarus had wounded him, 'sucking out the blood and applying soothing drugs'?[32] They didn't prescribe what he should eat and drink any more than for Euripylus. They knew the drugs were enough to cure anyone who had lived a healthy, orderly life before he was wounded
(even if he swallowed a potion at the time), and they didn't b
think that it paid for a naturally sick and self-indulgent man to go on living, worthless to himself and others, or that medicine was for people like that—they wouldn't treat them, even if they were richer than Midas."

"According to you, Asclepius's sons were very sophisticated."

"It's only fitting," I said. "Though Pindar and our tragedians don't believe us. They say Asclepius was the son of Apollo and that he was blasted by lightning for being bribed into curing a rich man who'd already been handed over to

[32]*Iliad* 4.218.

c Death. But after what we've said we won't accept both statements: if he was the son of a god we'll say he wasn't avaricious; and if he was avaricious, then he wasn't the son of a
god."

"Right," he said. "But don't you think we should have
good doctors in our city, Socrates? I should think a good
doctor would be one who's treated many sick people as well
d as basically healthy ones, just as a good judge would be one
who's associated with every type of nature."

"Good doctors, yes. Do you know what kind I think is
good?"

"I will if you tell me," he said.

"I'll try. But you're talking about things that aren't really
alike, Glaucon."

"How so?"

"Doctors become proficient by learning their skill from
childhood and associating with all sorts of corrupt bodies;
they ought to have had every disease themselves and be
e rather sickly by nature. This is because bodies are treated
not by the body—otherwise we could never permit it to be
or to have been bad—but by the soul which, to cure well,
409 must neither be bad nor ever have been so. But a judge, my
friend, rules soul with soul, which must not be permitted to
grow up or associate with corrupt souls and run through
every injustice so as to be sharp at inferring from itself
unjust acts in others like diseases in the body. A young soul
must be kept unsullied and have no experience of bad natures if it's to become beautiful and good and able to pass
sound judgments on just acts. That's why decent men appear 'good natured' and easily deceived when they're young;
b they have no patterns in them derived from experiences
similar to those of the corrupt."

"You're right," he said. "That's exactly what happens to
them."

"And that's exactly why a good judge must be old, Glaucon. He's a late learner at recognizing what injustice is,
because he can't observe it as something native to his own
soul. He has to work for years to see how great an evil it is,
using knowledge rather than direct experience, because it's
c something foreign to him, found only in other souls."

"It seems he'll be a noble judge, at least."

"A good one too, which is what you were asking about. A

man with a good soul is good. Your clever, suspicious rascal who has committed many crimes and thinks that he's wise appears clever for being wary around his own kind; he's looking at the patterns in himself. But as soon as he encounters good, older men he appears stupid, filled with untimely
suspicions and ignorant of sound disposition because he d
lacks a pattern. Since, however, he meets more bad men than good he appears wise rather than ignorant, both to himself and to others."

"That's absolutely true," he said.

"So we won't seek a good, wise judge in that kind of man, but in the other. Baseness will never know both itself and excellence; but excellence, if nature is educated, will with
time acquire knowledge of both itself and its opposite. Such e
a man, I think—not the bad one—becomes wise."

"I agree," he said.

"Then won't this be the kind of judiciary to legislate for your city, along with the kind of medicine we just discussed?
Both will care for citizens who are naturally good in body 410
and soul; those who are not will be allowed to die if the evil is in their bodies; if it's incurably grown into their souls they'll be put to death."

"At least we've shown that that would be best for both them and the city."

"And your young, using that simple poetry which we said breeds temperance, will clearly be cautious about being in need of the law."

"Certainly."

"The poetically educated man will pursue gymnastics b
along the same trail. If he wants, he'll capture it and have no use for medicine except in emergencies."

"It seems so to me."

"And when he struggles at the labors of gymnastics he works to arouse the spirited part of his nature rather than strength, as do other athletes who dabble in diets and labors."

"Exactly," he said.

"Even the ones who originally established education in
poetry and gymnastics didn't do so for the reason some c
people think, Glaucon—one to serve the body and the other the soul. I suspect they established both chiefly for the soul."

"How so?"

"Haven't you ever observed the state of mind of people who devote their lives to gymnastics without touching poetry? or the opposite?"

"What are you referring to?"

d "Hardness and savagery on the one hand," I said, "softness and tameness on the—"

"I know—the ones that just practice gymnastics get more savage than they ought to be, and the others turn out softer than is good for them."

"Indeed," I said. "And savagery comes from the nature's spirited part, which will be brave if properly trained, but hard and harsh, most likely, if overtightened."

"That seems true to me," he said.

e "And isn't there tameness in a philosophic nature, which if loosened too much becomes softer than it ought to be, but tame and orderly if properly trained?"

"That's correct."

"But we say our guardians must have both these natures, Glaucon—the spirited and the philosophic."

"Yes, they must."

411 "And the two must be tuned and adjusted to each other?"

"Of course."

"And the soul of an adjusted man will be brave and temperate, that of an unadjusted man cowardly and uncouth?"

"Very much so."

"Now when a man surrenders himself to poetry and lets
it flute to him and pour those sweet, soft, plaintive melodies
we discussed earlier through his ears as through a funnel
into his soul, and spends his whole life now moaning, now
radiant in song, then if he had any spirit to begin with, at first
it softens like iron and becomes serviceable instead of use-
b less and brittle. But if he's held spellbound and doesn't let
go, his spirit will melt and drip until he has melted it away
and cut out the very sinews of his soul and made it a 'soft
spearman.' "[33]

"Certainly," he said.

"That will happen quickly if he received a spiritless nature
from the beginning. If it was spirited, he'll make it feeble and
touchy, ready to flare up or die down at the slightest provo-
c cation. So instead of being spirited, he'll end up irascible
and grouchy, filled with discontent."

[33]Menelaus is called a "soft spearman" in *Iliad* 17.588.

"Completely."

"Suppose he labors greatly in gymnastics and feasts himself full deep, but touches not philosophy or poetry. Won't at first his body flourish and he be filled with spirit and big ideas and grow more courageous than he was?"

"Very much so."

"What if he does nothing else and holds no commerce
whatsoever with the Muse? If he had any love of learning in d
his soul, won't it—having never tasted learning or investigation or taken any part in discussion or other poetic things—
grow feeble, deaf, and blind, since it's never been awakened,
trained, or had its senses purged?"

"Exactly."

"Then I think he'll be museless and hate discussion, and
shunning the use of speech for persuasion, gain all his ends
by savagery and force, like a beast, and live a life of igno- e
rance and ineptitude coupled with lack of rhythm and
grace."

"That's just how he'll be," he said.

"So for these two parts, it seems—the spirited and the
philosophic—and not for the body and the soul (except,
perhaps, as a sideline), I'd say some god gave man two skills,
poetry and gymnastics, to bring the parts in tune by loosen- 412
ing and tightening them until they're just right."

"It certainly seems so," he said.

"Therefore we'll properly say that the man who most beautifully blends poetry and gymnastics and applies them moderately to his soul is perfectly musical and well adjusted, much more so than a man who can adjust the strings of an instrument."

"Very likely, Socrates."

"Then if our regime is to survive, won't the city need someone like that as a perpetual overseer?"

"It certainly will, Socrates." b

"Well, Glaucon, those are the patterns for our education and training. Why go through all the dances and hunts and athletic and equestrian events? It's clear enough that they must follow our patterns and wouldn't be hard to discover now."

"No, perhaps they wouldn't," he said.

"Well," I said, "I suppose the next thing to decide is
which of the guardians should rule and which should be
ruled. Now, isn't it clear that the older must rule instead of c

the younger, and that the rulers must be the best of the guardians?"

"Yes."

"Aren't the best farmers the ones most skillful at farming?"

"Indeed."

"Then since the rulers must be the best of the guardians, they'll be the ones most skillful at guarding the city. Therefore they must be knowledgeable in that, and also capable and concerned for the city."

d "True."

"Isn't a person most concerned for what he loves?"

"Necessarily."

"And he'll especially love something whose interests, he believes, coincide with his own—when he thinks he will do well when it does well, and vice versa."

"Correct," he said.

"Then we must examine the guardians and choose the
e ones who all their lives appear eager to do whatever they
think will be advantageous to the city and who refuse to do
anything harmful."

"Yes, they'll be suitable," he said.

"It seems to me they must be watched at every stage of life, to make sure they guard this conviction—always to do whatever seems best for the city—and not forgetfully drop it through beguilement or force."

"What do you mean, drop it?"

"It appears to me," I said, "that opinion leaves the mind
either voluntarily or involuntarily: false opinion voluntarily,
413 when a person learns better; all true opinion involuntarily."

"I understand voluntary dropping," he said, "but not the involuntary."

"Well, I suppose you agree that people are deprived of bad things voluntarily and of good things involuntarily. And isn't it bad to be deceived of the truth, but good to encounter it? Or isn't conjecturing the truth the same as encountering it?"

"Yes, it's the same, and I do think that people are deprived of true opinion involuntarily."

b "Which occurs through robbery, beguilement, or force?"

"You've lost me again," he said.

"I'm afraid I'm talking like a tragedian. By robbery I mean

forgetting and being dissuaded, because in one of them *time,*
in the other one *argument,* furtively robs you. Do you understand now?"

"Yes."

"And by force I mean changing your opinion because of
pain or suffering."

"I understand that too, and it's correct."

"I imagine you too call it beguilement when someone c
changes his opinion because he's enticed by pleasure or
terrified by fear of something?"

"Yes, it seems that whatever deceives, beguiles."

"Then, as I said, we have to seek out the best guardians
of this inner conviction to do always whatever seems best for
the city. From childhood up, therefore, we must set them
tasks that especially deceive and make one forget such convictions. We must watch them carefully and choose the one
who remembers and is hard to deceive, and reject the rest. d
Isn't that so?"

"Yes."

"We must also give them painful labors, struggles, and
contests, and watch for the same things in those."

"Correct."

"And they must compete and be watched in a third kind
of contest, involving beguilement. We must expose our
young guardians to both terrors and pleasures, the way they
expose colts to noises and uproar to see which take fright.
We must test them more rigorously than gold in fire, to see e
if they resist beguilement, keep their composure at all times,
and display good rhythm and harmony as proper guardians
both of themselves and of the poetry they've learned—precisely the kind of man who will prove the most useful to
himself and the city. The man tested and proven pure as a
boy, as a young man, and as an adult shall be appointed ruler 414
and guardian of the city, and shall receive honors both in his
lifetime and after he dies—the prize of a tomb and other
memorials. The ones who fail must be rejected. That, Glaucon, in outline, not in detail, is how I think we must select
and appoint our rulers and guardians."

"I agree; it should be something like that."

"So it's proper and true to call these the absolute guard- b
ians of friends within and enemies without, because they
keep the friends from wishing, the enemies from having the

power, to do wrong. The young ones, whom we've been calling guardians up till now, are properly auxiliaries[34] who help the guardians in their decisions."

"That seems right to me," he said.

"Now, can we contrive a scheme to make even our rulers, or at least the rest of our citizens, believe a single noble lie?
c —one of those lies we were just discussing, that come up when they're needed."

"What kind of lie?"

"Nothing new," I said. "The kind of Phoenician thing that used to happen all over—or so our poets have made us believe—but not in our time, and I'm not sure it can happen again, or at least not without lots of persuasion."

"You surely seem hesitant to tell it."

"With good reason, you'll say, after you've heard it."

"Speak, man—don't be afraid."

d "I will, though I don't know where I'll find the nerve and the arguments, Glaucon. But I'll try to persuade first the rulers and soldiers, then the rest of the citizens, that everything we've done in training and educating them took place as it were in a dream, and that all the while they were really being nurtured and molded, and their armor and equipment
e was being fashioned, underground in the earth; and because when they were fully developed the earth was the mother who bore them, they must now deliberate for their land as for their nurse and their mother, defend her against any attack, and regard the rest of the citizens as their earthborn brothers."

"No wonder you were so ashamed to tell us the lie!"

415 "I had good reason to be," I said. "But still, hear the rest of the myth: 'All of you in the city are brothers,' we'll tell them, 'but the most precious are the ones fit to rule, because when the god formed you at birth he mixed gold into them, silver into the auxiliaries, and iron and bronze into the farmers and craftsmen.[35] Since you are all related you will nor-

[34]First mention of auxiliaries, which means "helpers" or "allies." Plato has no distinct term for the class of guardians and auxiliaries together, and refers to it indifferently as either the guardian or the auxiliary class.

[35]Hesiod (ca. 700 B.C.) divides men on a historical basis into races named after these four metals, in *Works and Days* 109–201.

mally breed true, but a time will come when a golden b
offspring gives birth to a silver, the silver in turn to a gold,
and so on for the rest. Therefore the god commands that the
guardians' first and most pressing duty shall be for the offspring, to determine which metal is mixed in their souls, and
if one of their own is born with iron or bronze, they must
show him not pity but the honor befitting his nature and c
demote him to a farmer or craftsman; and if a child of gold
or silver should spring from the workers, he must be honored and elevated to the rank of guardian or auxiliary.' And
we'll pretend there's an oracle that predicts the downfall of
the city when she's guarded by the guardian of iron or
bronze. Can you think of a scheme to make them believe this
tale, Glaucon?"

"Not them," he replied, "but their sons and descendants d
and all later peoples."

"I think I know what you mean, but even that will help
increase their concern for the city and each other. Well, we'll
let that go wherever public opinion will take it. Now let's arm
our earthborn troops and march them out under the command of their rulers. When they arrive they'll have to search
out a place in the city to make camp, where they can best
restrain any citizen within from breaking the laws, and repel e
any enemy without who tries to come down like a wolf on the
fold. After they've pitched camp and sacrificed to the proper
gods, they must make their lairs, right?"

"Right," he said.

"Sufficient to protect them from heat and cold?"

"Of course. I assume you mean houses."

"Yes," I said, "—for soldiers, not businessmen."

"Now what do you mean by that distinction?" 416

"I'll try to explain. The most shameful and terrible thing
for a shepherd, I suppose, is to raise dogs as auxiliaries for
his flock and then, because of hunger, indiscipline, or some
other bad trait, have them try to harm the sheep and resemble wolves more than dogs."

"Yes, that would be terrible," he said.

"Then, since they're stronger, don't we have to take every b
precaution to keep our auxiliaries from acting like that toward the citizens and resembling cruel despots rather than
benevolent allies?"

"Yes."

"Won't the best precaution be to have them truly well educated?"

"But they already have been," he said.

"I wouldn't be positive about that, dear Glaucon. But I
would be about what we just said: that getting the proper
c education, whatever it is, will best make them gentle to each
other and to the people they guard."

"Yes, that's correct."

"Well then, besides this education, anyone with sense
would say that their houses and all their property must be
arranged so that it doesn't keep them from being the best
d guardians or incite them to harm the other citizens."

"And that would be true."

"Then," I said, "see if they mustn't live something like
this: They'll own no private property beyond the bare necessities. No one will have a house or a treasury that isn't open
to all. The provisions needed by brave, temperate military
e athletes will be levied from the other citizens and presented
to them as wages for guarding, enough so they'll neither run
short nor have any left over at the end of the year. They'll
share a common life and eat at a common mess as though
they were in camp. They must be told that with divine gold
and silver from the gods always in their souls they have no
need of the human kind, and that it's impious to pollute the
divine possession with mortal gold because many impieties
417 have been committed for the currency of the many, but
theirs is pure. To them alone in the city it is forbidden to
touch or handle silver and gold, to go under the same roof
with it, to wear it or drink from it. Thus they will be preserved as they preserve the city. If they ever possess private
land and houses and money, they'll become farmers and
b landowners instead of guardians, despots and enemies instead of allies to the citizens, and they'll live out their lives
hating and being hated, plotting and being plotted against,
fearing citizens within more than enemies without, and even
then skirting the brink of destruction for both themselves
and their city. For all of these reasons," I said, "let's legislate
that the guardians' houses and everything else be arranged
as we've said. Do you agree?"

"I certainly do," he said.

Book 4

Here Adeimantus interposed: "Socrates, what defense 419
would you give if someone accused you of not making these
men very happy? It's their own fault too, because even
though the city is in reality theirs they enjoy none of its
goods, as others do: owning farms, living in beautiful man-
sions with furnishings to match, making private sacrifices to
the gods, giving parties, possessing the silver and gold you
just mentioned—everything normally considered indispen-
sible to bliss. 'They seem,' he might say, 'to sit in the city like
paid mercenaries, with nothing to do but keep watch.' " 420

"They're not even paid," I said, "except food. So they
have no money to take private trips abroad if they like, to
give to mistresses, or to spend anywhere else they might
wish, like the seemingly happy. All that and much more you
left out of your indictment."

"Well, add it on," he said.

"Did you ask what defense we would make?" b

"Yes."

"I think we'll discover what to say by following the path
we've been on. We'll say we wouldn't be surprised if leading
that kind of life made them the happiest of men, even
though our object in founding the city wasn't the excep-
tional happiness of any one class, but the greatest possible
happiness for the whole city. We thought that in such a city
we could find justice, and injustice in the one governed the
worst; and that after looking at both we'd be able to judge
what we've been searching for so long. Thus, by making c
everyone happy rather than singling out a few, we think
we're molding a happy city. Later on we can examine the
opposite kind.

"It's as if we were painting a statue[1] and someone came up and criticized us for not painting the most beautiful parts in the most beautiful colors: 'You've painted the eyes—the

[1]Greek statues were painted.

most beautiful part—black instead of red!' I think we'd make
d a reasonable defense if we said: 'See here, you curious fellow, don't think we're supposed to paint the eyes so beautiful that they don't even look like eyes. Just see if we make
the whole thing beautiful by giving each part its appropriate
color. In the same way, don't force us to hang a kind of
happiness on our guardians that will make them anything
e but guardians. We know how to drape our farmers in robes
and gold and tell them to work the land for pleasure, how
to recline our potters around a fire at a banquet, passing the
cup left to right, with a wheel standing by in case one feels
like throwing a pot, and how to make the others blissful in
the same way, so that the whole city is happy. But don't give
us advice like that, because if we take it our farmer won't be
421 a farmer, our potter a potter, nor will anyone else keep to
one of the patterns from which a city is made. Of course
those others aren't so important: if the sandal stitchers de-
generate and pretend to be the craftsmen they aren't, that's
not so awful; but if the guardians of the laws and the city
aren't what they seem, you see that they'll utterly destroy the
whole city, just as they alone are crucial to happiness and
good government.'

"If we're making true guardians least likely to harm their
b city, then our objector with his happy quasi farmers decked
out like revelers at a festival rather than as citizens of a state
is thinking of something other than a city. We must therefore consider whether our aim in establishing the guardians
is to make them as happy as possible, or whether we're
looking for happiness to develop in the city as a whole, in
which case we must persuade or compel the auxiliaries and
c guardians, and also the others, to become the best craftsmen
of their own work. Thus the whole city will be well founded,
and as it grows each class must be left to that share of
happiness which nature apportions to it."

"That seems like a good argument to me," he said.

"I wonder if its sister will also seem reasonable?"

"What's that?"

d "Examine the other craftsmen too and see if two things
corrupt them and make them bad workmen."

"Which two things?"

"Wealth and poverty," I said.

"How?"

"Like this: if a potter gets rich, do you think he'll still be concerned for his craft?"

"Not at all."

"He'll become lazy and careless compared to what he was, and not as good a potter."

"No, much worse."

"Whereas if poverty prevents him from acquiring the
tools and materials of his trade he won't turn out good work, e
or teach his sons and apprentices to be good workmen."

"No."

"So both wealth and poverty cause bad work and workmen, and it seems we've found two more things for our
guardians to keep from slipping into the city: wealth, be- 422
cause it produces luxury and laziness; poverty, because it causes slavishness, crime, and bad work. Both encourage innovation and revolution."

"True," he said. "But look, Socrates, how will our city be able to fight without money, especially against a big, rich city?"

"It would obviously be hard against one; two would be
easier." b

"What do you mean?"

"Well, Adeimantus, our soldiers will be athletes of war fighting against rich men. Don't you think a superbly-trained boxer could easily fight two rich, fat nonboxers?"

"Probably not both at once."

"Not even if he could run away and keep turning around
to hit the closest one, and kept that up in the heat and the c
sun? Couldn't a boxer handle several that way?"

"Easily—that would be no feat."

"And don't you think rich men have more experience and knowledge of boxing than of war?"

"Yes."

"So we can expect our athletes to fight easily against two
or three times their number. And what if we sent an embassy d
to the other city to announce the plain truth: 'It is not permitted us, as you, to use silver and gold. If you join us, the spoils of the others are yours'? Do you think anyone who heard that would choose to fight tough, wiry dogs when he could join the dogs against fat, tender sheep?"

"I doubt it," he said. "But if all the money from the other

e cities collects in one, beware of danger to the moneyless town."

"What bliss," I said, "—to think that any place but the kind we're founding is worth calling a city!"

"Well, what would *you* call them?"

"They need a more grandiose designation," I said. "None is a city but 'many cities,' as they say in the game.[2] Each
423 consists of at least two cities at war, one of the rich and one of the poor, and each of these in turn consists of many cities. To treat them as one is a blunder, but if you treat them as many and offer the property, the power, and even the lives of the one party to the other, you'll always have many allies and few enemies. As long as your city is governed temperately as we have arranged, it will be the greatest, not in fame but in truth, even if it consists of only a thousand defenders. You won't easily find so large a city in Greece or anywhere
b else that is only one, though many that seem so, some many times larger than yours. —Do you disagree?"

"No, by Zeus, I don't," he said.

"Then isn't this the best size for our city? The rulers must fix this as its limit, mark off enough land to suffice when it's fully grown, and let the rest go."

"What limit is that?" he asked.

"Let it grow as long as it wants to stay one, but no further."

c "Very good," he said.

"So we have a further command to give to our guardians: Make sure that the city is neither small nor seemingly great, but sufficient and one."

"An insignificant little command," he said.

"We gave an even more insignificant one a while back," I said: "If an insignificant offspring springs from the guard-
d ians, pack him off with the others; and if a significant one comes from the others, put him with the guardians. That was to show that our other citizens also must get each the one job he's naturally fit for, one for one, so that by pursuing his one proper pursuit each will become one and not many, and the whole city will naturally grow to be one rather than many."

"You're right," he said, "—that's even more trivial."

[2] A reference to a board game called "Cities."

"It's not as people might think, Adeimantus: our commands will all be insignificant rather than big and many, so
that the guardians may guard the proverbial 'one big thing;'[3] e
or rather not 'big,' but 'sufficient.' "

"What's that?"

"Education and upbringing. If they're well educated and
become moderate men they'll easily discern this and everything we're leaving out, like marriage, mating, and the possession of wives, and see that all these must conform as
closely as possible to the old saying: 'The things of friends 424
are common.' "

"That would surely be proper."

"And if our regime once gets a good start it will continue
to grow like a circle.[4] Good education and upbringing, if
preserved, will produce good natures which in turn, if they
partake of good education, will grow better than their predecessors in breeding and everything else, like any other living
thing." b

"Very likely," he said.

"To sum up then: Those in charge of the city must cling
to this idea and stay constantly alert to keep corruption from
creeping in and to prevent innovation in gymnastics and
poetry, contrary to the established order. They must especially be on their guard when they hear 'That song turns
men's attention/ which falls newest from the singer's lips,'[5]
for fear that people may think the poet means 'new styles of c
song' rather than 'new songs,' and is praising that. That's
something that must never be praised or so understood.
They must guard against changing to a new form of music[6]
as against a universal danger. Ways of song are nowhere
disturbed without disturbing the most fundamental ways of
the state. So says Damon, and I believe him."

"Put me down as a believer too," said Adeimantus.

[3]Cf. Archilochus: "The fox knows many things, the porcupine one big one."

[4]An image from drawing a circle: it "grows" for the first half of its revolution, "declines" for the second. If the state grows like a circle, it must eventually decline like one, an idea here left unexpressed. Cf. 546a, p. 203–204.

[5]*Odyssey* 1.351–52.

[6]"Music" includes poetry.

d "Therefore, it seems, our guardians must found their guardhouse in music."

"Yes, that kind of waywardness easily slips in."

"Disguised as play that does no harm."

"Not much," he said. "It just settles down gradually and gently flows into people's dispositions and pursuits. From there it swells and bursts into business agreements and then, raging with depravity, sweeps down on laws and constitu-
e tions, Socrates, until finally it overthrows everything public and private."

"Oh," I said. "Is that what it does?"

"It seems so to me," he said.

"Then, as we've said from the beginning, our young must participate in a more lawful kind of play, because when it becomes wayward so will the boys, and we'll never get seri-
425 ous, law-abiding men from boys like that."

"Of course not," he said.

"Then if our boys begin by playing well and acquire lawfulness from their music and poetry, the opposite should happen: It attends and strengthens them in everything, and rights anything in the city that previously may have collapsed."

"That's surely true."

"So they'll rediscover all those seemingly trivial rules that their predecessors abolished."

"What rules?"

b "Things like the young keeping a respectful silence in front of their elders, standing up and making way for them, taking care of their parents, as well as hair style, clothing, shoes, deportment, and so on. I think it would be silly to legislate for those things—they won't catch on or last simply by being written down."

"No."

"I suspect that the direction set by education will deter-
c mine all that follows. Doesn't like always call up like, Adeimantus?"

"Of course."

"So I think we'll say that the result will be a single perfect and vigorous good or evil, and for that reason I wouldn't try to legislate for that sort of thing."

"A reasonable position," he said.

"And now, by the gods," I said, "what about all the mer-

cantile squabbles—contracts in the marketplace between
merchants and workmen, regulations for slander and as- d
sault, for filing suits and selecting juries, for collecting and
paying any necessary taxes in markets or ports, and all the
other urban, harbor, and market regulations—shall we
deign to legislate for that?"

"It's not worth it for men who are good. They'll easily
discover most of the minor things that need to be legis- e
lated."

"Yes, my friend—provided a god grants them the preservation of the laws we've gone through."

"If not," he said, "they'll spend their lives constantly making and adjusting these petty regulations, in hope of reaching the best."

"You mean like sick men too self-indulgent to give up a
vicious way of life? They too lead a charming life, constantly 426
being doctored and accomplishing nothing except to make
their disease worse and more complicated, while always expecting to be cured by whatever new medicine someone
suggests."

"A perfect description of that kind of invalid."

"And isn't it charming how they hate being told the truth:
that no medicine, cautery, surgery, or spell or amulet for
that matter, will do them any good until they stop drinking b
and overeating and give up sex and indolence?"

"Not very," he said. "There's no charm in getting angry when someone says the right thing."

"You seem not to admire that sort of man, Adeimantus."

"Not at all, by Zeus."

"Then you wouldn't admire a whole city that acted like
that. Or don't you think it's the same when a badly governed
city proclaims death to the man who tampers with the consti- c
tution, while the man who pampers the citizens as they are
and most pleasantly serves them, who ingratiates himself by
anticipating their desires and shrewdly catering to them, he
is proclaimed the good man, wise in important matters, and
is honored among them?"

"It seems the same to me, and I don't admire it at all."

"What about those willing and eager to serve such a city? d
Aren't you awed by their courage and complaisance?"

"Yes, except for the ones deceived by the applause of the many into thinking they're true statesmen."

"Shouldn't you forgive them? Do you think that a man
who doesn't know how to measure could disbelieve a mob
e of others like him who kept telling him he was six feet tall?"

"No, not in that case."

"Well then, don't be angry. They're really the most delightful fellows, constantly legislating and tinkering with the
trivia we just described, always hoping to put an end to these
squabbles and crooked business deals, unaware that they're
trying to cut off a Hydra's head."[7]

427 "You're right," he said, "that's just what it's like."

"Well, I wouldn't have thought it necessary for a true
lawgiver to fuss with such things in the laws and constitution
of either a badly or a well governed city, because in the one
it's useless and does no good, whereas in the other some of
these regulations would occur to anyone and the others will
flow of themselves from previous practices."

b "Well," said Adeimantus, "what's next to legislate?"

"For us, nothing; for Apollo at Delphi the first, foremost,
and most beautiful legislation."

"What's that?"

"Founding temples, sacrifices, and other sacred services
for gods, spirits, and heroes, as well as burial rites for the
dead and services to propitiate those over there. We don't
understand such things ourselves, and if we have any sense
c we won't listen to anyone else or use any interpreter but the
ancestral one. The ancestral interpreter of such things for all
peoples is the Delphic god who interprets while sitting on
the navel in the middle of the earth."

"Well said," he replied. "So be it."

"Son of Ariston," I said, "your city is founded. Now ask
d your brother and Polemarchus and the others here to help
you, and try to get enough light from somewhere to examine
it and see where justice and injustice are, how they differ
from each other, and which of them a man must possess to
be happy, whether or not he's noticed by all gods and men."

"Nonsense," said Glaucon. "You promised to search and
e said it would be impious not to defend justice with all your
might."[8]

"A truthful reminder," I said. "But you have to help."

[7]A mythical monster that grew two new heads for each one that was cut off.

[8]The reference is to 368b–c, p. 40.

"We will."

"Well, I hope to find it like this: if our city was properly founded it must be perfectly good."

"Necessarily," said Glaucon.

"Then it's obviously wise, brave, temperate, and just.[9] If we discover any of these in our city, therefore, what's left over will be the undiscovered."

"Of course." 428

"It's like searching for one of any four things in anything; if we recognize it first, that will do. If we recognize the other three first, we'll know by that what we're looking for, which must be the one left over. So we can use this method in our search."

"Correct," he said.

"The clearest thing here seems to me to be wisdom, but
there appears to be something strange about it." b

"What?"

"It seems to me that our city is truly wise because it has good judgment, and good judgment is clearly a kind of knowledge. I suppose men make good judgments by knowledge rather than by ignorance."

"Clearly," said Glaucon.

"Now there are many kinds of knowledge in our city. Should we call it wise and say it has good judgment because of the knowledge of its carpenters?"

"No, we should call it skilled in carpentry." c

"For its knowledge of furniture making, metal working, or any other skill in which its craftsmen show good judgment?"

"No."

"And knowledge of growing crops doesn't make a city wise but agricultural."

"It seems so to me," he said.

"What about the city we just founded? Do any of her
citizens have a knowledge, not of something in the city but d
of the city as a whole, that judges and deliberates how she may have the best relations with herself and other cities?"

"Yes," he said.

"What is it? Who has it?"

"Guardianship—those rulers we just called perfect guardians."

[9]The four Greek cardinal virtues, or "excellences."

"And what would you call the city because of this knowledge?"

"A truly wise city with good judgment," Glaucon replied.

"Do you think there'll be more smiths or more of these
e true guardians in our city?"

"Many more smiths."

"Would there be fewer guardians than any other group with some knowledge that gives them a name?"

"Far fewer."

"In a city founded according to nature, therefore, the
whole would be wise by virtue of its smallest part and of the
knowledge in it—the governing or ruling class. It seems that
429 this class, which is fit to partake of the only knowledge properly called wisdom, is by nature the smallest."

"Why, that's true," he said.

"Well," I said, "I don't quite know how, but we seem to have found one of the four and where it resides in the city."

"At least I'm satisfied with our discovery."

"And it shouldn't be hard to see where the city's courage is, by which we call her brave."

"How?"

b "Why, when someone calls a city cowardly or brave, what
does he look at but the part that she fights and defends
herself with? I doubt if the cowardice or courage of the
others would be decisive in making her one or the other."

"No."

"So a city is brave too by a part of itself, in which it has
the power to preserve under all circumstances the opinion
c that what must be feared are precisely the things and the
sorts of things that the lawgiver handed down in the citizens'
education. Isn't that what you call courage?"

"Please repeat that. I didn't understand it very well."

"I mean courage is a sort of preservation, Glaucon."

"Preservation? What kind?"

"Of the opinion of the things and of the sorts of things
that ought to be feared, imparted by law through education.
d By 'under all circumstances' I meant that a man will preserve
and not drop it in pains, pleasures, desires, or fears. I could
illustrate this with a simile if you'd like."

"Please do."

"Well," I said, "you know that when dyers want to dye wool purple they select from all the possible colors wool that

is naturally white, give it a long preliminary treatment to
make the color take, and only then dye it. Things dyed like e
that are permanent, and even detergent won't wash out the
dye. If some other color was used, or untreated white, you
know what will happen."

"Yes, it will wash out and look ridiculous."

"Then assume that when we selected our soldiers and
educated them in poetry and gymnastics we were trying, as
best we could, to do the same thing. What we did was devise 430
a scheme to persuade them to take our laws like a beautiful
dye so that, since they have the appropriate nature and upbringing, their opinion of terrors and other things will be
permanent and their dye won't wash out in those terrible
detergents—pleasure (stronger than the strongest detergent), pain, fear, and desire. This power to preserve under b
all circumstances the right, lawful opinion of what is and is
not to be feared I call courage, unless you tell me different."

"I won't, because it seems to be that if an animal or a slave
has right opinion in these things, not acquired by education,
you don't consider it very lawful or even call it courage."

"You're right," I said. c

"Then I accept your definition of courage."

"Accept it in the sense of 'courage of a citizen,' and you'll
have it right. We can go through this better some other time
if you'd like, but right now we're searching for justice, not
courage. I think what we've said will be sufficient for that."

"True."

"Then we still have two things left to see in the city:
temperance, and the object of this whole search, justice. d
How can we find justice without making a big fuss about
temperance?"

"I don't know, and I wouldn't want to do it. If you want
to do me a favor, examine temperance before justice."

"Of course, Glaucon—I'd be wrong to refuse. Now, seen e
from here temperance resembles a concord or a harmony
more than courage and wisdom did."

"How?"

"I suppose temperance is a kind of order, and control over
certain pleasures and desires, as is shown—I don't quite
know how—by expressions like 'mastering oneself,' which
are used for tracking it down."

"Absolutely," he said.

"Isn't that a ridiculous expression? A man master of him-
431 self would also be a slave, and a slave also a master. All these
phrases refer to the same person."

"Of course."

"What it apparently means is that a man has a good and
a bad part in his soul, and when the naturally better part
controls the worse it's praised as 'mastering oneself;' but
when bad company or upbringing allows the bad, mob part
to overwhelm the good part, which is smaller, that's cen-
b sured and blamed as 'being a slave to oneself,' and a man
in such a state is called 'intemperate.' "

"Yes, and reasonably so," he said.

"Now look at our new city and you'll find one of these
conditions in it. If a place where the better rules the worse
should be called 'temperate' and 'master of itself,' then you
can justly call our city 'mistress of herself.' "

"I'm looking," he said, "and it's true."

"Now the many, multifarious pleasures, pains, and desires
c exist mainly in women, children, slaves, and in those so-
called free men who constitute the worthless many; whereas
the simple, moderate ones, guided by reason together with
intelligence and right opinion, reside in the few that are best
by nature and education."

"True."

"Don't you see the same thing in your city? The desires
d of the worthless many are controlled by the desires and
knowledge of the decent few."

"Yes."

"So if any city ought to be called master of its desires,
pleasures, and itself, this would be the one. Doesn't that also
make it temperate in all these respects?"

"Very much so."

"And don't you think that in this city, if anywhere, both
e the rulers and the ruled will have the same opinion of who
should rule?"

"Absolutely."

"Then in which group would you say temperance exists in
a city like this: in the rulers or the ruled?"

"In both, I suppose."

"You see? our intuition was right—we said temperance
resembles a kind of harmony."

"But why?"

"Because unlike wisdom and courage, which reside in a

part to make the city wise or brave, temperance extends 432
through the whole and makes everyone—the weak, the strong and the in-between, in knowledge, strength, numbers, wealth, or however you want to judge them—sing the same song on key. So we can properly call this concord 'temperance:' the agreement between the naturally better and worse about which part should rule in both the city and the individual."

"I agree completely." b

"Well," I said, "we've seen three of the things in our city, at least well enough for an opinion. It's clear that the form left over, which would make the city partake of still another excellence, must be justice."

"Yes, that's clear."

"Now, Glaucon, we must circle the thicket like hunters
and pay close attention so justice doesn't elude us and disappear into the brush. It's clearly around here somewhere. So c
keep a sharp lookout and see if you can spot it first and point
it out to me."

"I wish I could. But you'll be acting fairly if you treat me as a follower who can spot what you point out."

"Follow then. But say a hunting prayer with me."

"I will. Lead on."

"Oh," I said, "what a dense, shady place! It's filled with shadows that hide the tracks. Still, we must push on."

"Go ahead," he said. d

I scouted around. "Look, Glaucon, look—I think we have the track—it won't escape us now."

"Joyous tidings!" he shouted.

"And yet," I said, "we've been acting like imbeciles."

"What do you mean?"

"My friend, it seems that it was really rolling around at our
feet all along, but like a couple of ninnies we didn't even
notice. We kept gazing out in the distance and missed it, like e
a man running around looking for something that's in his
hand."

"How come?"

"It seems we've been saying it all along and didn't realize that in a way we were saying it."

"This is a long prologue for someone eager to hear."

"Then see if this makes sense: What we established at the 433
very beginning of founding our city as necessary to do under

all circumstances—either it, it seems, or some form of it is justice. You remember we said over and over that each one must pursue the one pursuit to which his nature is most naturally suited."

"Yes, we did."

"And we've often heard it from others and said it ourselves, that justice is tending your own business and not
b meddling in others'."

"Yes we have."

"Well, my friend, I'll bet that in a certain way this will turn out to be justice: tending your own business. Do you know how I infer that?"

"No, tell me."

"It seems to me that the thing left over after examining
temperance, courage, and knowledge is what enables them
all to arise in the city and preserves them while it remains.
c And we said if we found the three, the one left over would
be justice."

"Necessarily."

"Now it would be hard to decide which of them does the
most to make our city good: the shared opinion of rulers and
ruled; the soldiers' preservation of their lawful opinion
about what is and what is not to be feared; the knowledge
d and guardianship of the rulers; or the principle embodied in
women and children, free men and slaves, merchants and
craftsmen, rulers and ruled—that each, being one, must
tend his own business and not meddle in many."

"Yes," he said, "it's a hard decision."

"Therefore, it seems, the ability of each to tend his own
e business rivals wisdom, temperance, and courage in making
the city excellent. And mustn't the thing that rivals those
three in contributing to the city's excellence be called justice?"

"Absolutely."

"Look at it in this way too and see if you agree: Will you appoint your rulers as judges in lawsuits?"

"Of course."

"And as judges won't they strive to make sure that no one has what belongs to another or is deprived of his own?"

"Exactly."

"Because that is just."

"Yes."

"So in this way too we agree that justice is having and
doing what is properly yours." 434

"True."

"Now suppose a carpenter attempts to do a shoemaker's
work, or a shoemaker a carpenter's, and they exchange their
tools and honors, or one man tries to do both—do you think
that would harm the city much?"

"Not very much."

"But when a man who is by nature a craftsman or any
other kind of moneymaker is induced by his wealth, b
strength, popular support, or anything else to enter the
military class, or when a soldier who is unworthy of it tries
to enter the deliberative, guardian class,[10] and they exchange tools and honors, or when one man tries to do all of
these things, I think you'll agree that this kind of exchange
and meddling will be the death of the city."

"Completely."

"So any interchange or meddling between its three classes
does the city the greatest harm and should properly be c
called the greatest wrongdoing."

"Absolutely."

"And wouldn't you call doing the greatest wrong to one's
own city injustice?"

"Of course."

"That, then, is injustice. Now turn it around: When the
moneymaking, auxiliary, and guardian classes each tend
their own business, that's the opposite condition and must
be justice and make the city just."

"I don't see what else it could be." d

"Let's not be too positive yet. If we agree that when this
same form enters an individual it is also justice there, then
we'll accept it—what else could we do? If not, we'll examine
something else. Now let's finish this examination. We
thought we could most easily see what justice is like in a man
if we observed it first in something large. Taking that to be
a city, we founded the best one we could, because we knew e
that a good city would have justice. Now let's apply what
we've found there to the individual. If it agrees, fine. If it

[10]Plato avoids rigid terminology. "Military class" = auxiliaries; "soldier" = an auxiliary; "deliberative class" = guardians. So in *c*, below, "moneymaking class" = craftsmen and farmers.

turns out to be different, we'll go back to the city for further tests. Perhaps by examining them against each other and
435 rubbing them together like sticks we can kindle justice, and once it flashes clear, confirm it for ourselves."

"A good method," said Glaucon. "Let's do it that way."

"Now when you apply the same term to something large and something small, are they like or unlike in the way they're called the same?"

"Like."

b "Then a just man won't differ from a just city as far as the form of justice is concerned."

"No, he'll resemble it."

"A city appeared to be just when it had three classes of people in it, each tending its own business, and it also appeared temperate, brave, and wise because of certain other states and conditions of these three classes."

"True."

"Then, my friend, if an individual has these same three
c forms[11] in his soul we'll expect him, because of the same conditions in them, to merit the same designations as the city."

"An absolute necessity," he said.

"Then we've stumbled onto another trivial investigation, my friend—whether the soul has these three forms in it or not."

"It doesn't seem so trivial to me. Maybe the old saying is true, Socrates: 'Beautiful things are difficult.' "

"Apparently," I said. "But this you can be sure of, Glau-
d con: in my opinion we'll never reach precision in this by inquiring as we have. A much longer path leads to it. But maybe we can at least reach something worthy of our foregoing talk and examination."

"Won't that do for now? It will for me."

"I'll be more than satisfied," I said.

"Don't hold back then—examine it."

e "Well, we surely have to admit that the same three forms or dispositions found in the city also exist in each one of us. They could hardly get there from anywhere else. It would be

[11]"Form" in Plato is not a specialized technical term used only of the eternal archetypes. Often, as here, it means merely "kind" or "class."

ridiculous to imagine spiritedness arising in a city from any
other source than the individuals who have this attribute, as
do people in Thrace, Scythia, and almost everywhere in the
North; or love of learning, which one might especially attribute to our region; or love of money, which might be 436
called prevalent among Phoenicians and Egyptians.[12] It's
not hard to see that this is so."

"No," he said.

"But this is harder: do we do everything with our whole
soul, or does it have three different parts, so that we learn
with one, feel emotions with another, and desire the pleasures of nourishment, procreation, and so forth with a third? b
That won't be easy to sort out. Let's first try to distinguish
whether the parts are identical with each other or different."

"How?"

"It's clear that the same thing will never suffer or do
opposite things in the same part at the same time toward the
same thing, so if we find that happening in the soul we'll
know it's not single but multiple. Examine what I mean: Can c
the same thing be both at rest and in motion in the same part
at the same time?"

"Never."

"Now let's agree more precisely so we don't disagree as
we move along. If someone were to say that a man standing
in one place but waving his arms is both in motion and at
rest at the same time, I think we'd reject the statement as
improper and say that part of him is moving and part is at d
rest. Right, Glaucon?"

"Right."

"And if our quibbler tries to be cute and dazzle us into
believing that a top, at least, or anything else that revolves
in the same place both moves and stands still as a whole at
the same time when it turns around a peg fixed in one spot,
we'll reject that too, because it moves and stands still in
different parts. We'll say that tops and so forth have both a e
straight and a circular part, and as long as they don't tilt
they're at rest in the straight but in motion in the circular,

[12]These three traits correspond to the three classes of the city: "spiritedness" to the auxiliary class, "love of learning" to the guardians, and "love of money" to the workers, or "moneymakers."

and if while spinning they incline from the vertical in any direction, then they're not at rest in any part."

"We'll be right too."

"So nothing like that will startle us into believing that the
437 same thing can ever do, suffer, or be opposite things in the same part at the same time toward the same thing."

"Not me, at least."

"Well then, to avoid drawing this out by disproving all sorts of such quibbles, can we continue with that as an assumption, taking for granted that should it prove false, all the conclusions depending on it will be invalid?"

"Yes, we must."

b "Then would you class as opposites things like consenting and refusing, striving to get and rejecting, drawing toward and pushing away, whether they're active or passive?—we're not interested in that distinction."

"Yes, they're opposites."

"What about hunger and thirst and the desires in general, as well as wanting and being willing? Wouldn't you put those
c somewhere with the forms we just mentioned and say that the soul of someone who desires always either strives for what it desires, or draws toward it what it wants to have, or, so far as it's willing to have something provided, consents to have it brought as if someone had asked it, and grasps for its attainment?"

"Yes."

"What about not wanting, being unwilling, and not desiring? Shall we class those with the opposites, among the soul's rejectings and pushings away?"

d "Of course."

"Then shall we say that the desires form a class, and that its most conspicuous members are the desire for food and for drink, which we call hunger and thirst?"

"Yes."

"Now is thirst in itself the desire for anything more than for what we say the soul desires? Is it desire for warm drink or cold, much drink or little or, in a word, for drink of a certain kind? Or does the addition of heat to thirst produce
e the desire for cold drink and of cold the desire for warm, and if by presence of magnitude the thirst is great, it produces desire for much drink; if little, for little? Isn't thirst itself the

desire only for that which it naturally desires—drink itself—just as hunger is the desire for food?"

"Yes, each desires only what it's the natural desire of. Additions produce desire of a certain kind."

"Let no man, therefore, rattle us when we're off guard by 438
saying we desire not drink but good drink and not food but good food, 'Because, you see, all men desire good things. Therefore if thirst is a desire it desires something good—drink, food, or whatever it's the desire of. And the same for the other desires.' "

"It might seem that he has a point, though."

"But it almost goes without saying that when things go
together, things of a kind go with things of a kind, and things b
in themselves go only with things in themselves."[13]

"I don't understand," Glaucon said.

"Don't you understand that the larger is the sort of thing that is larger *than* something?"

"Of course."

"Than the smaller."

"Right."

"And the much larger is much larger than the much smaller?"

"Yes."

"And the sometimes larger than the sometimes smaller, the eventually larger than the eventually smaller?"

"Well, obviously."

"Isn't the same true of more in relation to less, double in c
relation to half, and so on; of heavier to lighter and faster to slower; of hot to cold, and so on?"

"Certainly."

"Isn't it the same with knowledge? Knowledge itself is knowledge of learning itself (or whatever we ought to posit as the object of knowledge), but knowledge of a certain kind
is knowledge of learning of a certain kind. Here's what I d
mean: when the knowledge of building houses came about, wasn't it called housebuilding because it differed from all other knowledge?"

"Of course."

[13]Intentionally confusing, like much of this argument. The idea is that in pairs of relative things, neither or both must be qualified.

"In being a certain kind, unlike any other?"

"Yes."

"And it became a certain kind because its learning was of a certain kind. Isn't that true of all knowledge and skills?"

"Indeed."

"Then here's what I was trying to say, if you understand
me now: when things go together, things alone go only with
things alone, and things of a certain kind go with things of
e a certain kind. By which I don't mean that they're *like* what
they go with, as though knowledge of sickness and health
were itself sick and healthy, or knowledge of good and evil
itself good and evil, but only that when a knowledge arose
that was not of learning itself, but of a certain kind of learning such as sickness and health, then this knowledge also
turned out to be of a certain kind and could no longer be
simply called 'knowledge,' but by the addition of kind took
the name 'medicine.' "

"I understand," he said, "and it seems right."

439 "Then," I said, "wouldn't you put thirst with the things
that are what they are because they go with something? And
thirst, I suppose, goes with—"

"Yes," he said, "—drink."

"And thirst for drink of a certain kind is a certain kind of thirst, but thirst itself is not for much or little, good or bad or, in a word, for a certain kind: thirst itself is naturally only for drink itself."

"Absolutely," he said.

"Then as far as its thirst is concerned, a thirsty soul only
b wants to drink—that's all it grasps and rushes for."

"Clearly," said Glaucon.

"So if anything holds it back when it's thirsty, there must be something else in it different from the thirsty part that tries to lead it like a horse to water. We said that the same part of a thing can't act in opposite ways toward the same thing at the same time."

"Yes."

"So I imagine it's wrong to say that an archer's hands both push and pull the bow at the same time. We should say one hand pushes while the other pulls."

c "Correct," he said.

"Shall we say there are people who sometimes refuse to drink when they're thirsty?"

"Many frequently do."

"What should we say about them? that something in their soul urges them to drink while something else hinders them and overpowers the urger?"

"It seems so to me."

"And when the hinderer appears isn't it engendered by
reason, whereas the things that lead and drag the soul arise d
from certain states and diseases?"

"Apparently."

"So it won't be unreasonable to expect them to be two distinct parts, or to call the part with which the soul reasons the rational part, the one with which it loves, hungers, thirsts, and is flustered by the other desires the irrational or desiring part, the companion of pleasures and gorging."

"No, it will be quite reasonable," said Glaucon. e

"Well," I said, "two forms stand mapped out in the soul. Is the part with which we feel spirit[14] separate, or identical in nature with one of the others?"

"Probably with the desiring part."

"I trust in a story I once heard. Leontius, son of Aglaion, was walking up from the Piraeus outside the North Wall and saw some corpses lying at the executioner's. He wanted to look, but at the same time he felt angry and turned away in
disgust. He fought with himself and covered his eyes until
the desire overpowered him. Then with bulging eyes he ran 440
up to the corpses and cried: 'There, you damned eyes
gorge yourselves on the beautiful sight!' "

"I've heard it too," he said.

"This story shows that anger sometimes wars with desire, as though they were different things."

"Yes, it does."

"We see it often: a person's desires force him to something contrary to reason and he berates himself and gets b
indignant with the part that forces him, and his spirit allies with reason as though reason and desire were at civil war. But if reason says 'you mustn't,' I doubt if you've ever seen the spirit opposing it and siding with desire, in yourself or anyone else."

[14]I.e. strong emotions such as anger, resentment, and indignation. The spirit was the seat of these emotions, and the word is often applied to the emotions themselves.

"Never, by Zeus."

c "Suppose someone thinks he's committed injustice and
then suffers—justly, he believes—hunger, cold, and other
pains from the one he wronged. The more noble he is, the
less able he'll be to get angry with his tormentor—his spirit
will refuse to be aroused."

"True."

"But what if he thinks he's suffering unjustly? Won't he
boil and rage at this injustice and at the hunger, cold, and
pain, ally with what seems to him to be just, and conquer by
d enduring and refusing to abandon his noble cause until he
either accomplishes his purpose or dies, or until the reason
within him calls him back and soothes him like a shepherd
his dog?"

"It certainly resembles what you say. And we just appointed our auxiliaries to be like obedient dogs to the rulers, the shepherds of the city."

"You catch my meaning well, Glaucon. I wonder if you've thought of something else?"

e "What?"

"That the spirited part now appears the opposite of what it just seemed. We thought it was part of the desiring part, but now we say that in the soul's civil war it will bear arms on the side of the rational part."

"Absolutely."

"Then is it distinct, or a form of the rational part, so that
not three but two forms exist in the soul: the rational and the
desiring? Or as three classes held the city together—the
441 moneymaking, the auxiliary, and the deliberative—is there
also a third class in the soul; the spirited part, the natural
auxiliary of the rational part unless corrupted by bad upbringing?"

"The spirit is necessarily the third part," he said.

"Yes," I said, "if it turns out to be distinct from the rational part, as it did from the desiring part."

"It's not hard to see that—you can see it even in children:
they're full of spirit as soon as they're born, but some never
b seem to get reason, and most get it late."

"Good point, Glaucon," I said. "You can see it in animals too, and that line from Homer we quoted somewhere above testifies to the same thing: 'He struck his chest and rebuked

his heart.'[15] This clearly shows that Homer makes the part
that has reflected about better and worse reprimand the c
irrational, spirited part, as two separate things."

"You're absolutely right," he said.

"It's been a long, hard swim," I said, "but we've made it this far and pretty well agree that the same classes exist in both the city and the individual soul, and that the number in each is the same."

"True."

"Then isn't it a necessary conclusion that the individual is d
wise in the same part and in the same way as the city, that the city is brave in the same part and way as the individual, and so on for everything that pertains to excellence?"

"Absolutely necessary."

"Then I think we'll say that a man is just in the same way as the city, Glaucon."

"That's absolutely necessary too."

"I don't suppose we've forgotten that the city was just when each of its three classes tended its own business."

"No," he said, "I don't think that we have."

"So we must remember that each of us too will be just and
tend his own business if each of our parts tends its own e
business."

"We certainly must."

"And isn't it fitting for the rational part to rule, because it is wise and has forethought for the whole soul, and for the spirited part to obey it and be its ally?"

"Of course."

"Won't a blend of poetry and gymnastics make the two
harmonious, as we said, by tightening and nurturing the one
with beautiful words and studies, and by loosening and com- 442
forting the other, and taming it with melody and rhythm?"

"Absolutely."

"And when these two have been so nurtured and taught
what's truly their own business, they'll control the desiring
part, which is the largest part of every soul and by nature
insatiable for possessions, and keep it from gorging itself on
the so-called pleasures of the body and growing so big and
strong that it no longer tends its own business but attempts b

[15] *Odyssey* 20.17–18, quoted in 390d, p. 60.

to enslave and rule those which its birth does not fit it to rule, and so overthrow the whole life of them all."

"Of course," said Glaucon.

"Won't these two parts," I asked, "beautifully guard against outside enemies too on behalf of the whole soul and body, the one by deliberating, the other by following the ruler, fighting for it, and accomplishing by its courage what's been deliberated?"

"Yes."

"This is the thing, I believe, by which we call any individ-
c ual brave: when his spirited part preserves through both
pleasures and pains the commands of reason about what is
and is not to be feared."

"Correct," he said.

"And he's wise because of that little part which ruled in him and issued the commands, and which likewise had knowledge of what was advantageous both to it and to the whole community of three parts."

"Of course."

"And isn't he temperate because of the love and harmony
of these three, when both the ruling and the two ruled parts
d agree that the rational part must rule and don't rebel against
it?"

"Yes," he said, "that's exactly what temperance is, both in the individual and in the state."

"And he'll be just in the way we've so often said."

"Necessarily."

"Well," I said, "has the outline of justice been in any way blurred so as to seem different from what it appeared in the city?"

"It doesn't seem so to me," said Glaucon.

"If anything in our soul is still skeptical, we can completely
e confirm our conclusion by applying some vulgar tests to it."

"How?"

"Like this: if a man with a nature and upbringing similar
to our city's received a deposit of money and it was stolen,
do you think anyone would think he had done it rather than
443 someone unlike him?"

"Never."

"If a temple or a house were robbed, or a friend or the city betrayed, would he be a suspect?"

"No."

"He surely wouldn't be untrustworthy in an oath or in any kind of agreement, and adultery or neglect of gods or parents would pertain to anyone sooner than him."

"Absolutely," he said.

"And the reason for all this is that each of his parts tends b
its own business in regard to ruling and being ruled?"

"Exactly."

"So would you look for justice to be anything but the power to produce men and cities like that?"

"I wouldn't, by Zeus."

"Then our dream has come true. We said[16] we suspected
that some god had allowed us to come across a rule or
pattern of justice at the very beginning of founding our c
city."

"Completely."

"Therefore it really was a mirage of justice, Glaucon—which is why it was useful—the idea that a shoemaker by nature should properly make shoes and do nothing else, a carpenter build, and so on."

"Apparently."

"The truth, however, seems to be this: Justice, although
it resembles that mirage, is really concerned with internal
rather than external activity—with the true self and its busi- d
ness. It's the condition of a man who allows none of the
classes in his soul to tend another's business or to meddle
with the others. First he puts what are truly his own affairs
in order, arranges and takes command of himself, becomes
a friend to himself, and tunes his three parts like three notes
of a chord—high, middle, and low—[17] binding both them
and whatever may lie between them into one temperate, e
harmonious whole, one out of many. Only then does he act,
if he finds something to do in financial affairs, politics, private business, or the care of the body. And in all these
undertakings he will both think and call any act that produces or preserves this condition 'beautiful and just,' and
the knowledge that presides over such an act 'wisdom;' but
he will call 'unjust' any action that tends to dissolve this
condition, and 'ignorance' the opinion which presides in 444
turn over that."

[16]The reference is to 433a, pp. 99–100.

[17]I.e. the rational, spirited, and desiring parts, respectively.

"That's absolutely true, Socrates."

"I don't think we'd appear to be lying very much if we said we've discovered the just man and the just city, and also what the justice in them is."

"Not at all, by Zeus."

"Shall we, Glaucon?"

"Let's."

"So be it," I said. "Next, I believe, we must examine injustice."

"Clearly."

b "Wouldn't that have to be meddling and interference and a kind of civil war between the soul's three parts, and a revolt of one against the whole so that an unfit part might rule? All that, I think, as well as their confusion and wandering, we'll call injustice, intemperance, cowardice, ignorance and, in short, absolute evil."

"Precisely," he said.

c "If justice and injustice are clear, then acting justly on the one hand, and doing wrong and committing injustice on the other, must also be perfectly clear. They're like healthy and sick practices, in the soul instead of the body."

"How?"

"I suppose healthy practices engender health, sick ones disease."

"Yes."

"Then doesn't acting justly engender justice, acting un-
d justly injustice?"

"Necessarily," said Glaucon.

"And producing health means to establish the parts of the body so that they dominate and are dominated by each other according to nature, disease so that they rule and are ruled contrary to nature."

"True."

"Then," I said, "engendering justice means establishing the parts of the soul so that they dominate and are dominated by each other according to nature, injustice so that they rule and are ruled contrary to nature."

"Absolutely."

"So excellence, it seems, must be a sort of health and
e beauty and well-being of the soul; evil a disease, ugliness, and weakness."

"That's true."

"And don't beautiful pursuits lead to the possession of excellence, ugly ones to the possession of evil?"

"Necessarily."

"Then the last thing to examine is whether it pays to be
just, act justly, and pursue beautiful pursuits—whether one 445
be observed or not—or to be unjust and commit injustice,
as long as one isn't caught and made better by being punished."

"That would be ridiculous now that we've shown what
justice and injustice are like, Socrates. If life is considered
unbearable for a man whose bodily nature decays, even if
he's surrounded by all foods, drink, wealth, and power, then
how can life be worthwhile for a man whose nature is con- b
founded and corrupted in the very part by which we live,
even if he does everything he wants except what will rid him
of evil and win him excellence and justice?"

"It will be ridiculous," I agreed. "But still we can't give up now, when we've reached a place where we can clearly see how these things are."

"You're right," he said, "we can't hang back now."

"Come up here, Glaucon, so you can see how many forms c
I think evil has—the ones worth looking at, at least."

"I'm following," he said. "Just speak."

"We've climbed the argument this high, like an observation tower. From here it appears to me that excellence has one form, evil an unlimited number, but about four worth mentioning."

"How do you mean?"

"I suspect there are as many different types of souls as of
regimes—I mean generic types that constitute classes: five d
types of each."

"What are they?"

"One is the type of regime we just described, though it has two names. If one man emerges preeminent among the rulers, it's called a kingship; if there are many, an aristocracy."

"True," he said.

"So that's one form. If it has one ruler instead of many,
that won't disturb any of our laws that are worth mentioning, e
as long as he has the education and upbringing we've gone
through."

"Most likely it won't," said Glaucon.

Book 5

449 "Well then, such a city and regime I call right and good, as well as that kind of man. If this one is right, the others are mistaken and evil, in regard to both the administration of cities and the organization of the character of an individual soul. And the perversion takes four forms."

"What are they?" asked Glaucon.

I was about to give them in order, as I thought each
b emerges from the other. But Polemarchus, who was sitting
a little apart from Adeimantus, reached over and took hold
of his cloak up near the shoulder. He pulled him toward him,
leaned over and spoke with lowered head. All we caught of
it was: "Shall we let it go or not?"

"Certainly not," said Adeimantus, now speaking aloud.

"What won't you let go?" I asked.

"You," said Adeimantus.

c "Why? what did I do?"

"We think you're malingering and trying to cheat us out of a whole section of the argument, and not the smallest one either. You thought you could sneak by with some insipid comment about wives and children, as though anyone could see that the things of friends will be common."[1]

"Well, isn't that right, Adeimantus?"

"Yes," he said. "But like everything else this 'right' demands explanation—common in what way? There could be
d many, so explain the one you mean. We've been sitting here
waiting a long time, thinking you'd bring up the question of
mating and child rearing and what you mean by common
wives and children. We think the proper or improper arrangement of that will greatly, even decisively, affect the
regime. Now, since you're trying to attack a different regime
450 before adequately sorting this out, we passed the resolution
you heard—not to let you off till you explain it."

"Count me as voting with you," said Glaucon.

"Consider the resolution unanimous, Socrates," Thrasymachus said.

"Don't you see that this attack is unleashing a whole new discussion of the regime, right from the beginning? Just

[1]The reference is to 424a, p. 91.

when I was glad to be done with it, content if you'd accept
what we said then and let it lie, you bring it up again, unaware of the hornet's nest of words you're stirring up. I saw b
it then and passed it by, reluctant to set the swarm on
you."

"What?" cried Thrasymachus. "Do you think they came
here to pan for fool's gold or to hear a discussion?"

"A discussion," I said, "—in measure."

"A lifetime, Socrates," said Glaucon, "would be a sensible
man's measure for hearing discussions like these. Forget
about us—don't *you* give up. Tell us how you think our c
guardians will share in wives and children and in their upbringing while young, especially between birth and school
age, which is considered the most trying time. Try to explain
how it should be done."

"That won't be easy, my friend. This will be even more
unbelievable than what we've already gone through. One
may doubt whether these things are possible, and even if
they are, whether they'd be for the best. A person therefore
hesitates to touch them, for fear it will all seem nothing but d
a pious wish."

"Don't hesitate," he said. "Your listeners aren't mali-
cious, insensitive skeptics."

"Are you saying that to encourage me, Glaucon?"

"Yes."

"Well, you're doing just the opposite. If I were confident
that I knew what I was talking about, your reassurance would
be in place, because a man who knows the truth can speak
among intelligent friends about significant matters with
light-footed assurance. But when a man moves as I do, e
searching doubtfully as he speaks, that's a slippery, fearful
business. Not that I'm afraid of making a fool of myself—that 451
would be childish—but that I'll slip, miss the truth, and drag
my friends down with me in things where one least ought to
stumble. So I shall bow to Adrasteia,[2] Glaucon, to favor what
I'm going to say. I expect that deceit in good, beautiful, and
just institutions is a worse crime than involuntary murder.
It's better to risk a danger like that among enemies than
friends, so you were right to encourage me." b

Glaucon laughed: "Socrates, if your argument untunes us,

[2]A type of Nemesis, who punished proud words.

we'll absolve you of deceit as though you were only a murderer. So take heart and speak."

"The law does declare an absolved man to be pure."

"Of course," he said "So speak."

"Well, we must go back and pick up what we perhaps
c ought to have said then in its place. But maybe it's right to
present the women's drama after we've finished the men's,
especially since you challenge me to do so.

"People with the nature and education that we have described have, in my opinion, only one right way of possessing and treating their women and children, which must
follow the course we launched them on at the start. In our
discussion I believe we tried to appoint our men to be like
d guard dogs of a flock. So let's follow that up and give each
sex a similar birth and upbringing, and see if it suits us."

"How?"

"Like this: Do we expect female guard dogs to be partners with the males and to guard and hunt and do everything in common with them, or does bearing and rearing puppies prevent that, so that they sit inside and keep house while the males do the work and have full responsibility for the sheep?"

e "Everything in common," he said, "except that we treat
the females as weaker than the males."

"Is it possible with any animal to use them for the same tasks if you don't give them the same education and upbringing?"

"No."

"So if we're going to employ our women in the same tasks as the men, we must teach them the same things."

452 "Yes."

"Then we'll have to give them poetry and gymnastics, train them in warfare, and treat them the same."

"Most likely, from what you're saying."

"Perhaps much of what we're saying would appear ridiculous if put into practice because it goes against custom. I
suppose the most ridiculous thing would be to see the
women exercising naked with the men on the wrestling
b grounds—not just young ones, but the older ones too, like
the old men in the gymnasiums who still love to train even
when they're wrinkled and no longer pleasing to the eye."[3]

[3] The Greeks exercised nude.

"Yes, by Zeus, that would seem ridiculous, at least as things are now."

"Then since we've launched this discussion, we mustn't
fear the jokes of the sophisticates, who'll say the kinds of
things they always say when a great change takes place—
about their gymnastics and poetry, and of course about their c
bearing arms and riding horses."

"You're right," he said.

"But now that we've begun we must march through the
rough part of our law and ask the jokers not to tend their
own business but to be serious for a change, reminding them
that it hasn't been long since the sight of a naked man was
considered by Greeks, as by most barbarians still, to be
ridiculous and ugly, and when first the Cretans and then the
Spartans initiated gymnastics, the wits of the day were able d
to poke fun at it. Isn't that so?"

"Yes."

"But when experience revealed that undressing was better than covering things up, then I think what had appeared
ridiculous to the eye melted before the better disclosures of
reason. This shows that it's idle to consider anything ridiculous except foolishness and evil, and if a man tries to be
funny by looking at any other pattern of the ridiculous, he
has also set up a target of beauty for his seriousness to aim e
at, other than the good."

"Absolutely," Glaucon said.

"Then we must first decide whether or not all this is possible. The debate must be open to anyone, solemn or frivo-
lous, who is willing to debate whether female human nature 453
is able to join in all, none, or some of the tasks of the male,
and whether these include warfare. Wouldn't that be the
best beginning, most likely to lead to a good end?"

"By far," he said.

"Shall we also debate for the opposition so we don't lay siege to a deserted argument?"

"There's nothing to stop us," he said. b

"Then let's say this: 'You don't need anyone else to debate you, Socrates and Glaucon. You yourselves admitted when you began founding your city that each person must tend the one business that accords with his nature.' "

"I think we did—certainly."

" 'Isn't it true that a woman's nature differs completely from a man's?' "

"Of course it does."

" 'Then isn't it fitting to assign each a different work that
c accords with his own nature?' "

"Certainly."

" 'Then how can it be anything but a blunder and a self-contradiction when you now say that both men and women, with their totally distinct natures, must do the same things?' —Can you surprise me by finding a defense against that?"

"It's not easy to find one on the spur of the moment. I'll have to petition you to enter our plea too, whatever it may be."

"See, Glaucon?" I said. "This is just the sort of thing I
d foresaw, what made me hesitate and shrink from touching
this law about women and children."

"It doesn't look very friendly, by Zeus."

"No. But whether you fall into a swimming pool or the middle of the ocean, still you swim."

"Indeed."

"So we'll have to swim for it too and try to save ourselves from the argument. We can hope a dolphin picks us up, or some other prodigious rescuer."

e "It looks like we'll have to."

"Come on," I said, "let's try to find a way out. We admit that different natures must pursue different things, and that men and women have different natures. Now we say they must pursue the same things. Is that the indictment against us?"

"Exactly."

454 "Truly noble, Glaucon, is the power of the art of contradiction!"

"Why?"

"It seems to me that many fall into it even without wanting to and think they're discussing when they're wrangling, because they're unable to examine a subject by dividing it into its parts. They chase the opposite of what's been said by name alone, using disputation instead of dialectic."

"That does happen to many, but it doesn't apply to us now, does it?"

b "Absolutely," I said. "I'm afraid we've unwittingly slipped
into contradiction."

"How?"

"Valiantly but disputatiously and by name alone we've been chasing down the idea that different natures mustn't get the same pursuits. We didn't examine what form of sameness and difference we meant, or what we intended our definition to apply to when we gave different tasks to different natures, same to same."

"That's true, we didn't."

"By this reasoning we could just as well ask ourselves c
whether bald and hairy men have opposite natures and once we agree they have, forbid the hairy ones to be shoemakers if that's what the bald ones do, or vice versa."

"That would be ridiculous."

"Because we weren't referring to same and different natures in general, but only to that form of sameness and
difference that applies to pursuits. We meant, for example, d
that a man and a woman who are both doctors in their souls have the same nature. Don't you agree?"

"Yes."

"But a doctor and a carpenter have different ones?"

"Completely, I think."

"Then," I said, "if either sex excels the other in some skill or pursuit, that, we'll say, must be given to it. But if the only difference turns out to be that the female bears while the
male begets, we'll say we still haven't been shown that a e
woman differs from a man in what we're talking about, and go on believing that both our guardians and their women must pursue the same things."

"That will be right," he said.

"Shouldn't we next ask our disputatious opponent to tell
us in what skill or pursuit connected with the organization 455
of a city a woman's nature differs from a man's?"

"That would be fair."

"Maybe he'll say what you did a while ago, that it would be hard to give a decent answer on the spur of the moment, but easy if he had some time to think about it."

"He might."

"Then shall we invite him to follow us, and see if we can
show him that there's no pursuit connected with governing b
a city that's peculiar to women?"

"Of course."

" 'Look sharp,' we'll tell him, 'and answer this: When you

say one person has natural ability at something and another
does not, don't you mean that the one learns it easily, the
other with difficulty, that the one can discover much more
about the subject for himself after little study, while the
other can't even retain what he's learned after long study
and practice, and that the bodily constitution of the one
c adequately serves his mind while the other's opposes it? Is
there anything else by which you define native ability or lack
of ability in a thing?' "

"No one would claim that there was," he said.

"Can you think of anything practiced by humans in which
the male doesn't greatly surpass the female in all these respects? Shall we drag this out with weaving and watching
pots and pans, in which the female is thought to be some-
d thing and is ridiculed if she's outdone?"

"You're right," he said. "The one sex beats the other in practically everything. Still, many women excel many men in many things, though on the whole it's as you say."

"Then, my friend, there's no pursuit connected with governing a city that belongs to a woman because she's a
woman, or to a man because he's a man. The various talents
e are scattered throughout both sexes, and by nature women
take part in all pursuits, as do men, except that in all of them
the woman is weaker."

"Of course."

"So shall we assign them all to men and none to women?"

"How could we?"

"I think we'll say instead that one woman is medical, another not; one musical, another unmusical by nature."

"Certainly."

"And isn't one athletic and military, another not; one
456 philosophic, another not; one spirited, another spiritless?"

"I think so," said Glaucon.

"Then one woman is a guardian, another not. Isn't that the nature we selected in our guardian men?"

"Exactly."

"So both women and men have the same nature for guarding the city, except that the woman's is weaker."

"Apparently."

b "So women like these must be chosen to live with the men
and to be guardians with them, since they're capable and
related to them by nature. And mustn't identical pursuits be
given to identical natures?"

"Of course."

"Then we've circled back to where we were, and agree that it's not against nature to give poetry and gymnastics to the guardians' women."

"Absolutely not."

"So we didn't legislate impossibilities or merely pious
wishes, because we established our law in accordance with
nature. The customs now, which are contrary to our law, c
must also be contrary to nature."

"So it seems."

"We examined this to see whether our proposal was both possible and the best. We agree that it's possible, so we must now agree that it's the best."

"Clearly."

"And we won't need a different education to produce
guardian women, because they've received the same nature d
as the men. —Now what's your opinion of this?"

"What?"

"Of assuming that some men are better than others—or do you think they're all alike?"

"Not at all."

"Well, do you think education in cobbling makes the shoemakers the best men in our city, or does the education we've described make the guardians the best?"

"That's a ridiculous question," he said.

"I know," I replied. "They'll be the best of all the citizens, e
won't they, Glaucon?"

"By far."

"Then won't their women be the best of the women?"

"Yes."

"Can there be anything better for a city than to have the best possible men and women in it?"

"No."

"Isn't that produced by applying poetry and gymnastics as
we have described?" 457

"Certainly."

"So our institution is not only possible, but also the best for the city."

"Correct."

"Then the guardians' women, since they wear excellence in place of clothes, must undress and be partners in warfare and in all the other guard duties of the city, and do nothing else. Their tasks will be lighter because their sex is the

b weaker. And the man who laughs at them as they exercise
naked for the sake of the best 'shall reap a crop of fruitless
laughter,' because he knows not what he is doing nor what
he laughs at. For this is the most beautiful thing that will ever
be said: The helpful is beautiful; only the harmful is ugly."

"Absolutely."

"Shall we say we've escaped one wave of the women's law
and weren't completely pulled under for proposing that our
guardians and guardiennes pursue everything in common?
c Somehow our argument agrees with itself that this is both
possible and helpful."

"It certainly was no small wave you escaped from."

"You'll say it was when you see the one after it," I replied.

"Show me and I'll see," he said.

"Well, I think another law follows this one and all that
we've said: that these women shall all be common to all of
d those men, and none shall live privately with any. Children
too shall be common, and a parent shall not know his children, nor a child his parents."

"This wave tops the first for sheer incredibility, all right,
as to whether it's beneficial or even possible."

"I don't think anyone would deny the benefit of common
wives and children if it's possible. That's the point I expect
to see disputed."

e "You can be sure they'll both be hotly disputed."

"A conspiracy of arguments? I thought I could escape the
one and just discuss the possibility."

"You can't slip off like a runaway slave—we demand an
account of both."

"Well, I'll have to take my punishment, I guess. But do me
458 a little favor: Let me loaf and daydream the way lazy-minded
people do when they're walking by themselves. They think
of something they want and put off planning how to get it
so they don't wear themselves out deciding whether or not
it's attainable. They pretend they already have it and enter-
tain themselves by arranging the details and imagining what
b they'll do, and so make an already lazy soul even lazier. I've
gotten soft and lazy too, and want to postpone the question
of how this is possible, if that's all right with you. Let's
assume it's possible and I'll examine how our rulers will
work out the details and show that it will be the most advantageous practice for both our city and the guardians. Then

I'll try to examine the other question with you. Will that be all right?"

"Of course," he said, "go ahead."

"Well, if our rulers and their auxiliaries are going to be
worthy of their titles, I think the auxiliaries will carry out the c
commands of the rulers, who will follow our laws in some things and imitate them in others in which we permit them to do so."

"Most likely," he said.

"Now you, as their lawgiver, will choose the women as you did the men, as close to them in nature as possible, and then hand them over. Since they all share common houses, eat
together, possess no private property, and mingle in the d
gymnasiums and everywhere else, I think innate necessity will draw them to sexual intercourse with each other. Or don't you think that's a necessity?"

"Not a geometrical necessity," he said, "but the necessity of love, which is probably a keener goad for prodding and persuading the masses."

"It certainly is," I said. "But, Glaucon, any disorderly conduct, sexual or otherwise, is impious in a happy city and
must be forbidden." e

"Yes, because it's unjust," he said.

"Then we'll clearly arrange the most sacred marriages we can. Sacred means the most beneficial."

"Absolutely."

"How will they be beneficial, Glaucon? Look, I see that 459
you have hunting dogs and countless fighting birds at home —I wonder if you've ever noticed something about their mating and breeding?"

"What?"

"Though they're all well-bred, some are better than others. Do you breed indiscriminately from all, or only from the best?"

"Only from the best."

"From the youngest, the oldest, or those in their prime?" b

"Those in their prime."

"Otherwise your stock will deteriorate. Isn't that true of dogs, birds, horses, and every other animal?"

"It would be strange if it wasn't."

"Good heavens! What outstanding rulers we'll need if the same is true of humans!"

c “It is,” he said, “—why?”

“Because they’ll have to use lots of medicine. I suppose we agree that for bodies which respond to treatment without medicine any doctor will do. But when medication is required, the doctor must be brave.”

“True, but what does that apply to?”

“This: I’m afraid our rulers will have to use much lying
d and deceit for the good of the ruled. I think we said that such
lies were useful as a form of medicine.”

“And rightly,” he said.

“Well, I think this rightness will especially show up in our marriages and matings.”

“How?”

“It follows from what we’ve said that to develop a prime
herd our best men must come together with the best women
as often as possible, the worst with the worst as seldom as
e possible, that the offspring of the best must be reared, the
others not, and that all this must be hidden from all but the
rulers, to keep our flock of guardians free from civil war.”

“Right.”

“Then we’ll have to legislate certain festivals where we’ll
bring the brides and grooms together, with sacrifices and
460 with hymns composed by our poets, appropriate to the
forthcoming marriages. We’ll leave the number of marriages
up to the rulers so they can maintain a constant number of
men, adjusted against losses from war, disease, and so on,
to make sure that our city grows neither too large nor too
small.”

“Right.”

“Then we must rig an ingenious lottery so our worthless fellow will blame his luck and not the rulers every time he misses out on a get-together.”

“We certainly must,” he said.

b “The young men who prove good in warfare and elsewhere will receive, among other gifts and prizes, ungrudging access to the beds of the women, which will also be an
excuse for having such men conceive the most children.”

“Right.”

“Newborn infants will be taken up by officials appointed for the purpose, whether men, women, or both—all offices, I suppose, will be common to both men and women—and—”

"Yes."

"And offspring of good parents, I think, will be put in the c
pen with some nurses who live apart in a separate quarter
of the city. Offspring of inferior parents and any that are
deformed will be hidden away in mysterious obscurity, as is
fitting."

"They will be if we want to keep our guardian class pure."

"The officials will also supervise nursing and bring the
mothers to the pen when their breasts are full, contriving
every conceivable contrivance to keep any from recognizing d
her own baby. If a mother doesn't have enough milk, they'll
provide other women that do, make sure the mothers wean
their babies after a reasonable time, and turn the troubles of
sleepless nights and so forth over to nurses."

"You're making motherhood easy for the guardians' women."

"As is fitting," I said. "Now let's go through the rest of our
proposal. We said the offspring must be born from people
in their prime. Do you agree that the average length of a e
woman's prime is twenty years and of a man's thirty?"

"Which years?"

"That a woman shall bear for the state from her twentieth to her fortieth year; that a man shall begin to beget for the state when he has passed his sharpest running peak, continuing until age fifty-five."[4]

"That's the prime of mind and body for both," he said. 461

"Then if someone older or younger than that tampers
with communal breeding, we'll label the offense unjust and
impious, because he's sowing the city a child who, if he slips
by, will be born without the sacrifices and prayers offered up
at the wedding festivals by priests, priestesses, and the whole
city—that from good and useful parents may come ever
better and more useful progeny. He'll be born in dread b
incontinence under cover of darkness."

"Right," he said.

"The same law will cover any active breeder who tampers with eligible women without being paired by the ruler. We'll say he's presenting the city a child that's unauthorized, unsanctified, and bastard."

"Absolutely right," he said.

[4]Mock-legal language.

"But when they're past the breeding age, I think we'll set
c the men free to couple with anyone they wish, except mothers, daughters, grandmothers, and granddaughters, and the women with anyone but their sons and fathers and so on, urging them if they conceive not to bring a single pregnancy to light, or if the birth can't be prevented, to dispose of such a child as one that can't be reared."

"That's entirely reasonable," he said. "But how will they
d recognize their fathers and daughters and so on?"

"They won't," I said. "A man will count from the tenth or even the seventh month from the day he became marriageable, and call every child born after that date son or daughter, and the children will call him father, and the children of these children he'll call grandchildren, and so on; and all children born during the time their parents were breeding
e will call each other brothers and sisters. That will keep them from tampering with each other, as we said. But our law will permit brothers and sisters to sleep together if the lot so determines and the oracle at Delphi consents."[5]

"Absolutely right," he said.

"That, Glaucon, is how your city's guardians will have wives and children in common. Next we must ask our argument to confirm that this arrangement follows the rest of our
462 regime and is by far the best. Shouldn't we begin by asking ourselves what is the greatest good for the organization of a city, that which a lawgiver must aim at in framing his laws, and what is the greatest evil, and then examine the institution we just described and see if it matches the footprints left behind by the good?"

"That's exactly what we should do," he said.

"Can you think of a greater evil for a city than something
b that tears it apart and makes many out of one, or a greater good than something that binds it together into one?"

"No."

"Don't shared pleasures and pains bind it together? when all the citizens feel a common joy or sorrow at the same rise or fall of events?"

"Absolutely."

"But individualism in all this unbinds it—when some exult

[5]Since the rulers control the lottery and know who are true siblings, they will presumably prevent the mating of blood relatives.

and others weep at the same events as they affect the city and
its citizens." c

"Of course."

"Doesn't that happen when people in the city don't all utter words like 'mine' and 'not mine' and 'somebody else's' in unison?"

"Absolutely."

"Then the city where the most people apply these words to the same things in the same way will be the best governed."

"By far."

"Won't it also be the one most like the individual person?
When one of us smashes his thumb, for instance, the entire
partnership of body to soul, organized into a single community under its ruler, instantly feels it and suffers together as d
one with the hurt part, and we say '*the man* feels pain in his
thumb.' Don't we say the same of any part of a person,
concerning pain if it's suffering or pleasure if pain is abat-
ing?"

"Yes, and you're right—the best-governed city is arranged most like such an organism."

"Then when one citizen experiences something good or
evil, such a city will call the experience her own and the e
whole city will share his joy or his sorrow."

"Necessarily, in a city with good laws."

"Then it's time," I said, "to return to our city and see whether it or some other city most closely conforms to what the argument has made us agree on."

"Yes, we must."

"Well then, I imagine other cities as well as ours have both 463
rulers and people, who all address each other as citizens."

"Of course."

"What do the people in the other cities call their rulers, besides citizens?"

"In most of them despots; in democracies, the name we've been using—rulers."

"What about our city? What will the people call the rulers, besides citizens?"

"Preservers and allies." b

"And the rulers the people?"

"Wage-payers and providers."

"What do rulers in other cities call the people?"

"Slaves," he said.

"And each other?"

"Fellow rulers."

"What do ours call each other?"

"Fellow guardians."

"Now, Glaucon, can any rulers in other cities refer to some of their fellow rulers as belonging and to others as alien?"

"Many," he said.

"Do they regard and address the ones who belong as their
c own and the alien ones as not their own?"

"Yes."

"What about your guardians? Can any regard or address any of his fellow guardians as alien?"

"No. Each will regard everyone he meets as his brother, sister, father, mother, or some other relative."

"Very good," I said. "Now, will you legislate only names
of belonging, or must conduct correspond to the names, so
d that your citizens must accord what the law requires of filial
respect, consideration, and obedience to their fathers to escape the disapproval of gods and men for unjust and impious conduct? Will these be the sentiments that sing in a child's ears from childhood up from all citizens, directed both toward those he is told are his fathers and toward all other relations?"

e "Exactly," he said. "It would be absurd to have him mouth
names of belonging without acting accordingly."

"So in this city more than in any other when one citizen fares well or badly the others will chant in unison the words we just mentioned: 'It is my own that fares well, my own that fares badly.' "

"Completely true," he said.

464 "We said that these words and this conviction would make
their pleasures and pains be in common."

"And we were right."

"Won't our citizens have the same thing in common especially when they call it 'mine'? And by having the same thing in common, won't they be partners in pleasures and pains?"

"Very much so."

"Isn't that caused by the whole organization of the city, but especially by the guardians' having wives and children in common?"

"More than anything," he said.

"And we agreed that this unity was the greatest good for b
a city, likening good government to the relation of the body to its parts when they are in pleasure or pain."

"And it was a proper agreement," he said.

"Therefore we've shown that the auxiliaries'[6] possession of common wives and children is the cause of the greatest good for our city."

"Indeed."

"This also agrees with what we said earlier: that to be true guardians they must possess no private houses, land,
or other property, but receive their sustenance from the c
other citizens as wages for guarding, and all spend it in common."

"Right."

"Do you then, as I, think that this provision added to our earlier one will make them even truer guardians and keep them from tearing their city apart by each applying the word 'mine' to different things instead of to the same ones, each dragging off goods to his own home to possess apart from
the others, each with separate wives and children, and all d
introducing the private pleasures and private pains of private individuals? Won't they rather strive, with a single conviction about what belongs to them all, all for the same goal and all feel as fully as possible common pleasures and pains?"

"Absolutely," he said.

"Then won't accusations and lawsuits practically disappear from their midst because they possess everything in common and nothing in private except their bodies? Whence it redounds to them to live free from the civil strife
that besets other men from the possession of relatives, chil- e
dren, and property."

"They'll necessarily be rid of all that."

"Nor will there justly be any suits for assault or battery, because we'll call it just and honorable to defend oneself against peers, and force them to keep fit."

"Right."

"Here's another thing right about our law, Glaucon: if an 465

[6]= "guardians" in a, above. Plato calls the whole class of guardians and auxiliaries by either name.

angry man sates his spirit in a fight he's less likely to push
the quarrel any further."

"Certainly."

"Now we'll clearly direct elders to rule and punish the
young; but unless the rulers command it, no young man will
be likely to try to strike his elder or use any force with him
or show him any other disrespect. We have two strong
guardians to prevent that: fear and shame. Shame forbids
b molesting a parent, and fear warns that the others will rush
to the victim's defense as his sons, brothers, and fathers.
Thus in every way our laws will ensure that the men live in
peace with each other."

"Completely," he said.

"And as long as the guardians avoid civil war, there's no fear that the other citizens will quarrel either with them or with one another."

"None at all."

"For the sake of decorum I hesitate even to mention the
c minor evils they'll be rid of—the poor man's flattery of the
rich, the financial embarrassments that arise from having to
support a home and a family, the borrowings, the disavow-
als, the procuring of money by any means to hand over to
the women and servants to budget and spend—the indigni-
ties they suffer are clear enough, my friend, and they're both
ignoble and unworthy of mention."

d "Clear to a blind man," he said.

"They'll be rid of all that and lead a life more blissful than the blissful life of an Olympic victor."

"In what way?"

"A victor's happiness comprehends only a tiny part of
what accrues to the guardians, whose victory is more beautiful as their public maintenance is more complete. They win
the victory of preserving their whole city, they and their
children are crowned with all the necessities of life, they
e receive prizes from their city while living and a worthy funeral when they die."

"All of which are beautiful."

"Do you remember that someone—I forget who—startled
us earlier by objecting that we weren't making our guardians
466 happy, because they have nothing when they could have
everything in the city? We said we'd examine that later if it
came up, but for now we were making our guardians guard-

ians and our city as happy as possible, not looking at one class and molding it to be happy."

"I remember," he said.

"Well? If our auxiliaries' life now appears much better and more beautiful than an Olympic victor's, could it in any
way compare with the life of a farmer, a shoemaker, or any b
other craftsman?"

"I doubt it."

"So it would be fair to repeat here what we said then: If a guardian tries to be happy in any way that keeps him from being a guardian, and if a life so moderate, secure, and as we maintain, good doesn't content him, and if a senseless, childish notion of happiness seizes him and prompts him to
try to appropriate everything in the city for himself because c
he has the power, then he'll learn that old Hesiod truly was wise for saying that 'the half is somehow more than the whole.' "[7]

"If he takes my advice he'll stick to our way of life."

"Then do you agree to such partnership of women with men, to their having education, children, and the guarding of the other citizens in common; that both in the city and in battle the women must guard with the men, hunt with them
like dogs, and be partners in everything in every way possi- d
ble; and that thus they'll be acting for the best, not contrary to female nature compared with the male, but as both were naturally intended for partnership with one another?"

"Yes," he said.

"Next, Glaucon," I said, "we must decide whether it's possible for people, as for animals, to have such partnership; and if so, how."

"You took the words right out of my mouth, Socrates."

"Because I think it's obvious how they'll fight their wars." e

"How?"

"They'll campaign in common and take the hardier children into battle to observe the occupation that will be theirs when they grow up, like children of any other craftsmen.
Besides watching, they'll help in things connected with bat- 467
tle and serve their mothers and fathers. You've surely noticed that in other crafts, such as pottery, the potters' children look on as helpers for a long time before they touch

[7] *Works and Days* 40.

the wheel. Do you think potters should teach their children more carefully with observation and experience than the guardians?"

"That would be ridiculous."

"Besides, every animal fights harder with its offspring
b nearby."

"Yes, but Socrates, there's great danger that if they fail, as easily happens in battle, they'll destroy their children as well as themselves and make it impossible for the city to recover."

"True. But do you think we should eliminate danger altogether?"

"No."

"Then if they must take risks, shouldn't it be in something that will make them better if they succeed?"

"Clearly."

c "Do you think it's a small advantage, not worth the danger, for future soldiers to observe war?"

"No, it's a great one."

"So it stands: the children must be made observers of war. If we devise a means of safety for them, all will be well, won't it?"

"Yes."

"Now their fathers won't be totally ignorant but as knowing as humans can be about which campaigns will be danger-
d ous, and they'll shield the children from those and bring
them to the safer ones. I also assume they won't appoint
completely incompetent leaders and tutors for the children,
but ones qualified by age and experience."

"That would be fitting."

"Still, many things turn out contrary to what we expect."

"They surely do."

"Against such contingencies, my friend, the children must be winged so they can fly away if they have to."

e "What do you mean?"

"Horses," I said. "We must mount them as young as possible and bring them out to observe on swift but manageable horses after they've learned how to ride. Thus they'll best observe their own work and most safely escape if they must, following their older leaders."

"That seems proper to me."

468 "What about combat? How should our soldiers act toward

the enemy and one another? Do you agree with what I think?"

"I may if you tell me."

"If any soldier of ours deserts his ranks, throws away his sword, or commits any other cowardly act, we should set him up as a farmer or craftsman, and if the enemy takes one alive we'll give them their catch as a gift to do whatever they like with."

"Absolutely." b

"What about the man acclaimed the best fighter? Do you think each youth and boy that accompanies the army ought to wreathe him in camp?"

"Yes."

"And shake his hand?"

"That too."

"I doubt if you'll go along with this, Glaucon."

"What?"

"That he exchange kisses with each."

"Completely," he said. "I'll even amend your law to provide that for the duration of the campaign no one he desires c
to kiss has the right to refuse. That will make him even more eager to win the prize as the best if he should be in love with some boy or girl."

"Very good," I said. "And we've already said that a good man will be selected for more marriages than the others, so that the most children will come from such stock."

"Yes."

"Even Homer agrees that it's just to give honors like that to young men who are good. When Ajax was acclaimed the d
best fighter, 'they awarded him the full-cut backbone of boar,'[8] as a proper reward for a brave, vigorous man, from which he'd grow in strength as well as in honor."

"Right," he said.

"So we'll believe Homer in that much," I said. "We too will honor our good men, so far as they've proved themselves good, at sacrifices and other occasions with hymns and the privileges we've mentioned, and with 'seats and meats and brimming cups,' combining exercise with honor e
for our good men and women."

"Beautiful," he said.

[8]*Iliad.* 7.321. The next quotation is *Iliad* 8.162.

"And when an acclaimed fighter falls in battle, won't we
proclaim him of the race of gold and believe Hesiod, who
469 says that when men of this race pass away 'they become
hallowed spirits on the face of the earth:/ good, protecting
guardians of articulate mortals'?"[9]

"We certainly will."

"So we must learn from the god how to bury spiritual,
divine men, and with what distinctions, and then arrange it
as he directs. And we'll attend them as spirits and bow down
b to their tombs for all future time. Our observances will be
the same for any man whom we judge to have distinguished
himself in his lifetime, whether he died of old age or from
whatever cause."

"That would be just."

"Now how will our soldiers act toward the enemy? Do you
consider it just for a Greek city to enslave other Greeks? Or
should our city try to abolish this practice even in other cities
c and introduce the custom of sparing Greeks and guarding
against being enslaved by barbarians?"

"That would be preferable in every way."

"So they won't have Greek slaves themselves, and they'll advise other Greeks to abandon this practice also."

"Certainly," he said. "That will make them turn more against barbarians and leave each other alone."

"What about plundering the dead in a battle? Is it good
to take anything but their armor, or is that just an excuse for
d cowards to avoid facing the enemy by pretending to do
something necessary in poking around with the dead?
Hasn't such looting destroyed many an army?"

"It certainly has."

"Doesn't stripping a corpse strike you as slavish and
greedy, and isn't it small-minded and womanish to consider
the body the enemy when the real adversary has flown off
and left behind merely that which he fought with? Do you
think that's behaving any better than dogs who snap at the
e stones that hit them rather than at the people who throw
them?"

"Not a bit," he said.

"Then mustn't we stop this practice of stripping corpses and preventing the enemy from collecting their dead?"

[9]A paraphrase of *Works and Days* 122–23.

"Yes, by Zeus, we must."

"Surely we won't dedicate enemy armor, especially of
Greeks, in temples if we care about the good will of other
Greeks. In fact we'll fear that bringing kinsmen's armor into 470
a temple will defile it, unless the god should tell us otherwise."

"Right."

"What about ravaging the land and burning the houses of Greek adversaries? What will your soldiers do about that?"

"I'd like to hear your opinion."

"I think they'll do neither, Glaucon, but only take the
year's crops. Do you want to know why?" b

"Yes."

"It seems to me that war and civil war aren't just two different names, but two realities denoting disagreement in two different spheres; one related and kindred, the other foreign and alien. Hostility in the foreign sphere is called war; in the kindred sphere civil war."

"That doesn't depart from accepted usage."

"See if this also conforms: I maintain that the Greek race c
is kindred and related to itself, but foreign and alien to
barbarians."

"Well said."

"Then we'll say that Greeks and barbarians are natural
enemies and when they fight it must be called war. But
Greeks are natural friends even when they fight, and when
they do we'll say Greece is sick with strife and call it civil
war." d

"I'll surely agree to that definition," he said.

"Then observe that when civil war as now defined arises
in a city and sets it against itself, people consider it an abomi-
nation if the two parties destroy each other's fields and
houses, and they condemn both sides as unpatriotic for
ravaging their nurse and mother; whereas they consider it
moderate for the winners to take the crops of the losers and
to think of them not as permanent enemies, but as people e
they'll eventually be reconciled with."

"That's certainly a gentler, more civilized attitude."

"Won't your city be Greek, and your men good and gentle, lovers of Greece who regard her as their home and who share a common religion with other Greeks?"

"Absolutely."

471 "Then they'll regard disagreements with Greeks—their
kin—as civil war and not even speak of it as war. They'll treat
them as friends with whom they'll be reconciled, and discipline them with kindness rather than punish them with slavery or death, because they're disciplinarians, not enemies."

"Exactly."

"And being Greeks, they won't ravage Greece, burn
houses, or assume that every man, woman, and child in a city
is their enemy, but only the few that instigated the dispute.
b Since they regard the majority as their friends, our men will
refuse to ravage their land or raze their houses, and they'll
pursue the quarrel only far enough to force the innocent to
punish the guilty for making them suffer."

"I agree: our citizens must deal with their Greek opponents like that and treat barbarians the way Greeks now treat
one another."

"Then shall we make it a law for our guardians not to
c ravage land or burn houses?"

"Certainly," he said, "—and assume that it and our other
laws are good. But, Socrates, if we let you go on like this I'm
afraid you'll never get to what you put off earlier and show
how it's possible for such a regime to come about. I agree
that every good thing would come to a city where this happened, and I'll even fill in what you left out: they'll fight the
d best because they'll desert each other the least, and they'll
view as well as address each other as father, son, and
brother. If the women join their campaigns, in the same
ranks or in rear ranks of their own to frighten the enemy and
help the men when necessary, I'm sure their army will be
totally invincible. I also see all the good things they have at
e home, which you didn't mention. So don't dwell on this any
longer. Try to persuade us that this regime is possible and
show us how, and let the rest go."

472 "I see you've no patience with someone who dawdles, the
way you sweep down in this sudden raid on my argument.
I guess you don't know you're bringing on the third and
biggest wave of all, after I just barely escaped the first two.[10]
When you see it and hear it you'll more than forgive me for

[10]See 457b-d, p. 122. The third wave was the one that drowned you (cf. English "go under for the third time"). Here the waves are of laughter and disbelief.

fearing and hesitating to argue such a paradoxical argument."

"The more you talk like that, Socrates, the less chance you
have of getting off. So quit stalling and speak." b

"Well, first we must recall that we got here because we
were inquiring what justice and injustice are like."

"What of it?"

"Nothing. Just that if we find out what justice is like, will
we expect the just man to be exactly like it in every way, or
will we be satisfied if he comes as close to it as possible and c
participates in it more than anyone else?"

"Yes, we'll be satisfied with that."

"So by inquiring what justice and injustice themselves are
like and what a perfectly just or unjust man would be like if
he came into being, we were seeking a model—so that by
looking at the men and seeing what they're like in regard to
happiness and misery we can then look at ourselves and be
forced to admit that whichever of us most resembles one of
these men will also receive a life most resembling his. We d
didn't do it to prove that the models themselves can come
into being."

"That much is true," he said.

"Do you think a painter who has painted an adequate
model of what the most beautiful human being would look
like would be a poorer painter for being unable to prove that
such a man can be born?"

"Not at all, by Zeus."

"Well, weren't we making a model in words of a good
city?" e

"Certainly."

"Do you think we'll be poorer modelers if we can't prove
it possible to govern a city as we've said?"

"Not a bit."

"Then that's the truth of the matter, Glaucon. But if for
your sake I must be eager to demonstrate how this might
most nearly be possible, then to further the demonstration
give me your agreement again on the same point."

"What point?"

"Can anything be done exactly as said, or is it the nature 473
of practice to catch less of the truth than does speech, contrary to what people may think?"

"You've got my agreement on that," he said.

"Then don't force me to show that everything we've described in words can be realized completely in practice. If
we're able to discover how a city may be governed as closely
as possible to what we've said, we'll say I've proved what you
b demand: that this is possible. Will you be satisfied with that?
—I will."

"So will I."

"Next, it seems, we must try to point out what's being done wrong in the cities now to keep them from being so governed, and what would be the smallest change that would bring a city to our kind of regime—preferably only one or two, but at any rate the fewest in number and smallest in effect."

c "Absolutely," he said.

"I think we can point out one change," I said, "that would transform everything. It isn't small or very easy, but possible."

"What is it?"

"Now I'm on top of what we compared to the biggest wave. Still I shall tell it, though it drown me in laughter and disrepute, like a cackling billow. So examine what I'm going to say."

"Speak," Glaucon said.

"Until either philosophers become kings or those now
d called kings and regents become genuine philosophers, so
that political power and philosophy coincide and the many
natures that now enter exclusively on one or the other are
constrained from so doing, there will be no end to the evils,
dear Glaucon, for cities nor, I think, for the human race, and
e this regime we've gone through in words will never grow
into possibility and see the light of the sun. This is what
made me hesitate so long—I knew what I'd say would be
completely contrary to opinion. It's not easy to see that
nothing else will bring happiness to the individual or to the
state."

"Socrates," he said, "you've tossed out a proposal that
474 will incite a horde of respectable men to throw off their
cloaks, grab the first weapon they find, and stampede you
down intent on some horrible mischief. If you don't have an
argument to defend yourself with, your penalty will be hoots
and scurrility."

"Aren't you responsible, Glaucon?"

"I acted honorably. But I won't betray you—I'll defend
you with all that I have: good will, encouragement, and a
willingness, perhaps, to answer more civilly than another. So
with these reinforcements try to show the disbelievers that b
things are as you say."

"I'll try, since you offer such a powerful alliance. If we
want to be acquitted by that mob, I think we must define who
we mean by philosophers when we have the nerve to say they
should rule. When this is made clear, we can defend ourselves by pointing out that they are fitted by nature both to c
grasp philosophy and to lead in the city, while the others are
fitted neither to grasp nor to lead, but to follow."

"The time has come," he said, "to define."

"Follow me then—maybe we can run this thing down somehow or other."

"Lead on," he said.

"Need I remind you," I asked, "or do you remember that when we say someone loves something we must, to speak properly, say he loves the whole and not just a part?"

"You'd better remind me, I guess. I don't seem to have d
it very well."

"Nay, Glaucon," said I, "what you say befits rather another. It ill beseems a loving man to forget that every youth
in his bloom somehow bites and stirs up an erotic, boy-
loving man by appearing worthy of his attention and em-
braces. Isn't that how you fellows act toward the beauties?
One has a snub nose, you praise it as 'cute;' another a beak
and you call it 'royal;' while the one in the middle is 'balanced.' This dark-complexioned beauty is 'manly;' that e
white one 'a child of the gods.' And where do you think
'honeyskin' came from if not from the brain of some simper-
ing lover determined to charm away pallor if only it graces
a youth? In a word, you fellows dream up any excuse, any
endearment to keep from having to reject any flowering 475
boy."

"If," he said, "you choose to speak of me in describing the doings of lovers, then I assent for the argument's sake."

"What? don't wine lovers do the same thing? use every excuse to enjoy every wine?"

"They certainly do."

"What about lovers of honor? If they can't make general they'll serve as lieutenants, content to be honored by the

b small and insignificant if not by the great and the proud.
Their desire is for honor, in whatever form."

"Absolutely."

"So is it correct to say that when someone desires something he desires the whole class and not just a part?"

"Yes."

"Then so with the lover of wisdom.[11] We'll say he desires it all and not just a part."

"True."

"So if someone is finicky about learning, especially a
c young man who doesn't yet know what's useful or not, we
won't call him fond of learning or a lover of wisdom, any
more than we'd call someone finicky about food a good
eater, or say he's hungry and desires food."

"Correct."

"But if he's not squeamish and willingly swallows all learning with insatiable gusto, then we'll justly call him a lover of learning, right?"

d "You'll have lots of strange birds if you do," Glaucon
replied. "All lovers of sights strike me as being so because
they delight in learning, and lovers of sounds are surely a
rare set to put with philosophers—they avoid discussions
and pastimes like that, but run around to every festival in city
and town, listening to the choruses as though their ears had
been hired. Do you really want to call learners like that, as
e well as students of hobbies, lovers of wisdom?"

"No, but they resemble them."

"But whom do you call true lovers of wisdom?"

"Those," I said, "who love the sight of the truth."

"That's correct too, but how do you mean it?"

"It would be hard to explain to anyone else. But you, I think, will agree with me in this—"

"What?"

"Since the beautiful and the ugly are opposites, they are two."

476 "Of course."

"Since they are two, each is one."

"True."

"So with the just and the unjust, the good and the bad, and all the other forms: each itself is one, but by their part-

[11]I.e. the philosopher, which means "lover of wisdom."

nership in actions, bodies, and one another, they show up everywhere and each appears to be many."

"Right," he said.

"Well, that's how I divide them up: on one side your lovers of sights and hobbyists and men of action; on the
other the ones we're concerned with, the only ones rightly b
called lovers of wisdom."

"How do you mean?"

"Well, I suppose the lovers of sounds and sights embrace beautiful tones and colors and figures and whatever is fashioned from them, but their mind is incapable of seeing and embracing the nature of the beautiful itself."

"That's just how it is," he said.

"And only a few can approach the beautiful itself and see it by itself?"

"Very few." c

"What about a man who believes there are beautiful things but neither believes in the beautiful itself nor is able to follow another who leads him to the knowledge of it? Is he awake or living a dream? Look, isn't it dreaming when a person asleep or awake takes the resemblance of something for the thing it resembles?"

"I at least would say such a person is dreaming."

"How about the opposite case—thinking there is a beautiful itself and being able to see both it and the things that d
participate in it, not supposing the things to be it or it the things—is that living awake or a dream?"

"Wide awake."

"Then won't we properly call the state of mind of the one 'knowledge' because he knows; that of the other 'opinion' because he conjectures?"

"Certainly."

"What if the one who we say conjectures and doesn't
know gets angry with us and disputes what we say? Can we e
soothe and gently persuade him without making it too obvious that he's nearly out of his mind?"

"We'd better, by Zeus!"

"Come on, let's see what we'll tell him—or would you rather we question him, to show that we don't begrudge him if he should know something, in fact would be delighted to see that he did?—'So tell us: does a knower know something or nothing?'—You answer for him, Glaucon."

"I'll answer that he knows something."

"Something that *is* or *is not?*"[12]

477 "That *is.* How could something that *is not* be known?"

"So even if we examined it further, this would still be sufficiently clear: What completely *is,* is completely knowable; what in no way *is,* is totally unknowable."

"That's clear enough."

"Then if there's something that both *is* and *is not,* it must lie between what purely *is* and what totally *is not.*"

"It must."

"If knowledge pertains to what *is* and ignorance necessarily to what *is not,* then we must find something between knowledge and ignorance for this in-between thing, if
b there's anything like that."

"Certainly."

"Do we say that opinion is something?"

"Of course."

"The same or a different power than knowledge?"

"Different."

"Then knowledge and opinion each align with a different thing, each according to its own power."

"Right."

"Knowledge, therefore, naturally pertains to what *is,* to know how it *is*—but wait, I think we have to sort something out first."

"What?"

c "We'll describe powers as a class of the things that *are,* by which we and everything else are empowered to do whatever we do. I call sight and hearing, for instance, 'powers.' Do you understand the class I mean?"

"Of course."

"Then here's my notion of them: In a power I see neither color, figure, nor any other feature that I might look at in the
d other many things to distinguish one as different from another. In a power I look only to this: what it pertains to and what it effects. It's by this that I call it a power, and if it pertains to and effects the same thing I call it the same; if not, different. How about you?"

[12]Forms of the verb "to be" are italicized when used in the sense of "exist" or "have real being," a use more common in Greek than in English.

"I do the same."

"So back to you, my excellent fellow: 'Do you call knowledge a power, or in what class do you put it?' "

"In that one. It's the strongest power of all."

"Then shall we rank opinion as a power, or put it in some e
other class?"

"No, it's the power by which we conjecture."

"But just a moment ago you agreed that knowledge and opinion are not the same thing."

"No one with sense would call the fallible and the infallible the same."

"Good," I said. "Then we clearly agree that opinion is
different from knowledge." 478

"We do."

"And being different powers, each naturally pertains to a different thing: knowledge pertains to what *is*, to know how it is; whereas opinion, we say, conjectures."

"Yes."

"The same thing that knowledge knows? Is the same thing both knowable and conjecturable? Or is that impossible?"

"Impossible from what we've agreed on. If knowledge and opinion are really both powers, and different powers, as we said, and if each power naturally pertains to a different thing,
then it follows that the same thing cannot be both knowable b
and conjecturable."

"So if the knowable is that which *is*, then the conjecturable must be something else."

"Indeed," he said.

"Well, can opinion conjecture what *is not?* Or is that impossible even to conjecture? Think about it, Glaucon: Doesn't a conjecturer relate his opinion to something? Or is it possible to conjecture, yet conjecture nothing?"

"No."

"So a conjecturer conjectures some one thing?"

"Yes."

"And what *is not* surely can't be called some one thing, but
nothing." c

"Of course."

"Weren't we forced to hand knowledge over to what *is* and ignorance over to what *is not?*"

"Yes, and rightly."

"So opinion conjectures neither what *is* nor what *is not*."

"Correct."

"Then opinion is neither knowledge nor ignorance."

"It doesn't seem to be."

"Does it lie outside of them, surpassing knowledge in clarity or ignorance in obscurity?"

"No."

"Well, does opinion strike you as being darker than knowledge, but brighter than ignorance?"

"Much."

d "So opinion lies within them, between knowledge and ignorance."

"Absolutely."

"Didn't we say earlier that if something showed up that both *is* and *is not* at the same time, this would lie between what purely *is* and what totally *is not,* and that neither knowledge nor ignorance would pertain to it, but whatever showed up between knowledge and ignorance?"

"Right."

"And what's showed up between them is what we call opinion."

"Yes."

e "Then this remains to discover, it seems: what is it that participates both in what *is* and what *is not,* yet itself can be properly called neither, so that if it shows up we can justly call it conjecturable. That way we'll assign extremes to extremes and the in-between to the in-between. Isn't that so?"

"Yes."

"With that established then, let me question our good
479 man, that lover of sights who believes there are many beautiful things, but not a beautiful itself or a *shape*[13] of beauty itself, always the same in every respect; who won't even put up with someone saying that the beautiful and the just and so on are one: 'O excellent man,' we will say, 'is there one of these many beautiful things that won't also appear ugly? or one of the just or the holy that won't also appear unjust or unholy?' "

[13]The Greek word is *idea,* a synonym for "form." It has been consistently translated as "shape" rather than "idea," which in English suggests something that exists only in the mind. The root of both Greek words is "see;" they denote something seen, an appearance or outline.

"No," said Glaucon, "they'll necessarily appear somehow b
both ugly and beautiful, and so on."

"How about the many doubles? Don't they appear to be halves as well as doubles?"

"Yes."

"And large things and small, light ones and heavy—can't they all be called their opposites as well as what we say they are?"

"Yes," he said, "each always has something of both."

"Then each of these manys both is and is not what we call it."

"It's like those party puzzlers," he said, "or the children's
riddle about the eunuch throwing at the bat: who hit what c
with what and what was the bat sitting on.[14] So with the
things: they equivocate, and none can be firmly thought to
be or not to be, or to be neither or both."

"Do you know what to do with them then? Can you find
a better place for them than between existence and nonbeing? I doubt they'll appear brighter than being, that they
should more be, or darker than unbeing, that they should d
more un-be."

"Most true," he said.

"Then we've discovered, it seems, that the many's many standards of beauty and of everything else roll around somewhere between what purely *is* and *is not.*"

"We certainly have."

"And we agreed earlier that if something like this showed up it would have to be called conjecturable not knowable, the in-between wanderer caught by the power between."

"We're agreed."

"So those who watch the many beautiful things without e
seeing the beautiful itself, and who can't even follow another
who leads them to it—or the many just things without the
just itself, and so on—we'll say they conjecture them all and
know nothing of what they conjecture."

"Necessarily," said Glaucon.

[14]RIDDLE: A man who was not a man threw and did not throw a stone that was not a stone at a bird that was not a bird sitting and not sitting in a tree that was not a tree. ANSWER: A eunuch threw a piece of pumice at a bat clinging to a reed and didn't hit it ("throw" and "hit" are the same word in Greek).

"What about the ones who watch every 'itself,' each always the same in every respect? Don't they know and not conjecture?"

"That's necessary too."

"Then won't we say that they love and embrace what knowledge pertains to, the others what opinion pertains to?
480 Do you remember saying that the others love beautiful tones and colors and so on, but won't put up with the beautiful itself as even existing?"

"I remember."

"Then we won't be off key in calling them lovers of opinion[15] rather than wisdom. Will they get terribly angry with us for calling them that?"

"Not if they listen to me," he said. "It's unlawful to be angry at the truth."

"So the ones who embrace each thing itself that *is* ought to be called philosophers: lovers of wisdom rather than of opinion."

"Absolutely."

Book 6

484 "Well, Glaucon," I said, "after marching them through a rather long argument, we've somehow managed to show who are the philosophers and who are not."

"It might not have been easy to do in a short one."

"Apparently not. Though I think we'd have shown them more clearly if we'd only had that to discuss, and there weren't so many other things left to go through to see how
b the just life differs from the unjust."

"Well, what's next?"

"Why, what's next in line. If philosophers are the ones who can reach what always stays the same in every respect, and nonphilosophers the ones who cannot, who wander among the many things that go in every direction, then which should rule in the city?"

"What would be a reasonable reply?"

[15]"Opinion" in Greek also means "appearance," "illusion."

"Whichever are shown capable of guarding the laws and
pursuits of a city." c

"Right," he said.

"If you have a sharp-eyed man and a blind one, it's clear which ought to be a guardian to watch over something."

"It's hardly unclear."

"Do people truly deprived of the knowledge of each thing
that *is,* who lack a distinct pattern of it in their souls, who
are unable to look at absolute truth like painters and constantly refer to it over there and contemplate it as accurately
as possible, and then either set up standards here, if they
must, of beauty, justice, and goodness, or guard and pre- d
serve the existing ones—do people like that seem better
than blind men?"

"Not very much, by Zeus."

"Then which shall we make guardians—them, or the ones who equal them in experience and every other part of excellence, and have also recognized each thing that *is?*"

"If they really equal them in the other things," he said, "it would be odd to choose anyone else, because that knowledge would make them excel in almost the greatest thing of all."

"So shall we discuss how they can have both knowledge 485
and the rest?"

"Certainly."

"Then, as we said at the beginning of this discussion,[1] we must first understand their nature. If we can agree on that, I think we'll also agree that not only can they have both, but that no one else should lead in the cities."

"How can we do that?"

"We may take it as established that philosophic natures
always love the learning which reveals something of the b
essence that always *is,* that never wanders through generation and decay."

"Yes, that's been established."

"And also that they'll love all of it and never willingly renounce any part, great or small, more or less respectable, just like those lovers we discussed earlier."

"Right," he said.

"Next, see if they mustn't also have this in their nature." c

"What?"

[1] 474b, p. 139.

"Truthfulness—love of truth, hatred of lies, and an aversion to ever accepting one voluntarily."

"Most likely."

"Is it only likely, my friend, or absolutely necessary that a man who's passionately in love should cherish everything related or belonging to his sweetheart?"

"Absolutely necessary," he said.

"Could you find anything more closely related to wisdom than truth?"

"I doubt it."

d "Then can the same nature love both wisdom and lies?"

"Never."

"So from earliest childhood the true lover of learning must grasp above all for all truth."

"By all means."

"And when a person's desires tilt sharply to some one thing, we know they weaken toward everything else, as though the stream had been diverted there."

"Of course."

"And when they've been channeled toward learning and all that goes with it, I think they'll be concerned with the pleasure of the soul itself by itself; they'll recede from pleasures that come through the body, if the man's a true
e philosopher and not an impostor."

"An absolute necessity."

"Such a man, therefore, will be temperate and not at all greedy or interested in spending money for the things it can buy."

"Indeed."

486 "Another thing to observe when you judge whether a nature is philosophic or not: be sure it has no slavishness in it. Nothing is so inimical as pettiness to a soul that always strives to reach the whole of everything human and divine."

"Most true," he said.

"Do you suppose a mind endowed with grandeur and the ability to view all time and all being can think much of this human life?"

"Impossible."

b "Will such a man regard death as a terror?"

"Not at all."

"Then a slavish, cowardly nature, it seems, has no part in true philosophy."

"I think not."

"An orderly man—not greedy, slavish, cowardly, or boastful—could he ever be unjust or hard to deal with?"

"No."

"So to determine whether a soul is philosophic or not, Glaucon, you'll examine it from childhood up to see whether it's gentle and just or savage and unsociable."

"Certainly."

"I doubt if you'll overlook this." c

"What?"

"Whether it learns easily or hard. Or do you expect someone to cherish something that brings him great pain and small accomplishment?"

"Never," he said.

"What if he can't retain anything he learns? If he's full of forgetfulness won't he be empty of knowledge? And if he struggles in vain, don't you think he'll finally end up hating both himself and the activity?"

"Of course."

"Therefore we won't admit a forgetful soul to the philo- d
sophic ones; we'll seek out the one that remembers. We'll also say that an awkward, museless nature can lead nowhere but to lack of measure and proportion."

"Correct."

"Do you think truth is related to measure or its lack?"

"To measure."

"Then let's also seek a mind naturally measured and agreeable, whose self-nature allows it to be easily led to the shape of each thing that *is*."

"All right."

"Do you think the qualities we've mentioned accompany e
each other and are necessary for a soul that aspires to partake perfectly and sufficiently of that which *is?*"

"Absolutely," said Glaucon. 487

"Could you in any way criticize a pursuit that can be adequately pursued only by those who have native memory, ease of learning, grandeur, and agreeableness, who are friends and relatives of truth, justice, courage, and temperance?"

"Blame himself could find no fault in a thing like that."

"Then when such men are perfected in age and education," I said, "won't you turn the city over to them alone?"

b Here Adeimantus spoke up: "Socrates, no one could dispute what you say—your listeners are in the same position
as always when you talk about this. They think that because
of their inexperience at question and answer the argument
leads them astray a little bit at a time until finally, when all
the bits are collected, they find themselves lost in apparent
contradiction to what they said at the start, like an uninitiated player trapped by an expert in checkers and left with
c no place to move; except that they've been trapped and left
with nothing to say in a game where the pieces are words.
But the game has nothing to do with the truth. I say this in
reference to the present discussion. A person might say that
while he has nothing to reply to each of your questions in
words, still in practice he sees that of the men who charge
into and stay with philosophy instead of practicing it for
d education while young and then giving it up, the majority
turn out to be cranks—not to say scoundrels—while the few
that seem decent still are made useless to their cities by this
pursuit that you recommend."

"Do you think he'd be telling a lie?" I asked.

"I don't know. I'd like to hear what you think."

"I think he's telling the truth."

e "But if we admit that philosophers are useless to their
cities, how can it be right to say that evils won't end for the
cities till the philosophers rule?"

"I'll have to answer that with a simile, Adeimantus."

"And I thought you never used similes!"

"How can you joke when you've caught me in something
488 so hard to explain? Listen to this and see how I can strain
for an image. I'll have to, because the condition of decent
philosophers toward their cities is so acute that there's nothing else like it, and to make an image of it and a defense for
them I'll have to gather materials from all over and slap
them together like a painter who paints goatstags and other
mixed monsters.

"Imagine a situation like this, on one ship or many: a
b captain[2] who outstrips everyone on board in size and in

[2]The captain represents the people, to whom the ship of state belongs and who ought to maintain order so that the navigator (statesman) can steer. Greek captains owned their own ships. The sailors are the politicians and political parties. This long sentence straggles just as badly in Greek. Presumably Plato intends it to illustrate the chaos it describes.

strength, but nearsighted, partially deaf, and with knowledge of sailing to match; sailors in mutiny over the navigation, each thinking that he ought to steer, though none has
learned the skill or can point to his teacher or to the time
when he learned it, who deny in fact that navigation can even
be taught and are ready to cut down anyone who says that
it can, always swarming around the captain begging for the c
wheel and sometimes, if one group persuades him and another does not, the one kills off the other or pitches them
overboard, and, having stupified the noble skipper with
drugs or wine, they take over and revel and party on the
ship's stores and sail as you'd expect of such rowdies, and
on top of it all they praise as a navigator and sailor with d
knowledge of shipcraft the man who's sharpest at persuading or coercing the captain into letting them rule, but denounce as useless a man who lacks this ability, refusing even
to hear that a navigator must necessarily study the seasons
and climates, the sky, the stars, the winds and everything
else that pertains to his craft if he's to become a true ship-
master, and that he will be a navigator whether anyone wants e
it or not, and disbelieving that there is a skill or practice of
steering that can be acquired along with navigation. In such
a state of affairs, is it any wonder that the true navigator is
called a useless, babbling stargazer by the crews of such 489
topsy-turvy ships?"

"Not at all," said Adeimantus.

"I don't think you'll ask me to examine the simile—you
understand that it represents the attitude of the cities toward
the true philosophers."

"I certainly do."

"Then teach it to that fellow who was surprised that
philosophers aren't honored in the cities and try to convince
him that it would be much more surprising if they were." b

"I will," he said.

"And also that he was right in saying decent philosophers
are useless to the many. But tell him to blame it on the ones
who don't use them, not on the philosophers. It's not in the
nature of things for a navigator to ask sailors to let him rule
them, or for 'wise men to go to the doors of the rich.' The
subtle fellow who said that was a liar, because the true nature
of things is that a sick man, rich or poor, must go to the door c
of the doctor, and everyone who needs to be ruled must go
to the door of the one who can rule him. No ruler worth

anything asks his subjects to let him rule them. So you won't go wrong if you liken political rulers now to these sailors, and the ones they call useless stargazers to the true navigators."

"Right," he said.

"Under these circumstances it's hard for the noblest pursuit to be held in repute by those who pursue the opposite.
d By far the gravest prejudice comes to Philosophy from the
people who claim to follow her ways—the ones you say her
accuser was referring to when he called most of her suitors
scoundrels, the few decent ones useless, and I agreed.
Right?"

"Yes."

"We've explained why the decent ones are useless. Shall
we next discuss why most of them are necessarily scoun-
e drels, and try to show that philosophy isn't the cause of that
either?"

"Certainly."

"Then let's recall the nature we said a man must acquire
490 at birth to grow beautiful and good. His leader, you'll remember, was truth, which he must pursue entirely wherever
it leads, or else be an impostor cut off from all intercourse
with true philosophy."

"That's what we said."

"So this is one thing that drastically contradicts current opinions about the philosopher."

"It surely does."

"Then will it be a reasonable defense to say that the true
lover of learning is disposed by nature to court what *is* rather
b than to dally with each of the manys conjectured to be, that
his passion neither dulls nor abates until he has clasped the
nature of each thing itself that *is* with the part of his soul
suited to clasp it—the part related to it—and that when he
has approached it and has been in reality wedded to reality
and has begotten intelligence and truth, he truly lives and
knows and is nourished, and only then ceases from the
pangs of labor, and not before?"

"Entirely reasonable," said Adeimantus.

"Will such a man cherish falsehood, or on the contrary
hate it?"

c "Hate it."

"And with truth as his leader, I doubt if we'd say a chorus

of evils will follow, but rather a healthy, just disposition,
accompanied by temperance."

"Right."

"Why reassemble the whole chorus of a philosophic nature all over again? You'll remember that some of its members turned out to be courage, grandeur, ease of learning,
and memory. Then you objected that though a person might
be forced to agree with our words, still by looking at the d
people they applied to, he'd say that some are useless and
most totally evil. In examining the cause of this prejudice we
got to our present question—why most are bad—and therefore took up the nature of the true philosopher again and
defined it as it must necessarily be."

"True," he said. e

"Then," I said, "we must first contemplate how this nature gets corrupted and in most destroyed, so that only a tiny
part escapes to be called useless rather than evil. Next, what
kinds of natures imitate the philosophic one and usurp its 491
pursuit which, being too high for them, completely untunes
them, so that they've stuck the reputation you mentioned
onto philosophy among peoples everywhere."

"What do you mean by corrupted?" he asked.

"Well, Adeimantus, I think anyone would agree that natures with all the parts we just assigned to one that may
become perfectly philosophic will be few and far between. b
Do you agree?"

"Completely."

"Now observe how many powerful corrupters these few
have. The most surprising thing is that each of the parts
we've praised in a philosophic nature destroys the soul that
has them and tears it away from philosophy. I mean courage,
temperance, and so on."

"That does sound strange."

"So do all the so-called goods—beauty, wealth, physical c
strength, influential relations in the city, that sort of thing.
You get the pattern I mean."

"Yes, but I'd like to hear it in detail."

"Well, if you properly grasp the whole, it'll all become
clear, and what we said about the parts won't seem so
strange."

"How do I do that?"

"We know that any seed or growth, animal or vegetable, d

must find proper nourishment, climate, and place, or else the stronger it is the more it will lack in the qualities appropriate to it. Evil is probably more opposed to the good than to the no-good."

"Of course."

"So I think it makes sense: in alien surroundings the best nature will end up worse than a poor one."

"Yes."

e "Therefore, Adeimantus," I said, "shall we also say that the best-natured souls turn out exceptionally bad if they get a bad schooling? Great crimes and pure evil come only from vigorous natures perverted by upbringing; a weak nature never does anything great, good or evil. Or do you think so?"

"No, it's as you say."

492 "So if the nature we posited as philosophic finds its appropriate learning it will necessarily grow to attain every excellence. But if it was planted and grew in the inappropriate, and is brought up there, it will arrive at just the opposite, unless a god comes to its aid. Or do you, like the many, believe that some young men are corrupted by sophists—that there are teachers corrupting people privately to any notable extent—or are the ones who make this allegation
b themselves the greatest sophists, perfect teachers who fashion young and old, men and women, into exactly what they want them to be?"

"When do they do that?" he asked.

"Whenever great numbers are gathered to sit in the assembly, in courts, in the theater, in camp, or in any of the mob's communal gatherings where with stupendous uproar they cheer and jeer actions and speeches, both to excess,
c shouting and applauding till even the echoing rocks and the place where they're sitting join in to redouble the racket of their cheering and jeering.[3] How do you think a young man's heart will react to all that? What private education could hold up and not be washed down the river of cheering and jeering, carried wherever the current may take it, so that he calls what they call beautiful and ugly, pursues what they do, and becomes like them?"

d "An absolute necessity, Socrates," he said.

[3]Communal gatherings (courts, theaters, etc.) were held outdoors, usually in amphitheaters on the side of a mountain.

"And yet, Adeimantus, we still haven't mentioned the greatest necessity."

"What?"

"The one that these sophists and teachers impose in deed upon the ones they can't persuade in word. Or didn't you know that they punish people who don't listen to them with fines, disfranchisement, and death?"

"They certainly do."

"What sophist or private argument could prevail against that?"

"None that I know of." e

"No," I said, "even the attempt is senseless. There is not,
never has been, nor will there ever be a divergent disposition educated in excellence contrary to the education given
by the many—a human one, my friend; we'll follow the prov-
erb and exempt the godlike from the argument. Because in
such a state of political affairs, if anything is preserved and
becomes what it should be, you won't go wrong by saying 493
a god's dispensation preserved it."

"That's my opinion too," he said.

"Here's something else for you to conjecture: Each of
these paid private teachers, whom they call sophists and
regard as competitors, teaches nothing but the convictions
of the many, which they conjecture when they gather together, and which these teachers call wisdom. It's as if a man
had observed the moods and desires of a huge, powerful
beast and had learned how to approach it and handle it, b
when it is savage or gentle and what makes it so, what sounds
it normally makes on different occasions, and what sounds
a person must make to soothe or enrage it. He then takes
what he has learned from this long association and calls it
wisdom, organizes it into a science, and takes up teaching;
even though he has no true knowledge about which of these
desires and convictions may be good, bad, beautiful, ugly,
just, or unjust, but makes these words depend on the whims c
of the creature, so that he calls whatever delights it 'good,'
whatever angers it 'bad,' and can give no further explanation
of them. He therefore terms necessities just and beautiful
because he's never been a spectator of, nor can he point out
to another, the nature of the necessary and the good, how
much in reality they differ from each other. Wouldn't a man
like that, by Zeus, strike you as a strange educator?"

"He surely would."

"Does it seem any different when a man has observed the
d moods and pleasures of the assembled many and multifarious concerning painting, music, or even politics, and then
considers it wisdom? If a man consorts with the many and
makes them his masters more than is necessary by displaying
his poetry or other works to them, or his service to the city,
then the legendary 'necessity of Diomedes'[4] will force him
to do whatever they approve. Have you ever heard such a
man give an argument for the true goodness and beauty of
this that wasn't utterly contemptible?"

e "No, and I don't think I ever will."

"Keeping all that in mind," I said, "remember this: the
beautiful itself and not the many beautiful things, or every
'itself' and not each of the 'manys'—will the mob ever put
494 up with that or think they exist?"

"Not in the least."

"So it's impossible for the mob to be a philosopher."

"Yes."

"And they'll necessarily denounce those who are."

"Necessarily."

"Then so will those private teachers who consort with the crowd and desire to please it."

"Clearly."

"Then do you see anything that will preserve a philosophic nature so it can stay in this pursuit till it reaches the
b end? Judge from what we've said: it has ease of learning,
memory, courage, and grandeur. Won't he therefore be
from the first the first of the boys, especially if his body
grows to resemble his soul?"

"How could he help it?"

"Then I suppose his family and the citizens will want to
use him for their own affairs when he grows up, so they'll
c grovel before him in supplication and respect, flattering him
in anticipation of his power."

"There is that tendency," he said.

"Then how do you think he'll behave, especially if he comes from a great city and is rich and well-born, perhaps even handsome and tall? Won't he be stuffed with wild ex-

[4]A proverbial expression for excessive force. Once, after Odysseus had tried to kill him, Diomedes bound him and drove him back to camp by beating him with his sword.

pectations, think he's up to handling the affairs of Greeks
and barbarians alike, set himself up on a pedestal and be d
filled with vacuous posings and grandiose ideas empty of
sense?"

"He certainly will."

"Now if somebody should approach him while he's in this
state and gently tell him the truth—that he's got none of the
sense he should have and won't get it unless he works for it
like a slave, do you think he'll readily listen, surrounded by
so many evils?"

"Not at all."

"But if he does listen because of his good birth and nature
and his affinity with the advice, and is turned and drawn to e
philosophy, what will we expect of those others who think
they're losing his usefulness and companionship? Won't
they say and do anything to prevent him from listening and
his advisor from being able to persuade him, by hatching
private plots and public prosecutions?"

"Necessarily." 495

"Is there any way he can become a philosopher?"

"Not very easily."

"You see?" I said. "We weren't far wrong when we said
that the parts of a philosopher's nature, if they fall in evil
surroundings, themselves somehow cause his exile from the
pursuit, as do so-called goods like wealth and other appurte-
nances."

"No, we were quite right."

"Then that, surprisingly enough, is what corrupts and
destroys the best natures—few enough to begin with, as we b
said—for the noblest pursuit. From them come the ones who
wreak the greatest evil on cities and individuals, as well as
the ones who do good, if their stream should flow in that
direction. A small nature never does anything great, for a
man or a city."

"True."

"Thus the ones most suited to Philosophy fall away from
her, leave her unwed and forsaken, and lead a false, inappro- c
priate life while unworthy strangers move in on her after
she's been left without relatives like an orphan, defile her
and hang on her that reproach you said her detractors make
against her: that some of her companions are good for nothing, and most of them only for evil."

"So they say, at any rate."

"With good reason. Other paltry fellows, who have
achieved the greatest distinction in their own little crafts, see
d the abandoned field ripe with impressive words and poses,
and like runaway slaves taking refuge in temples, they glee-
fully leap from their trades into philosophy. Even as now
practiced, philosophy has the grandest reputation compared
to other crafts; and many, aspiring to that even though
their natures are incomplete and the menial labor of their
e trades has left them as broken in soul as deformed in body
—or isn't that necessarily so?"

"It certainly is."

"Don't fellows like that remind you of a bald little blacksmith with money, just out of prison and fresh from the baths, in a new cloak and decked out like a bridegroom, about to marry his master's daughter because she's been left forsaken and destitute?"

496 "They're not very different."

"What sort of children will a couple like that most likely produce? Won't they be worthless bastards?"

"Necessarily."

"What about suitors unsuited to education who unworthily court Philosophy? What kind of notions and opinions shall we say they'll produce? Shouldn't we properly name them 'sophisms' because they're illegitimate and have nothing to do with true knowledge?"

"Absolutely."

"Then only a very few of Philosophy's worthy suitors re-
b main, Adeimantus—perhaps a noble and well-reared disposition caught in exile where no corrupters can unnaturally
separate him from her, or a great soul growing in a small city
and scorning its provincial affairs; and maybe a few good
natures come to her from some other craft which they justly
despise. Our companion Theages has a 'bridle' that may also
c curb some. Theages was all prepared for his exile from
Philosophy, but nursing his sickly body restrained him by
keeping him out of politics. My own divine sign[5] barely
deserves mention, because I imagine it has come to hardly
anyone before me. Now when a man has become one of
those worthy few and has tasted that sweet and blissful pos-

[5]Socrates' famous "divine voice," which warned him against doing certain things. Mentioned in *Apology* 31d and elsewhere.

session, when he has seen on the other hand the madness
of the many—how scarcely any does anything sound for his
city, and how there's no one among them to help him defend d
justice and to offer him safety—and when, like a man fallen
among beasts, unwilling to join in their crimes but too weak,
being one, to stand against all when they are all wild; they
would kill him before he could help his city or his friends,
and they would thus make him useless both to himself and
to others—when one of those few has comprehended all
that, he steps aside, as under a little wall in a storm when the
winds drive the dust and the sleet; he keeps his peace and
tends his own business; and observing the lawlessness of
others, he is content if he can somehow live this life free
from injustice and impious actions and depart from it gra- e
ciously, with kindliness and good hope."

"Yet, you know, his accomplishment won't be the smallest 497
by the time he departs."

"Nor the greatest, without finding a community suited to
him. There he'd flourish more fully and preserve both his
own and the commonwealth. But I think we've adequately
discussed the reasons for Philosophy's prejudice and why
it's unjustified, unless you have something to add."

"Not about that," he said. "But which of the present
regimes is suited to her?"

"None," I replied. "That's my complaint, Adeimantus— b
none of our present constitutions is worthy of the philosophic nature. Therefore it alters and turns, and as a foreign
seed planted in alien soil tends to be overwhelmed and
disappear into a native type, so at present this nature fails
to retain its own power and is banished into an alien disposition. If ever it finds the best regime—best as *it* is the best
—it will reveal that it was truly divine and all other natures c
and pursuits merely human. Obviously you're next going to
ask which regime this is."

"Wrong," he said. "I was going to ask whether it's the one
we've been founding."

"In all other respects, yes. And we did mention that there
must always be an element in our city with the same understanding of the regime that you as lawgiver had when you d
established the laws."[6]

"We did say that."

[6]Apparently a reference to 412a, p. 81.

"But not clearly enough, for fear of what your objections have shown will be a long, hard demonstration. What's left won't be so easy."

"What is it?"

"How a city can handle philosophy without destroying itself. All great things are precarious, and the old saying is true—beautiful things really are difficult."

e "Still, we must finish our demonstration by making this clear."

"If we don't, it won't be from lack of desire but ability. Watch and see how eager I am. Note the reckless enthusiasm with which I declare that a city must take up philosophy contrary to the way it's done now."

"How?"

"If people now take it up at all they do so as adolescents
498 before going into business. They flirt with its hardest part
—discussion—drop it, and are made out to be complete
philosophers. In later life they may, if invited, agree to listen
to others discuss, and consider it a wonderful thing if they
do, because they think of it as an avocation to pursue in
spare time. In old age all but a very few are extinguished
b even more completely than Heraclitus's sun, because they
never rekindle."[7]

"How should they do it?"

"Just the opposite—engage in adolescent philosophy and
education as boys and young men, and give special attention
to their bodies as they grow up, to acquire a helper for
philosophy. As the soul begins to mature with the passing
years, tighten up its exercise, and when their strength declines and exempts them from military and political duties,
c then be turned out to pasture to do nothing—except as a
sideline—but practice philosophy, if they're to live happily
here and crown their lives when they die with their fitting
portion over there."

"You do seem to be speaking enthusiastically, Socrates. But I think most of your listeners will resist even more enthusiastically and remain completely unconvinced, beginning with Thrasymachus here."

[7]Heraclitus was an early Ionic philosopher (ca. 500 B.C.), who wrote startling aphorisms. The reference is to his saying, "the sun is new every day."

"Don't estrange Thrasymachus and me when we've just
become friends, not that we were enemies before. We won't d
give up our attempt until we either convince him and the
others or make some useful contribution to that life when
they'll be born again and encounter discussions like these."

"A short time you address yourself to!"

"Nothing at all compared to the whole," I said. "But it's
no wonder the many disbelieve what we say—they've never
seen 'the implementation of our recommendation;' they've
only heard jargon like that, rhymed and balanced on pur- e
pose instead of falling out naturally, as here. But a man
rhymed and balanced to the highest perfection of excellence
in word and deed and holding sway in a city like himself— 499
that they've never seen, one or many. Nor, my friend, have
they heard enough beautiful, liberal speech, which strives in
every way to search out truth for the sake of knowledge and
only greets from afar that subtle disputation which strains
purely after rivalry and opinion in courts and private gatherings."

"No," he said, "they haven't."

"Those are the facts that we then foresaw with dread. b
Nevertheless, truth compelled us to say that neither a city
nor a regime nor even a man will grow to perfection until
some necessity thrown by chance enmeshes those few
philosophers now called not evil but useless into taking care
of their cities whether they want to or not, and the cities into
obeying them, or until true love for true philosophy falls c
from divine inspiration into some reigning king or regent or
into one of his sons. To say that either or both of these
alternatives cannot occur makes no sense, I maintain. If it
did, they could justly laugh us to scorn for mouthing pious
wishes, don't you think?"

"Yes."

"But if in boundless time gone by, some necessity to care
for a city has ever befallen eminent philosophers, or is upon
them now in some barbarian land far beyond our view, or
will befall in the future, then we'll be prepared to contend d
that this regime was and is and will again come to be whenever the Muse of philosophy masters a city. It isn't impossible, nor are we discussing impossibilities, though we
ourselves admit that it's difficult."

"It seems so to me too," he said.

"But not to the many, you say?"

"Probably not."

"Ah, my friend, don't be so hard on the many. They'll
e have a different opinion if you encourage them rather than argue with them, and if you dispel their prejudice by pointing out who you mean by philosophers, distinguishing as we
500 did their nature and pursuit so that they don't imagine you mean who they think. And even if they keep on viewing them as they do, don't you think they'll change their minds and answer differently? Or do you think that someone mild and ungrudging will be angry or envious toward one who is neither angry nor envious? I'll forestall your reply by saying that though a few people may have such harsh natures, I don't think it's true of the crowd."

"I fully agree," he said.

b "Do you also agree that the cause of their indignation with philosophy are those riotous party-crashers who burst in from outside, abusing and quarreling with each other and forever indulging in personalities, doing what least comports with philosophy?"

"I certainly do."

"I suppose a man with his mind truly on reality has no time to look down at human concerns, Adeimantus, or to
c fight with these people and fill himself with rancor and envy, but in watching and contemplating ordered things that always stay the same in every respect, that neither suffer nor commit injustice toward one another but keep a rational order, he starts to imitate and resemble them himself. Or do you think a man can associate with something he admires and yet not imitate it?"

"Impossible."

"Therefore by associating with the orderly and divine, the philosopher becomes as orderly and divine as a human be-
d ing can be, though prejudice occurs in everything."

"Absolutely."

"Now if some necessity befalls him to practice what he sees over there and to stamp it individually and collectively on human dispositions instead of molding only himself, do you think he'll become a poor craftsman of temperance, justice, and all popular excellence?"

"Not at all."

"And if the many see we were telling the truth about him,

will they be angry with the philosophers and disbelieve us e
when we say that a city will never be happy unless it's been
painted by painters who use the divine model?"

"Not if they see it," he said. "But what kind of painting do
you mean?" 501

"They'll take a city and human dispositions as if they were
a slate and first clean it off, which isn't so easy. You'll note
that right here they differ from others in refusing to touch
a man or a city or to draw up laws unless they either receive
a clean slate or clean it themselves. Next they'll sketch an
outline of the regime and then fill it in, constantly looking b
back and forth to that which by nature is the just, the beautiful,
the temperate, and so on, and to that which they're
trying to paint into the men, mixing and blending from all
pursuits to get the true complexion of man, basing their
judgment on what Homer too called divine and god-complexioned
whenever it appeared in a human. And often,
I suppose, they'll rub out a part and repaint it, until they c
create human dispositions as dear to the gods as can be."

"At least they'll produce a beautiful picture," he said.

"Are we somehow persuading the ones who you said were
stampeding us down that this is the regime-painter we recommended
to them when they got angry with us for handing
the city over to him? Will they calm down now that they've
heard this?"

"They will if they have any sense."

"What do they have to carp at? that the philosophers d
aren't lovers of truth and what *is*? or that their nature as
we've presented it isn't akin to the best?"

"That would be a strange cavil."

"And won't this nature, if any, become perfectly good and
philosophic if it finds its proper pursuits? Or will they say it's
those others that we rejected?"

"Hardly." e

"Will they still be indignant at us for saying that until the
philosopher class masters the city there'll be no end to the
evils for her or her citizens, nor will the regime we've spun
out in words find fulfillment in deed?"

"Less, perhaps."

"Instead of 'less,' can't we say they've been completely
calmed and persuaded and will agree with us now out of 502
shame, if nothing else?"

"Yes."

"Then let's assume they're persuaded of that. Now will anyone dispute that kings or regents could by chance produce offspring with philosophic natures?"

"No."

"And if born, Adeimantus, could anyone prove that they
must necessarily be corrupted? We ourselves admit that
b their preservation would be difficult, but who could say that
of all the princes in all of time not one could be preserved?"

"No one."

"And one would suffice," I said, "if he had an obedient city, to accomplish all this that now seems incredible, because if a ruler established the laws and pursuits we've gone through, it isn't impossible that the citizens might be willing to carry them out. And would it be impossible or surprising if someone else had reached the same opinion of this that we have?"

c "I don't think so."

"I think we've already sufficiently shown that if all this were possible it would be for the best."

"Yes."

"Then the result of our inquiry, it seems, is that our legislation would be for the best if it came about, and that it would be hard to bring about, but not impossible."

"That's the conclusion, all right."

"Well, we've managed to finish that and must now discuss
what remains: how to produce preservers of the regime,
d what studies and pursuits will produce them, and at what age
they should take up each one."

"Yes, we must."

"I cleverly dodged these unsavory topics before—possession of wives, mating, and the way to appoint the rulers—
because I knew the absolutely true way would arouse envy
and be hard to achieve. But my cleverness did me no good
e because now we must go through it anyway. We've finished
with the women and children and must now go back to the
rulers as though starting from scratch. We said, you'll recall,
503 that they must prove themselves patriotic by being tested in
pleasures and pains, and show that they won't drop this
conviction in fear or suffering or any other vicissitude, or
else be rejected. The one who emerges from all that as pure
as gold tested in fire must be appointed ruler and receive
prizes and gifts both while living and after he's dead. Some-

thing like that is what the argument dropped as she slipped past in a veil, in dread of stirring up the present discussion." b

"That's true," he said, "—I remember."

"I was hesitant then, my friend, to suggest what now has been ventured. But let it now be said: as our most exacting guardians we must appoint philosophers."

"Yes, let it be said."

"Notice how few you're likely to have, Adeimantus. They must have the nature we described, whose parts seldom occur together, but tend to grow scattered."

"How do you mean?" he asked. c

"You know that shrewd, quick, retentive minds which learn easily and also possess vigor and grandeur seldom are found in natures disposed to lead orderly, quiet, and stable lives—their alacrity carries them hither and yon, and all their stability vanishes."

"True."

"Whereas stable, unchangeable dispositions that inspire confidence and refuse to be budged by the fears of battle are d
the same in their studies—when they face an assignment they're hard to budge and slow to learn, full of sleep and yawns, as numb as if stung by a stingray."

"That's true too."

"But we say our men must duly participate in both of these natures, or else have no share in the most exacting education, in honor, or in rule. Won't that be a rare combination?"

"Certainly."

"Then they must be tested in those pleasures, pains, and e
fears we mentioned, as well as in other things we'll now add: We must exercise them in many subjects and observe whether they'll be able to endure the highest studies or shrink back, the way some athletes shrink back from their 504
events."

"That would be fitting," he said. "But what studies do you mean by the highest?"

"I suppose you remember," I said, "that after separating out three forms in the soul we concluded what justice, temperance, courage, and wisdom are."

"If I didn't I wouldn't deserve to hear the rest."

"Do you also remember what we said before that?"[8]

[8]The reference is to 435d, p. 102.

"What?"

b "That these four could best be seen by taking a detour, a longer way that would make them all clear, but that we could also tack on proofs that followed our previous discussion. You said that would be fine, so we discussed them like that. I thought the discussion lacked accuracy, but if it was precise enough for you, you may say so."

"I think you gave us good measure," said Adeimantus, "and these others seem to agree."

c "My friend, in something like this a measure that falls short of what *is*, by even the slightest amount, can hardly be good. Nothing imperfect is the measure of anything. But some seem satisfied even with that and think there's no need to search further."

"That happens to many from laziness."

"But a guardian of the laws and the city ought to be immune to such an affliction."

"Most likely."

"Then, my friend, he must take the longer path and work
d as hard at learning as at gymnastics. Otherwise, as we said, he'll never reach the end of the highest studies, which most properly belong to him."

"You mean there's something higher than justice and all we've gone through?"

"Not only higher," I replied, "but it demands to be contemplated in a finished portrait rather than in outline, as we've been doing. Wouldn't it be absurd to sweat and strain
e to get these less important details as clean and exact as possible and then not insist on the greatest precision in the highest things?"

"It certainly would," he said. "But do you think anyone would let you go without asking what this highest learning is and what it's about?"

"Not really, so ask me. But you've heard it many times, so either you're not thinking or you intend to pester me as
505 before by not letting me go. I think that's it, because you've often heard that the highest learning is the shape of the good, which everything just, beautiful, and so on must use in order to become useful and beneficial. You probably also know that I'll say we don't have sufficient knowledge of it, and that knowing everything else is useless without knowing the good, just as possessing anything is useless without it.

Or do you think there's profit in having or knowing every- b
thing without the beautiful and the good?"
"No, by Zeus, I don't."
"And you also know this: The many imagine the good to
be pleasure; the more refined call it knowledge."
"Of course."
"But the latter can't specify which kind, and finally are
forced to say 'knowledge of the good.' "
"Absurdly enough."
"Yes," I said. "They berate us for not knowing the good c
and then turn around and speak as if we knew it. 'Knowledge
of the *good,'* they say, as though we'll catch their meaning if
only they utter the word."
"True," he said.
"What about the ones who define the good as pleasure?
Aren't they filled with wandering too? They're forced to
admit that there are bad pleasures, and end up identifying
the good with the bad. Isn't that so?"
"Yes." d
"Controversial as this subject clearly is, isn't this, at least,
clear? That concerning the just and the beautiful, many people might choose to do, possess, or imagine things that *seem*
like that, even if they *are* not; whereas no one would consent
to have things that seem *good;* they seek what *is* good, and
at this point everyone despises the seeming."
"Very clear," he said.
"What every soul pursues and for which it does all that it
does, divining that it exists but baffled and unable to grasp e
what exactly it is, lacking firm belief to rely on as in everything else and therefore missing whatever benefit may come
from anything else—in a matter of such size and merit are
we to say that our city's best men, to whom everything shall 506
be entrusted, should grope around in the dark?"
"Absolutely not."
"I should think just and beautiful things won't have much
of a guardian in a man ignorant of how they are good. I
predict that no one will know them sufficiently until he
knows that."
"A good prediction," he said.
"Then won't our regime be completely ordered when it's
watched by a guardian who knows that?" b

"Necessarily," he said. "But, Socrates, what do *you* say the good is—knowledge or pleasure or what?"

"What a man!" I exclaimed. "You made it clear long ago that you wouldn't be satisfied with other people's opinions of this."

"I don't think it's right, Socrates, to give the convictions of others without telling your own, when you've been in-
c volved with this for such a long time."

"What? do you think it's right for a person to speak as if he knew about things that he doesn't?"

"Not as if he knew, but he might tell what he thinks about them."

"But haven't you seen how ugly all opinions are without knowledge? The best are blind—or do people who conjecture some truth without using intelligence strike you as better than blind men who take the right road?"

"Not a bit."

"Then why do you want to see my blind, crooked, ugly
d opinions, Adeimantus, when you could hear beautiful, clear ones from others?"

"By Zeus, Socrates," said Glaucon, "don't stop now as though you were at the finish. We'll be satisfied if you explain the good the way you explained justice and temperance and all that."

"So would I, Glaucon—more than satisfied. But I'm afraid that for all my eagerness I'd stumble around and look like a fool. So, my friends, for now let's leave the question of
e what the good is—I don't think we have enough of a start even to reach my opinion of it. But I am willing to tell who I think is the *offspring* of the good and most in its likeness, if you wish. If not, let it go."

"Speak," said Glaucon, "you're holding our interest. You can stay in debt to us for the father's account till some other time."

507 "I wish I could return, and you could collect, the principal and not just the interest. As it is, accept this as the interest and offspring of the good. Just be careful I don't unintentionally deceive you—don't credit my account if it's counterfeit."

"We'll be careful—just speak."

"I will, after I remind you of what we said a while ago and many times before, and get your agreement on it."

"What?" he asked. b

"We say beautiful things and good things and so forth are many, and so define them in our speech. Then we turn around and say there's a beautiful itself, a good itself, and so on for all the things we then classed as many—we posit one shape for each class, on the grounds that a shape is one, and call it 'that which *is.*' "

"Right," he said.

"And we say the manys are visible but not intelligible; the shapes intelligible but not visible."

"Absolutely."

"What do we see visible things with?" c

"Sight."

"And hearable things with hearing, and all sensible things with our senses."

"Of course," said Glaucon.

"Have you noticed how the craftsman who fashioned the senses made the power of seeing and being seen the most priceless of all?"

"Not really."

"Well, look: do hearing and sound need some third thing
as a medium to enable them to hear and be heard?" d

"No."

"The same with the other powers: I can think of few if any that need a medium. Can you, Glaucon?"

"No."

"Except seeing and being seen."

"How so?"

"If someone has sight and tries to use it, then even if colors are present you know his eyes will see nothing and the
colors be dark without the presence of a third kind of thing e
that naturally exists just for this."

"What is it?"

"What you," I said, "call light."

"That's true," he said.

"So the sense of sight and the power of being seen are
harnessed together by a yoke more precious in kind than 508
those that join other teams, if light is no cheap thing."

"Far from it!"

"Then which of the gods in the sky do you proclaim lord of this, whose light causes our sight most beautifully to see, and visible things to be seen?"

"The same as you and everyone else. Clearly you mean the sun."

"And isn't sight related to this god in such a way that
b neither it nor its organ, which we call the eye, *is* the sun?"

"Yes."

"But of all the organs of sense, I think, the eye is the most sunlike."

"By far."

"And it holds its power as an overflow dispensed by the sun?"

"Of course."

"So too the sun is not sight, but the cause of sight, which sees him."

"Exactly."

"That's what I meant by the offspring of the good. The
good begot the sun as a proportion to itself: as is the good
to intelligence and to intelligible things in the intelligible
c realm, so is the sun to sight and to visible things in the visible
realm."

"What? Explain that more fully."

"When you look at things whose colors are covered not
with sunlight but moonlight, you know your eyes darken and
seem almost blind, as though there were no pure sight in
d them. But in sunlight they see clearly and clearly have sight."

"Of course."

"Then think of it as the same with the eye of the soul, Glaucon. When it rests on the place lit by truth and what *is,* it perceives it and knows it and seems to have intelligence. But in the place mingled with darkness, the region of becoming and passing away, it darkens and conjectures, changes its opinions up and down, and now appears to have no intelligence."

"That's how it appears."

e "This, then, which lends truth to things known and gives
to knowers the power to know, you may call the shape of the
good. As cause of knowledge and truth, you may think of it
as apprehended by knowledge and yet, beautiful as truth and
knowledge both are, you will be right in considering the
good to be something other and even more beautiful than
they. Just as before it was proper to regard light and seeing
509 not as the sun, but as sunlike, so now it is proper to regard
both knowledge and truth not as the good, but as good-

like; higher honors must be reserved for the state of the good."

"What fabulous beauty," he cried, "if it imparts truth and knowledge, yet exels them in beauty! I guess you don't define the good as pleasure."

"Hush!" I said. "Now examine the image further: I think b
you'll agree that the sun lends to visible things not only visibility, but also generation, nurture, and growth, though the sun himself is not generation."

"Of course."

"Then you must also agree that because of the good not only is knowability present in knowable things, but also existence and being, even though the good is not being, but beyond being, surpassing even it in dignity and power."

"Apollo!" Glaucon cried comically. "What divine transc- c
endence!"

"Well, it's your fault for making me give my opinion of it."

"Don't stop," he said. "At least go on with the simile of the sun, unless you're already up to the end."

"Oh, I'm hardly up to that."

"Don't drop a thing."

"I'm afraid I'll drop a lot, but I'll try to keep it up as far as present circumstances permit. I won't let you down intentionally."

"No, don't."

"Then regard them as two,[9] the one reigning over the d
realm of the intellect, the other over the realm of the eye—I avoid saying 'sky' so you don't think I'm playing on words. Anyway, do you have these two classes, the visible and the intelligible?"

"Yes."

"Then take a line divided into two unequal segments—one for the visible, one for the intelligible class—and divide

[9]I.e. the good and the sun. The pun on "eye" and "sky" below is more involved in Greek. If the Greek word for "sky" is taken as three separate words *(ou-ra-nou),* it means "of no intelligence." Socrates pretends to avoid saying "realm of the sky" (or "of no intelligence") so as not to be accused of deriving his scheme from a pun.

each segment again in the same ratio.[10] Your segments, arranged by relative clarity and obscurity, will be: First, in
e the visible class, images.[11] By that I mean shadows, appari-
510 tions in water or other dense, smooth, bright surfaces—everything like that, if you see what I mean."

"I see."

"As the next segment[12] take the things that they image: animals around us and the whole class of natural and man-made things."

"All right."

"Would you say this division expresses a proportion in regard to truth and its opposite?—as the conjecturable is to the knowable, so is the likeness to the original."[13]

b "I certainly would."

"Now observe how we must divide the intelligible segment."[14]

"How?"

"Into two parts: one[15] that the soul is obliged to investi-

[10]The divided line might look something like this:

b
forms, shapes (objects of intellection)
intelligible class (truth, knowledge)
e
mathematical objects (objects of understanding)
c
things (originals of ad, objects of trust)
visible class (opinion, conjecture)
d
images (objects of imaging)
a

ac/cb = ad/dc = ce/eb, and dc is the same length as ce. Also cb/ac = eb/dc = ce/ad (see 534a, p. 193–194.). It is impossible to tell which segment Plato intended to be the larger, but it should be the intelligible, since it contains everything in the visible segment as well as concepts (such as numbers) that do not exist in the visible segment.

[11]ad in footnote 10 above.

[12]dc in footnote 10.

[13]ac/cb = ad/dc in footnote 10. "Knowable" = "intelligible."

[14]cb in footnote 10.

[15]ce in footnote 10.

gate from assumptions, using as images what in the previous
segment[16] were originals and proceeding not to a source[17]
but to a conclusion; another[18] where it goes from an assumption to an unassumed source and uses no images, but
only forms themselves by themselves."

"I don't quite understand."

"Try again," I said. "This may be easier. I think you know c
that geometers and arithmeticians and so forth assume the
odd and the even, the figures, the three kinds of angles, and
all the other things that pertain to each field. They posit
these as assumptions, as if they were known, and consider
them so self-evident that they needn't give any further account of them either to themselves or to others. Starting
from these, they go through the rest of their inquiry and d
finally reach the logically consistent conclusion they were
looking for when they began."

"I know that very well," he said.

"Then you also know they use visible forms to illustrate
what they mean, though they're not thinking of them but of
the originals they represent—the rectangle itself and the
diagonal itself, rather than the ones that they draw. They use e
the figures they mold and draw, which themselves throw
shadows and images in water, as images, striving to see the
figures themselves, which only the understanding can see." 511

"True."

"I called this class[19] intelligible then, even though the soul
is forced to investigate it by means of assumptions without
going to a source—as though unable to climb above the
assumptions—and uses as images things imaged by things
below them, compared with which the higher are honored
as clear and distinct."[20]

"I understand you mean the class studied by geometry b
and related sciences."

[16]dc in footnote 10.
[17]*Arche*, the same word as political "rule." But it also means "source" or "beginning," in contrast to "conclusion," which in Greek literally means "end."
[18]eb in footnote 10.
[19]ce in footnote 10.
[20]"Things imaged by things below them" = dc, imaged by ad in footnote 10. "The higher" = dc.

"Then understand that by the other intelligible segment[21] I mean the one that reason[22] itself grasps by the power of dialectic, taking assumptions not as sources, but in the literal sense—as starting points or rungs—to climb to the unassumed up to the source of the whole, grasp it, and then, clinging to the consequences clinging to it, climb back down to a final conclusion, using nothing perceptible at all, but
c only forms themselves by themselves to themselves, ending at forms."

"I understand," he said, "though not well enough—it seems like a gigantic task you're relating—that you wish to define the segment contemplated by the dialectical knowledge of the intelligible and of what *is*[23] as being clearer than the one studied by the so-called sciences,[24] where the observers, though forced to observe with understanding instead of the senses, treat assumptions as sources; and since
d they examine down from assumptions rather than up to a source, they seem to you not to have intelligence of their subjects, which are, however, intelligibles with a governing source. And I think you call the geometrical or mathematical state of mind not intelligence but understanding, as standing under intelligence, between it and opinion."

"You've got it well enough," I said. "Now for these four segments take four states that arise in the soul and give intellection to the highest segment, understanding to the
e second, trust to the third, and imaging to the last.[25] Arrange them in a proportion and regard each as participating in as much clarity as its object does truth."

"I understand, concur, and arrange them as you say."

Book 7

514 "Next," I said, "compare human nature in its educated and uneducated state to the following situation: Imagine

[21]eb in footnote 10.
[22]Also "argument;" both reason and its operation.
[23]eb in footnote 10.
[24]ce in footnote 10.
[25]eb, ce, dc, and ad respectively in footnote 10. "Imaging" is a nonce word used to designate the perception of images *as images.*

men in a cavelike underground dwelling with a long entrance, as wide as the cave and open to the light. The men have been chained foot and neck since childhood. The chains keep them in place and prevent them from turning b
their heads, so that they only see forward. Light comes to them from a fire burning at a distance above and behind them. Between the fire and the prisoners, higher than they, imagine a road with a low wall built alongside, like the screen set in front of puppeteers, over which they show their puppets."[1]

"I see," said Glaucon.

"Then see people walking along the road carrying things on their heads, including figures of men and animals made c
of wood, stone, and other materials. These extend over the 515
top of the wall and, as you might expect, some of the people are talking, while others are silent."

"Strange is your image," he said, "and your prisoners strange."

"Like us," I said. "Do you think such prisoners would ever see anything of themselves or each other except their shadows thrown by the fire on the facing wall of the cave?"

"How could they if their heads were held still all their lives?" b

"What would they see of the things carried by?"

"The same."

"Now if they could talk to each other, don't you think they'd believe what they saw was reality?"

"Necessarily."

"What if the prison had an echo from the front? Whenever a passerby spoke, wouldn't the prisoners think it was the passing shadow that spoke?"

[1]The cave would look something like this:

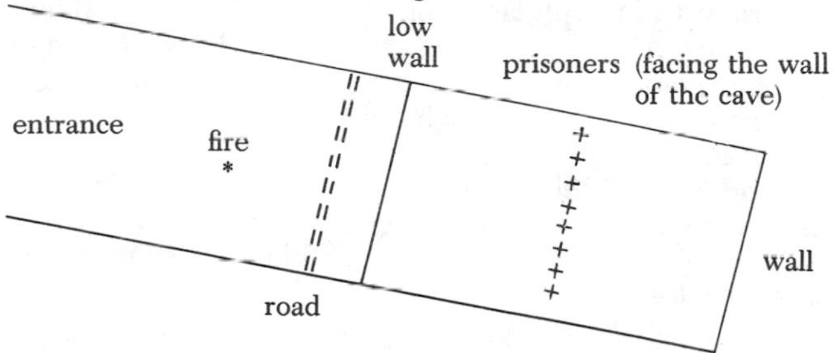

"They certainly would."

c "So men like that," I said, "would firmly believe truth to
be the shadows of artificial objects."

"An absolute necessity," he said.

"Now look: what if they could be freed from their bonds
and cured of their unreason by some natural happening like
this? One is released and suddenly forced to stand up, turn
his head, walk and look up to the light of the fire; all this
causes him pain and the glitter blinds him to the things
d whose shadows he formerly saw—what do you think he'd say
if someone told him he used to see nonsense and now sees
more truly because he's turned to what more nearly *is* and
to things more nearly real? What if the things passing by
were pointed out to him and he was forced to say what each
of them was? Don't you think he'd be baffled and believe that
the things then seen were truer than the ones now pointed
out?"

"Much," he said.

e "And if forced to look at the light itself, it would hurt his
eyes and he'd turn away and run back to the things he could
see, and believe that they were in reality clearer than the
ones pointed out."

"True."

"Suppose someone forcibly dragged him out of there, up
that steep, rugged incline, and didn't let go till he'd dragged
him clear out to the light of the sun. Wouldn't such treat-
516 ment pain and outrage him, and the beams fill his eyes and
make him unable to see any of the things that now are called
true?"

"At first it would."

"I think he'd have to become habituated to see the things
above. At first he'd most easily make out shadows, then
apparitions of people and things in water, then the things
themselves. After that he'd contemplate the heavenly bodies
b and heaven itself by night, finding starlight and moonlight
easier to look at than sunlight and the sun."

"Of course."

"And finally, I think, the sun—not an apparition in water or in some other foreign setting, but himself by himself in his own place—he'll be able to see him and contemplate what he's like."

"Necessarily," he said.

"And here he'll conclude that this is the giver of seasons
and years, curator of all in the visible sphere, the cause c
somehow of all that he used to see."

"Clearly he'll come upon this after that."

"What if he thinks back on his former dwelling, on the 'wisdom' there and on his fellow prisoners? Won't he pity them and congratulate himself on his transition?"

"Very much."

"Suppose they conferred offices, honors, and prizes down
there on the one sharpest at spotting the passing shadows,
at remembering which normally precede, follow, or accompany each other, and at being able to divine from that what d
will come next—do you suppose he'd covet such prizes and
strive with the men holding honors and power down there,
or would he with Homer much rather 'follow a plow as the
serf/ of a land-hungry, indigent peasant,'[2] and prefer to
suffer anything rather than conjecture those things and live
like that?"

"Yes," he said, "I think he'd suffer anything rather than e
live like that."

"Now think about this," I said: "If he again went down and sat down in his old place, wouldn't darkness fill his eyes after suddenly coming in from the sun?"

"Completely."

"And if again he had to 'evaluate' those shadows down
there in competition with the perpetual prisoners, then in
that not short time of habituation in which his eyes were 517
dimmed and unrecovered, he'd make a fool of himself, and
they'd say he came back from above with ruined eyes and the
trip wasn't even worth the attempt. And if they could get
their hands on the one who was trying to release them and
lead them upward, wouldn't they kill him?"

"Most violently."

"Then take this image, dear Glaucon, and apply it all to
all that we've said. Liken the prisoners' cave to the region b
apparent to sight, and the light of their fire to the power of
the sun. If you regard the upward journey and the viewing

[2] *Odyssey* 11.489–90 (quoted above, 386c, p. 56). The passage continues: "than be king over all these exhausted dead" (in the underworld).

of the upper world as the soul's ascent to the intelligible you
won't mistake my expectation, which is what you wanted to
hear. A god, perhaps, knows if it's true. But here is my
vision: the shape of the good is finally and with difficulty
c seen in the knowable[3] realm, and when seen it must be
reckoned the cause of everything upright and beautiful in
all, begetting in the visible world light and the Lord of Light,
itself the lord giver of truth and intelligence in the intelligible world, that which a man must see to act rationally for
himself or his community."

"I assent," he said, "as well as I'm able."

"Then assent to this too," I said, "and don't be surprised
if the ones who have been there don't want to tend to human
concerns, but their souls always strive upward to pass time
d there. I suppose that will happen, if this part also comports
with our image."

"Very likely," he said.

"Do you wonder that a man returned from divine contem-
plations to human evils should cut a poor figure while still
dazzled and unaccustomed to the present darkness? Won't
he look clumsy and ridiculous if forced to contend in court
or elsewhere about the shadows of justice—or rather about
e the figurines that throw the shadows—and about how men
interpret them who have never seen justice itself?"

"He certainly will."

518 "If a person has sense he'll remember that two things
confuse the eyes: moving from darkness to light and from
light to darkness, and believe that the same happens to the
soul. Therefore he won't thoughtlessly laugh when he sees
a soul stunned and unable to see, but examine whether it's
darkened by unfamiliarity after coming from a brighter life
b or dazed by the glitter in moving from deeper ignorance to
greater brightness; then congratulate the first on its state
and life, but pity the other. And if he feels like laughing
at it, his laughter won't be as contemptible as when a man
laughs at a soul come down from the light above."

"That's quite reasonable."

"If it's true, we mustn't believe that education is as some
people proclaim: that the soul has no knowledge and they
c put it in, like sight in blind eyes."

[3]= intelligible.

"That is what they say."

"But our argument indicates that the power of learning inheres in everyone's soul. It's as if we couldn't turn our eye from the dark to the bright without turning our whole body around; so here we must turn the whole soul and its organ of learning[4] away from becoming until it faces being and can endure contemplating the brightest of what *is.* We call that
the good, don't we?" d

"Yes."

"Then," I said, "education would be the art of turning this organ around in the easiest, most effective way—not of implanting sight, which it already has, but of contriving to turn the organ around to look where it should."

"So it seems," he said.

"The other excellences said to belong to the soul are
probably close to those of the body—really absent at first e
and then implanted by habit and practice. But the excellence of understanding, it seems, is definitely something more divine; it never loses its power, but becomes useful and helpful or useless and harmful depending on how it's
turned. Have you ever seen people called wise but vicious? 519
Their little soul peers out shrewdly and keenly discerns whatever it's turned to, as though its sight were not poor. But since it's forced to serve evil, the sharper it sees the more damage it does."

"Yes, I have."

"If this part of such a nature had been hammered from childhood, then the relatives of becoming, which grow on to
it through eating and similar gluttonous desires and plea- b
sures and turn the soul's vision downward, would have been struck from it like lead weights. Then, rid of those and turned around to things that are true, the eyes of those same souls would have seen truth the most sharply, just as now they see sharply whatever they're turned to."

"Most likely," he said.

"Doesn't everything we've said make it both likely and necessary that neither the uneducated with no experience of
truth nor people allowed to continue their education to the c
end will ever adequately manage a city? The uneducated have no single target in life at which to aim all their activity

[4]= "eye of the soul," i.e. mind or intelligence.

in public and private; the others won't willingly act at all—while still alive they think they've been settled on the Isles of the Blest."

"True," he said.

"Then our job as founders," I said, "is to force the best
natures to reach the learning we called the highest—to climb
that ascent and see the good, and when they've climbed and
d sufficiently seen, not to permit them what's permitted them
now."

"What?"

"To linger there and refuse to climb back down to those prisoners and take part in their labors and honors, whether serious or trivial."

"But won't we be doing them an injustice, forcing them to live a poor life when they could live a better?"

e "You've forgotten, my friend, that the law doesn't care
about any one class doing exceptionally well, but is trying to
devise this for the whole city by fitting the citizens together
through persuasion and necessity, by making them share
520 whatever benefit each can contribute to the common good,
and by engendering beneficial men in the city—not so each
may do as he likes, but so the law may use them to bind the
city together."

"You're right," he said, "I had forgotten."

"Then, Glaucon," I said, "observe that we won't be doing
our philosophers an injustice—we can justify forcing them
to care for the others as guardians. 'Philosophers born into
b other cities,' we'll say, 'can reasonably decline to share in the
chores because they've arisen spontaneously, against the
will of their governments, and a natural growth is obligated
to no one for its nurture and has no just debt to repay. But
we've bred you like queen bees to lead the hive and yourselves, educated you better and more completely than those,
and made you more capable of participating in both tasks.
c Down you must go, therefore, each in your turn to that cave
with the others and accustom yourselves to viewing the
things of darkness. Once you do you'll see them infinitely
better than they and recognize each phantom and its original, because you've seen the truth about just, beautiful, and
good things. Thus your city and ours will be governed awake
and not in a dream as most cities now, whose citizens fight
with each other about shadows in civil war over rule, as

though rule were some great good. But the truth is probably d
this: A city whose future rulers are the least eager to rule will
necessarily be the best governed and freest from strife, and
the one with opposite rulers the worst.'"

"Certainly," he said.

"Do you think they'll disobey us and refuse to join in the work of the city each in his turn, though living together most of the time in the pure?"

"Impossible: we issue just commands to the just. But each e
above all will accept rule as a necessity to be endured, the
opposite of all rulers now."

"True enough, my friend. If you discover a life better than
ruling for those destined to rule, a well-governed city will be 521
possible, because only in it will the rulers be truly rich—not
in gold, but in the wealth that a man must have to be happy:
a good and sensible life. If they're beggars who enter public
life because they're starved of personal goods and think they
have to steal their good there, it will be impossible. When
rule becomes hotly contested, civil war settles down and
destroys rulers and city alike."

"True," he said.

"Do you know of any life except a true philosopher's that b
despises public office?"

"No, by Zeus," he said.

"And Rule must be courted only by non-lovers. Otherwise her suitors will fight."

"Of course."

"Then will you force anyone else to accept the guardianship of your city but those who know what makes a city the best governed, and who have other honors and a better life than the political?"

"No."

"Would you like to examine how such men can be brought c
into being and led up to the light, the way they say some
have gone from Hades up to the gods?"

"Of course I would."

"It seems this will be no chance spin of the shard, calling it 'light or dark,'[5] but a turning around of the soul from a

[5] A piece of pottery painted white on one side and black on the other was spun or flipped and would be called "light or dark," i.e. "heads or tails."

day like night to the true day, the upward climb to what *is*, which we call true philosophy."

"Certainly."

d "Then shall we examine which learning has this power?"

"Of course."

"What study serves as a winch to lift the soul from becoming to being? Something occurs to me as I speak, Glaucon. Didn't we say that while still young our guardians must be athletes of war?"

"Yes."

"So the study we're looking for must also be useful for warriors."

"Yes, if that's possible."

"They've already been educated in gymnastics and po-
e etry. Gymnastics putters around with becoming and passing
away, supervising the body's growth and decay. So that's not
522 what we're looking for. How about the poetry we went
through earlier?"

"That was the counterpoint to gymnastics," he said.
"You'll remember it educated our guardians by habit, its
melody and rhythm imparting good harmony and grace, not
knowledge. Its words, fictitious or more true, had certain
sister habits, but nowhere did it have a learning that led to
b the sort of good you're looking for now."

"An accurate reminder, Glaucon—it really didn't. But what else could it be, for heaven's sake? The skills all seemed rather menial."

"Of course. And what study is left besides poetry, gymnastics, and the skills?"

"If we can't find something outside them, let's get one that applies to them all."

"What?"

c "Something common, which all skills, knowledge, and
thought use—one of the first things we all must learn."

"What's that?"

"The trivial business of distinguishing one, two, three—number and calculation, I mean. Isn't it true that every skill and science is forced to participate in number?"

"It surely is."

"Even military science?"

"An absolute necessity."

d "That's how Palamedes makes Agamemnon look like an

ass in all the tragedies.[6] Haven't you noticed? They say he invented number and then marshalled the army in ranks at Troy and counted the ships and everything, as though they were uncounted before. Agamemnon must not have known how many feet he had if he didn't know how to count. How's that for a general, Glaucon?"

"A rather odd one, if it's true."

"Then we'll establish another learning as necessary for a e
military man—the ability to count and calculate."

"Absolutely, if he's supposed to know anything about marshalling troops or even be a human being."

"Do you see what I see in this learning?"

"What?"

"It seems to be one of the studies we're looking for—it 523
naturally leads to intellection, though no one uses it properly, as a winch to absolute being."

"How do you mean?"

"I'll try to make my opinion clear. Observe how I distinguish the things that lead up there from the ones that do not and agree or disagree so we'll clearly see whether or not I intuit this correctly."

"Show them."

"I will if you watch: some things that strike the senses
don't invite the intellect to examine them because they're b
sufficiently judged by perception, whereas others encourage examination because perception yields no sound result."

"Clearly you mean things seen from afar and in perspective drawings."

"You don't quite have it," I said.

"What do you mean then?"

"By 'not inviting' I mean things that don't issue in a simultaneous contrary impression; those that do I class as inviting c
—whenever perception reveals both a thing and its contrary, whether it strikes the senses from near or far. This will make it clearer: these, we say, are three fingers—the little, the middle, and the one in between."

"All right."

"Assume that I speak of them as seen from close up. Now observe that each appears to be as much a finger as the

[6]Agamemnon led the Greek army at Troy. Palamedes was credited with the invention of numbers and the alphabet.

d others, whether seen as between or outside, black or white, thick or thin, and so on. In none of these cases does the soul in most people compel the intellect to ask what finger is, because sight nowhere gives it a simultaneous signal that the finger contradicts finger."

"No, it doesn't," he said.

"Therefore we wouldn't expect a thing like that to invite
e or awake intellection."

"No."

"But what about their largeness and smallness? Does sight suffice to see that—whether the finger lies between or outside? And is the sense of touch able to feel their thickness and thinness or hardness and softness? Aren't all the senses deficient in revealing that sort of thing? Doesn't each of
524 them function like this: the sense directed to hardness is necessarily also directed to softness and reports to the soul that it perceives the same thing as both hard and soft?"

"Yes," he said.

"So in this situation," I said, "the soul is necessarily baffled about what touch means by signaling hard when it calls the same thing soft, and about what the heavy and the light can be when the sensations of light and heavy report the heavy as light and the light as heavy."

b "Yes, these communications puzzle the soul and demand examination."

"In such cases, it seems, a soul first summons calculation and intellection and tries to examine whether each of the things reported is one or two. If they appear two, then each appears to be one and different, and if each is one and both two, then intellection thinks of the two as separate, because
c if they weren't separate it would think not of two but of one."

"Right."

"Similarly sight, we say, saw the large and the small; not separated, but jumbled together. Isn't that so?"

"Yes."

"And to clear this up the intellect was also forced to see the large and the small; not jumbled, but separate, the opposite of sight."

"True."

"So it's in situations like this that it first occurs to us to ask 'What is the large?' and 'What is the small?' "

"Absolutely."

"Therefore we called the one class intelligible and the other visible."

"Right." d

"That's what I was just trying to say: some things invite understanding and others do not. And I defined things that strike the senses along with their contraries as inviting the intellect, those that don't as not inviting it."

"Now I understand and agree," he said.

"Then in which class do you put number and one?"

"I've no idea."

"Well, figure it out from what we've said. If one itself is
sufficiently seen, or grasped by some other sense, then it's e
not a winch to being, just as we said finger is not. But if one is never seen without its contrary, so that it always appears to be its contrary as well as itself, then it demands judgment because it baffles the soul and forces it to investigate. The soul stirs up its mind and asks what one itself is. Thus the
study of unity would be one of the studies that lead the soul 525
and turn it to the contemplation of what *is.*"

"Certainly the sight of it especially does that—we see the same thing simultaneously as one and as limitless in quantity."[7]

"If that happens with one it must happen with every number."

"Of course."

"And arithmetic and calculation deal with number."

"Certainly."

"And they appear to lead to truth." b

"Incredibly."

"So calculation, it seems, is one of the studies we're looking for: a soldier must learn it to marshal troops, a philosopher to emerge from becoming and seize being, or never become a rational[8] being."

"That's a fact," he said.

"And our guardians are both soldiers and philosophers."

"Certainly."

[7]I.e. as infinitely divisible.

[8]Also "calculating," the same word in Greek. This makes it easy to maintain that calculation awakens the calculating ("rational") part of the soul. So "Calculation," below, also means "reason."

"Then it would be fitting, Glaucon, to make a law and
persuade the ones destined to participate in the highest
c things of the city to court Calculation and clasp her to them;
not in the popular way, but until they come to contemplate
the nature of number with pure intellect; and not for the
sake of buying and selling, like merchants and shopkeepers,
but for war and for ease in turning the soul itself around
from becoming to being and truth."

"Beautifully put," he said.

"Now that arithmetic has come up," I said, "I notice how
d elegant and how comprehensively useful it is for what we
want, if pursued for knowledge rather than shopkeeping."

"In what way?"

"In the way we just said: it powerfully leads the soul upward somewhere and forces it to discuss numbers themselves; it firmly rejects any proposal to discuss numbers that
have visible or tangible bodies. I suppose you know that if
e you try to divide the one itself in an argument, the adepts
will laugh and refuse to accept it—if you split it they'll multiply it and make sure it never appears to be not one but many
parts."

"True."

526 "Suppose someone asked them, 'What kind of numbers
are you discussing, you strange people, in which the ones
live up to your expectations—each of them equal to every
other without any divergence and without any parts?' What
do you think they'd reply, Glaucon?"

"That they're susceptible only of thought, and can be handled in no other way."

"You see, my friend? Arithmetic really seems a necessity
b for us because it imposes the added necessity on the soul to
use the intellect itself to reach truth itself."

"And a truly powerful necessity it is."

"Have you ever observed that natural arithmeticians are naturally quick in almost every subject, whereas slow people educated in calculation at least improve and get quicker, if nothing else?"

"That's true," he said.

c "And I don't think you'll find many studies that involve
more hard work for the student. For all of these reasons we
mustn't let arithmetic go but educate the best natures in it."

"I agree."

"That's one then," I said. "For the second let's examine the subject that follows it and see if it suits us."

"What do you mean? geometry?"

"Exactly," I said.

"Well, it's clearly suited to warfare. Geometry would make d
a man a better officer for occupying territory, making encampments, forming ranks and columns, and for all the other formations made in battle and on the march."

"But a small part of geometry and arithmetic would be sufficient for that. We have to decide whether the large,
more advanced part tends to make it easier to see the shape e
of the good. We say anything tends there which forces the soul to turn around to that region where it can see what it must see above all—the happiest of what *is.*"

"You're right," he said.

"Therefore geometry is suitable if it forces the soul to contemplate being; if becoming, it's not."

"So we say."

"No one with the slightest acquaintance with geometry 527
would deny that it completely contradicts the ridiculous language geometricians are forced to use in dealing with it. They speak as if they were *doing* something and all their words refer to actions—squaring, adding, applying, and all the other terms they use—whereas in reality, I think, the
whole study is pursued for the sake of knowledge." b

"Absolutely," he said.

"Shouldn't we agree on something else?"

"What?"

"That it's the knowledge of what always *is,* not of something now becoming, now passing away."

"That's an easy agreement," he said: "Geometry's the knowledge of what always *is.*"

"Then, my friend, it would serve as a winch to hoist the soul to truth, producing a philosophic state of mind to lift upward what we now perversely keep down."

"More than anything," he said.

"So more than anything," I said, "we must direct the c
citizens of your lovely city not to neglect geometry. Even its side benefits are considerable."

"What are they?"

"Besides the military things you just mentioned, we know it makes one beautifully receptive to every study, so that a man who has grasped geometry differs completely from one who has not."

"Completely," he said.

"Then shall we put geometry down as the second subject for our young?"

"Yes."

d "The third will be astronomy, don't you think?"

"Yes, because in making the phenomena of seasons, months, and years more easily perceptible it suits not only farming and sailing, but soldiering too."

"Delightful," I said. "You seem afraid that the many will
think you're prescribing useless studies. But though it may
be hard to believe, this is no trivial thing. Each of us has in
his soul an organ blinded and ruined by other pursuits,
e though more worth preserving than ten thousand eyes (for
it alone sees truth), which in studies like these is cleansed
and rekindled. Those who share this opinion will think you
speak marvelously well, but those who have never seen it will
reasonably think you talk nonsense, because they see no
other benefit in these studies. So stop right here and decide
528 which group you're addressing. Or is it neither? Do you
speak chiefly for yourself, without of course begrudging another if he can profit from it?"

"That's my choice," said Glaucon: "to speak mainly for myself by asking and answering."

"Fall back then," I said. "We didn't take up the subject that rightly follows geometry."

"What do you mean?"

"After plane geometry we took up solids in revolution
b before the solids themselves. The right way is to take the
third dimension after the second. That would be solid geometry: the dimension of cubes and of everything with depth."

"True, but I don't think it's been developed yet, Socrates."

"For two reasons," I said. "First, it's investigated feebly
because of its difficulty and because no city holds it in honor;
secondly, to develop it the investigators need a director, who
would be hard to find and, as things are now, couldn't man-
c age its arrogant investigators. But if a whole city honored it
and supervised it with him, they'd cooperate and study solids continuously and intensively until the truth came to light.

Even now, though dishonored by the many and pruned by
investigators who have no idea how it is useful, it pushes
through everything and grows by its charm, and it wouldn't
be surprising if it came to light."

"Grace and charm it surely has," he said. "But explain this d
more clearly. You defined geometry as the study of planes
and first followed it with astronomy and then took it back."

"Yes, I made waste in my haste to get everything done.
The next dimension was depth, but I skipped over the study
of solids because of its laughable state of neglect and followed geometry with astronomy, solids in motion." e

"You're right," he said.

"So we'll put astronomy down as our fourth study; the one we left out will be there if a city pursues it."

"Very likely. And since you rebuked me for praising astronomy in a vulgar way, Socrates, I'll praise it the way you
approach it: I think anyone can see that it forces the soul to 529
look up and leads it from things here to things there."

"Anyone but me, I guess. That's not my opinion."

"Then what is?"

"That those who would now lead us up to philosophy treat astronomy in a way that makes us look down."

"How do you mean?"

"How nobly you seem to take the study of things above!
I'll bet if someone leaned back and tried to learn something b
by staring at the patterns on the ceiling, you'd think he was
contemplating with intellect instead of his eyes. Maybe
you're right and I'm being silly, but I can't believe that any
learning makes the soul look up except the one that deals
with what *is* and with the invisible. If a man tries to learn
anything perceptible, I say he'll never do it, no matter if he
gapes upward or stares down with his mouth closed, because
there's no knowledge in that kind of thing, and his soul will c
look down and not up, even if he's floating on his back on
the sea or the land."

"I had that coming," he said, "—you were right to rebuke me. But how should they study astronomy to make it useful for what we say they must learn?"

"Like this," I said. "The patterns in the sky, in that they
bedeck the visible world, must be held the fairest, most
precise of their kind, though far inferior to the true ones: to d
the motions, in true number and in all true figures, of speed

that *is* and slowness that *is* as they move in relation to each other and carry what is in them, grasped by reason and understanding, not by sight. Or do you think so?"

"Not at all."

"Then the heavenly embroidery must be used as a model
for the learning that leads to those others. It's as if you came
e across diagrams exquisitely drawn by Daedalus or some
other great artist. An experienced geometrician would probably admire their workmanship but think it ridiculous to
study them seriously to learn the truth about equals or dou-
530 bles or any other proportion."

"That would be ridiculous," he said.

"Don't you think a real astronomer will feel the same way
when he looks at the movements of the stars? He'll believe
that the craftsman of heaven has arranged it and the bodies
in it as beautifully as such works can be arranged. But the
proportion of night to day and of day to month and of month
to year, of the other stars to the sun and the moon and to
b one another—wouldn't he think it odd to believe that these,
though bodily and visible, occur always the same without
deviation, and to seek in every way to get truth from them?"

"I think he would, now that I've heard you."

"Then," I said, "if we're going to participate in real astronomy to make the naturally thinking part of our soul
c useful, we'll dismiss the stars and pursue astronomy like
geometry—by means of problems."

"That would certainly multiply the work."

"If we're going to be any good as lawgivers at all, I think we'll prescribe everything else the same way. But what can *you* suggest as a suitable study?"

"Nothing at the moment," he said.

"But motion, I think, surely has more than one form.
d Maybe someone wise could name them all, but two at least
should be apparent to us."

"Which two?"

"Astronomy and its counterpoint."

"What's that?"

"Just as the eyes are fashioned for astronomy, the ears are fashioned for harmonic motion; and don't we agree with the Pythagoreans in calling astronomy and harmonics sister sciences, Glaucon?"

"Yes."

e "Then we'll save ourselves a lot of work by asking them

their opinion of harmonics and of anything else they may have. But in all these studies we'll stay alert for what we're after."

"What?"

"That our charges attempt to learn none of them incompletely, without always arriving where they all must arrive, as we just said about astronomy. Or don't you know they do the same thing in harmonics as in astronomy? They struggle endlessly to measure audible[9] sounds and consonances 531
against each other, and accomplish nothing."

"Yes, by the gods—it's ridiculous how they hunt for something they call 'minimals' and strain their ears as if trying to eavesdrop on their neighbors. Some insist they overhear a note between two others and that this is the smallest interval and must be made the unit of measurement. Others deny it and say the strings are making identical sounds. Both sides put the ear above the mind." b

"You're referring to those noble gentlemen who stretch strings on pegs with torture and interrogation. I won't strain the image with blows from the pick, denunciations, and the strings' high-strung bravado, but simply say I didn't mean them, but the Pythagoreans, who do the same thing as the astronomers. They search for numbers in these audible har- c
monies instead of ascending to problems and examining which numbers are harmonic and which not, and why in each case."

"That would be a superhuman task," he said.

"Useful," I said, "for investigating the beautiful and the good; useless if hunted differently."

"I suppose," he said.

"If all these studies are pursued far enough to see their mutual relationships and to infer what they have in common d
and how they're related, I think their study will somehow lead to the desired end and the effort won't be wasted. Otherwise it will."

"I predict so too," he said. "But the work will be stupendous, Socrates."

"You mean in the prelude, or what? Or didn't you know that all this is merely the prelude to the song they must learn? Surely accomplished mathematicians don't strike you as sharp at dialectics?" e

[9]In contrast to "true" sounds, inaudible and intelligible.

"No, by Zeus, except for a very few that I've met."

"And will people who can't examine or explain their views in discussion ever know what we say they must know?"

"No again," he said.

532 "Then isn't this the song performed by dialectics, Glaucon?—the song which, though intelligible, we represented
by the power of sight when we said the prisoner tried to look
first at animals themselves, then at the stars themselves, and
finally at the sun itself. So for anyone who uses dialectics
alone without any of the senses and attempts to storm each
thing itself that *is* with rational discourse and doesn't stop
b until he seizes the good itself that *is* with the intellect itself;
he arrives at the end of the intelligible world, as the prisoner
arrived at the end of the visible."

"Absolutely," he said.

"Wouldn't you call this journey dialectics?"

"Of course."

"Being freed from those chains and turned around from
the shadows to the phantoms[10] and the firelight; climbing up
from the cave to the sun and being temporarily blinded and
unable to look directly at plants, animals, and the light of the
c sun, but only at their divine[11] apparitions in water and at
shadows—not at shadows of phantoms shadowed by a light
which is itself a phantom compared to the sun, but at shadows of real things—just as there the body's clearest part was
led to the contemplation of the brightest thing in the bodily
and visible region, so here the study of all the subjects we've
gone through has the power to lead the soul's best part up
d to the sight of the best of the things that *are.*"

"I'll accept that," he said, "though it seems to me altogether hard to accept, and in another way hard not to
accept. But still, since we'll have to return to this topic many
times again, let's assume it's as you say and go on to the song
itself and describe it as we did the prelude. Tell us the
manner of dialectic's power, what parts it consists of, and
e what again are its paths. They, it seems, would lead the
wanderer to a resting place on the road and to the end of
his journey."

533 "No longer, dear Glaucon, will you be able to follow,
though not for lack of enthusiasm on my part. I'd have to

[10]I.e. the figures that threw the shadows on the wall of the cave.
[11]"Divine" because reflected by the sun, a god.

show you not an image of what we're discussing, but the truth itself as it appears to me—whether it's so or not I wouldn't presume to assert. But we will assert that something like this is what we must see. Isn't that so?"

"Of course."

"And also that only the power of dialectic will reveal it, and only to those experienced in the studies we just went through?"

"That's worth asserting too," he said.

"At least no one will quarrel with us when we say that b
some other method methodically attempts in every case for every 'itself' to grasp what each of them is. All other skills are directed either toward human opinions and desires or toward composites that come into being or toward the care of growing or composite things. As for the remaining studies —geometry and the ones that follow it—which we said catch hold of something of being, we see that they merely dream about reality and will never glimpse it while waking as long c
as they use assumptions they don't disturb and can't explain. When someone begins with a source he doesn't know and weaves his intermediate strands and final conclusion out of this unknown, his reasoning may be consistent, but how could it ever be knowledge?"

"It couldn't," he said.

"Therefore," I said, "dialectics is the only method that advances this way—by demolishing assumptions—up to the source itself to secure confirmation; it gently drags the eye d
of the soul out of the odious ooze in which it lies buried and leads it upward, using the studies we've gone through as helpers for turning the soul around. We've been referring to them as 'knowledge' out of habit and for want of a better word to describe something more distinct than opinion but murkier than knowledge—I guess we defined it earlier as 'understanding'—but I suppose people with such important e
things to examine shouldn't haggle over a word. We'll be satisfied if it indicates clearly enough the state of soul that we mean."

"Indeed," he said.

"Then as before[12] we'll be content with calling the first

[12] 511d-e, p. 174. See diagram of divided line, footnote 10, p. 172. Here "knowledge" is substituted for "intellection" (eb), and "intellection" refers to the whole intelligible class (cb). Plato dislikes consistent terminology.

part knowledge, the second understanding, the third trust
534 and the fourth imaging. The first two are both intellection, the other two both opinion. Opinion concerns becoming, intellection being. As being is to becoming, so is intellection to opinion; and as intellection is to opinion, so is knowledge to trust and understanding to imaging.[13] As for the proportion of their objects to each other, and the division of each class—the objects of intellection and of opinion—into two, we'd better let that go, Glaucon, to avoid a longer discussion than the one we've already had."

b "Well, as to the rest," he said, "I agree, as far as I'm able to follow."

"Would you also call someone a dialectician who can grasp and explain the essence of each thing? As for one who cannot, would you say the less able he is to give an account of a thing to himself or another, the less intelligence he has of it?"

"What else could I say?"

"Then the same with the good. He who cannot define the shape of the good in argument by sorting it out from every-
c thing else and pass through every examination as in battle, eagerly testing his position by essence, not opinion, and march out of all this with his argument unthrown—won't you say that he knows neither the good itself nor any good thing, that if he clings somehow to a phantom of something, he clings to it not by knowledge but by opinion, and that he drowses and dreams his present life away and won't wake up
d until he gets to Hades and falls asleep forever?"

"Yes, by Zeus, I'll say all that."

"Now you've been raising and educating these children of yours in word, but if you ever have to do so in deed, I doubt if you'll let them be rulers in charge of the greatest things in the city if they're incapable of expression, like irrational numbers."

"Of course not," he said.

"Then won't you legislate that they take part in the education that makes them able to question and answer most knowingly?"

[13] "As intellection is to opinion, so is knowledge to trust and understanding to imaging": cb/ac = eb/dc = ce/ad. See diagram of divided line, footnote 10, p. 172.

"Yes, together with you." e

"Do you think dialectic caps our studies like a cornice so
that we can't properly set another study higher than it? Has
our discussion of studies reached its end?" 535

"Yes," he said.

"Next then," I said, "you must decide whom we shall give
these studies to, and in what way. Do you remember the kind
of men we chose earlier when we were selecting our rulers?"

"How could I forget?"

"Then assume that those must be the natures we have to
select. We must prefer the bravest and most stable, who are
as well-formed as possible and have not only tough, noble b
dispositions, but also natural parts suited to our education."

"What are you setting down now?"

"Why, keenness toward their studies, of course, as well as
ease of learning. A soul will much sooner shrink from severe
studies than from athletics, because the work is more kindred and personal to it, not shared by the body. He must c
also be retentive, dogged, and fond of all kinds of work. How
else could anyone work through all those physical labors and
also master such a great study and discipline?"

"No one, without having natural talent."

"That's the error now, and the reason Philosophy has
fallen into dishonor, as we said; people don't embrace her
by merit. Her embracers should be legitimate, not bastards."

"How do you mean?" he asked.

"Well, for one thing," I said, "they shouldn't limp and be d
half fond of work and half not, as when a person loves work
in gymnastics, hunting, and all bodily labors, but hates it in
learning, listening, and searching. Someone whose fondness
for work runs the opposite way is also a cripple."

"Very true," he said.

"In the same way, won't we class a soul as maimed for
truth if it hates voluntary lies and can hardly bear one itself e
or choke back its indignation when someone else tells one,
but cheerfully accepts an involuntary lie and doesn't get
indignant at being trapped somehow in ignorance, but wal-
lows in it as complacently as a hog?"

"Absolutely." 536

"The same for temperance, courage, grandeur, and every
part of excellence; we must be on our guard for those legiti-

mate in them and for the bastards. When anyone, a man or a city, doesn't know how to examine a person for such things, they unwittingly employ cripples and bastards for whatever occasion arises, as friends in the one case, rulers in the other."

"That's a fact."

"Then we must be cautious about all this, because if we
b admit quick-limbed, quick-witted people and educate them
in so great a study and so great a training, Justice herself
won't reproach us and we'll preserve regime and city alike.
If we bring in a different kind we'll do just the opposite and
dump even worse ridicule on Philosophy's head."

"That would be shameful," he said.

"It would," I agreed. "But I think I just made myself look ridiculous again."

"How?"

c "I forgot we were playing and spoke too intently. I
glanced at Philosophy as I spoke, and seeing her spattered
with mud unworthily, I think, I got indignant and addressed
the culprits too seriously, as though I had lost my temper."

"It was none too serious for me as a listener, by Zeus."

"But for me as the speaker," I said. "—Now let's not
forget that though in our earlier selection[14] we chose older
d men, we won't do so here. We won't let Solon persuade us
that 'an old man can still learn,' any more than he can win
a race. All great and difficult labors belong to the young."

"Necessarily," he said.

"Arithmetic, geometry, and the whole preliminary education that prepares for dialectics must be presented to them as children; but we mustn't teach them in any way that uses force."

"Why not?"

e "Because a free man mustn't learn anything slavishly. Enforced bodily labors do the body no harm, but enforced
learning doesn't stay with the soul."

"True," he said.

"Therefore, Glaucon, make sure you raise your children
537 by having them play in their studies, and don't use force.
That way you'll also more easily see what each of them is
naturally fit for."

[14]The reference is to 412c, p. 81–82. Solon, below, was an Athenian lawgiver and poet, ca. 640–560 B.C.

"That makes sense," he said.

"You'll recall that we said they must be brought out to battle as observers on horseback, and that whenever it was safe we should bring them up close to taste blood, like pups. The one who consistently proves the most agile in all these labors, studies, and terrors must be selected and enrolled on a list."

"At what age?" he asked. b

"When they're freed from enforced gymnastics. During that period of two or three years it will be impossible for them to do anything else, because sleep and exhaustion are inimical to study. At the same time this will be one of our best tests, to see how each of them does in gymnastics. After that time the ones chosen from the twenty-year olds will receive greater honors than the others, and the studies given
them promiscuously as children will now be unified into a c
comprehensive view of the relation of these studies to one another and to the nature of what *is.*"

"That's the only learning that stays with the ones who receive it."

"It's also the best test for a dialectical nature. A comprehensive man is dialectical; others not."

"I agree," he said.

"Then you must examine which of your candidates are
especially like that and also unyielding in their studies as d
well as in battle and other lawful duties. These, when they've passed their thirtieth year, you must choose from out of the chosen, appoint to higher honors than the others, and examine, testing them by the power of dialectic to see which can let go of his eyes and the rest of his senses and approach being itself and truth. Here, Glaucon, the job demands the greatest alertness."

"Why?"

"Haven't you noticed how great an evil has grown up e
around dialectics?"

"What evil?"

"Its adepts seem infected with lawlessness."

"They certainly do."

"Do you think that's surprising? won't you forgive them?"

"Why on earth should I?"

"Because they're like a man raised as an adopted child in
a large, powerful family and surrounded by wealth and flat- 538

terers, who upon reaching manhood learns that his parents aren't his parents at all, but can't discover his real ones. Can you surmise his attitude toward those flatterers and toward his adoptive parents, both in the time when he doesn't know he's adopted and after he does? Or would you rather hear my surmise?"

"I'd rather hear yours."

"Well," I said, "I surmise that while still ignorant of the
b truth he'll honor his father and mother and his other seeming relations more than the flatterers, be less willing to see his parents in need, less willing to disobey them in anything important, and less willing to say or do anything lawless to them than to those toadies."

"Very likely," he said.

"But after he learns his true situation, I surmise that his honor and seriousness will relax toward his parents and
c intensify toward the flatterers—he'll listen to them more attentively, begin to fashion his life after theirs and to associate with them openly, and unless he's unusually decent by nature, care not at all for that father of his and for his other adoptive relations."

"You're telling it as it would be," he said. "But what does this simile have to do with people who take up discourse?"

"This: from childhood on we have certain convictions about just and beautiful things, in which we're brought up as though under parents, which we honor and whose commands we obey."

"Indeed."

d "And then there are certain contrary practices, which produce pleasure, flatter the soul, and drag it to them, though they're unable to persuade anyone moderate, who honors the paternal teachings and obeys their commands."

"True."

"Now what happens to someone like that when a question comes up and asks 'What is the beautiful?' and he answers what he heard from the lawgiver and the argument refutes him, and after being refuted many times in many ways he's finally reduced to the opinion that this is no more beautiful
e than ugly—and so for the just and the good and everything he once held in honor—after all that, what do you think his attitude toward those convictions will be?"

"He'll necessarily neither honor nor obey them as much."

"And when he no longer honors and obeys them as relatives, but can't discover the true ones, is he likely to go over
to any life but the flattering one?" 539

"No."

"So I think he'll seem to have grown lawless instead of law-abiding."

"Necessarily."

"Then the condition of people who approach discourse like that is reasonable and deserves forgiveness, as I said."

"Pity too," said Glaucon.

"To keep this pity from applying to your thirty-year olds, won't you be cautious how they take up dialectics?"

"Extremely."

"Wouldn't one of the best precautions be to make sure b
they don't taste it while young? Surely it hasn't escaped you
that when young fellows first encounter discussion they treat
it as a plaything to use for contradiction. They imitate the
cross-examiners and refute others, delighting like puppies
in tearing and dragging anyone around in an argument."

"Fantastically."

"And when they've refuted and been refuted many times,
they quickly and vehemently fall to doubting all their former c
beliefs. From this they and philosophy both fall into disrepute among others."

"True."

"But an older man would refuse to participate in such
madness and imitates people who use dialectics to examine
the truth rather than as a toy for play and contradiction.
He'll be more moderate himself and bring the pursuit honor d
instead of disgrace."

"Right."

"Hasn't everything we've said been for the sake of this precaution, so that the ones who partake of discussion may have stable, orderly natures, and so that not any random misfit may approach it, as now?"

"Certainly," he said.

"Will it suffice if they intensively persevere in dialectics to the exclusion of everything else, exercising antiphonally to those bodily exercises for twice as long as in them?"[15]

[15]They were to spend "two or three years" in enforced gymnastics. See 537b, p. 197.

e "Six years, you mean, or four?"

"I don't care—make it five. After that you must march
them back down to that cave and force them to rule in the
military and in offices fit for the young, so that they don't lag
behind the others in experience. Here too you must test
540 them to see if they hold firm when pulled in every direction
or if they somehow give way."

"For how long?"

"Fifteen years," I said. "At fifty you must take the ones
preserved and proved best in work and in knowledge and
lead them up to the end, forcing them to bend the rays of
their souls upward to look at that which imparts light to all;
and after they've seen the good itself they must use it as a
model and spend the rest of their lives taking turns at order-
b ing the city, the individuals, and themselves, though spending most of their time in philosophy. When their turns come
they must rule and endure political labors for the sake of the
city, not as something beautiful but as a necessity, constantly
educating others like them to leave behind as guardians of
the city when they pass on to live on the Isles of the Blest.
And the city will make public memorials and sacrifices to
c them as to spirits, if the Pythia[16] consents; if not, then as to
happy, divine men."

"You're finishing off beautiful men for your rulers, Socrates, just like a sculptor."

"Women too, Glaucon. Don't think I've been speaking of
men any more than of all women born with natures equal to
the task."

"You're right, if they're going to be equal partners with
the men in everything, as we said."

d "Well," I said, "do you all agree that what we've said
about the regime and the city hasn't been entirely a pious
wish? It would be difficult but in a way possible, though only
in the way that we said: When true philosophers, one or
many, come to power in a city and despise everything now
held in honor as slavish and worthless but prize above all the
e right and the honors that come from it, considering justice
the greatest necessity and in serving and magnifying that,
put their city in order."

"How?"

[16]Apollo's prophetess who delivered the oracles at Delphi.

"They'll send everyone in the city older than ten out to the
farms and take over the children, remove them from their 541
parents' habits, and raise them in their own customs and
laws, such as we have described. Won't that be the quickest
and easiest way to institute the city and regime we've been
discussing, so that it will be happy and bring the greatest
benefit to the people in which it occurs?"

"By far. And it seems to me, Socrates, that you've well
described how it'll come about if it ever does." b

"Have we talked enough about this city and the man who resembles it? I suppose it's obvious what we'd say he must be like."

"Yes. As to your question, I think that we're finished."

Book 8

"Well then, Glaucon, it's agreed: in the consummately 543
governed city women will be common, children and all education common, pursuits likewise common in peace and war, and the ones who turn out the best in both war and philosophy will be kings."

"It's agreed," he said.

"We also agreed that after being appointed rulers they'll b
lead out the soldiers and settle them in houses such as we described, all common to all and with nothing private to any. Besides houses, I think we agreed what other kinds of possessions they'll have, if you remember."

"I remember we thought they should own none of the
things that others do now, but live as guardians and athletes
of war, receiving their yearly sustenance from the others as c
wages for guarding, and devote themselves to the care of
themselves and the city."

"Right," I said. "And now that we're finished with that, let's recall where we turned off to get here, so we can go back to the road we were on."[1]

"That's not hard. You were speaking almost as you are

[1]The digression occurred at the beginning of Book 5, 449b, p. 114.

now, as though you had finished describing the city, and you
were positing that city as good, as well as the man who
d resembled it, though it seems you had a still more beautiful
544 city and man to describe. And you called the others mistaken
if this one is right. As for the remaining regimes and the men
who resemble them, I recall that you said there are four
kinds worth discussing, whose defects we should observe in
order to agree which is the worst man and which the best
and then examine whether the best is the happiest and the
worst the most wretched, or the other way around. I was
b asking which four regimes you meant when Polemarchus
and Adeimantus interrupted and you took up the argument
that brought us to where we are now."

"You recall correctly," I said.

"Then offer me the same hold again, like a wrestler: I'll ask the same question and you try to say what you were about to say then."

"If I can," I said.

"Well, I'm eager enough to hear which four regimes you meant," said Glaucon.

c "It isn't hard to hear them," I said. "Of those with names
I mean first the one praised by the many, your Cretan or
Spartan regime. Second in favor and order is oligarchy, a
regime with numerous evils. Its adversary, democracy,
emerges next, with noble tyranny fourth, surpassing them
all as the city's ultimate disease. Can you name any other
d type of regime that forms a distinct class? Hereditary dicta-
torships, purchased monarchies, and so forth are probably
intermediate types, and as common among barbarians as
among Greeks."

"Yes, one hears of many strange types," he said.

"And you know that the human character must have the
same number of forms as the regime. Or do you think
regimes come from 'sticks or stones'[2] or something, rather
than from their citizens' dispositions, which sink like the
e scale of a balance and drag everything else along with
them?"

"No, that's where they come from."

"Then if there are five types of city, there must also be five arrangements of soul. We've already described the best man, who resembles aristocracy, and rightly called him just

[2] *Odyssey* 19.163, *Iliad* (a proverbial expression) 22.126, etc.

and good. Shall we now go through the others—the honor 545
and victory-loving man who corresponds to the Spartan
regime, the oligarchic man, the democratic, and the tyrannical—to see the most unjust man and contrast him with the
most just?[3] That would complete our examination of how
pure justice and injustice compare in the happiness or misery of their possessors. Then we can either believe
Thrasymachus and pursue injustice, or follow our emerging
argument and practice justice." b

"That's exactly what we should do."

"We began before by first examining the dispositions of
regimes, as being more distinct, and then of individuals.
Shall we do the same thing now and first examine the honor-
loving regime? —It doesn't have a common name; we could
call it "timocracy' or 'timarchy,' I suppose. Then shall we
examine the same type of man against it, go on to oligarchy c
and the oligarchic man, look next at democracy and the
democratic man, and fourth go to tyranny and the tyrannical
soul and so try to become competent judges of this issue
we've proposed for ourselves?"

"If we do, we'll be looking and judging in a logical way."

"Come on," I said, "let's try to say how timocracy, rule by
honor, might arise from aristocracy, the rule of the best. Or
is it simply a fact that every revolution comes from the ruling d
class, when civil war arises in it? As long as that class remains
single-minded, no matter how small it may be, the city cannot be disturbed."

"Yes, that's a fact."

"Then how will disturbance come to our city, Glaucon, to
make our auxiliaries and rulers fight in civil war with themselves and each other? Shall we, like Homer, invoke the
Muses to tell 'how Faction first fell among men,' and make e
them rant in a high-flown, tragical style, as if they were
serious and not teasing and playing with us as though we
were little boys?"

"How?"

"Something like this: 'A city so constituted will be hard to 546
disturb. But since all that becomes must fall to decay, even

[3]Aristocracy in Greek means "the rule of the best," timocracy "rule by honor," oligarchy "the rule of the few," democracy "the rule of the people," and tyranny "dictatorship." These definitions have sometimes been added in the translation.

such a constitution endures not for all time but dissolves. Its dissolution is this: Bearing and barrenness of bodies and soul come to all animals and plants of the earth whenever the turning circle for each species joins its circumference, winding close for the short-lived, wide for the long.[4] As for your race, the leaders you have educated, wise as they are,
b will nevertheless fail at some time to achieve either good offspring or none by combining perception and calculation, and they will beget children when they ought not to.

" 'The period for a divine progeny is embraced by a perfect number, but for a human it turns out to be this: The first in which increases, dominating and being dominated, taking three distances and four limits, of likes and unlikes and of things waxing and waning, exhibit all things as rational and
c conversant with one another. Of these, the basic raised third wedded to the fifth produces two harmonies when thrice increased, one equally equal so many times one hundred, the other equal in one way, but oblong—one side of one hundred squares of the rational diameter of the fifth, each diminished by one, or by two for the irrational, the other side one hundred cubes of the third.[5]

[4]The period of gestation is compared to drawing a circle. Its beginning is conception. Birth or miscarriage occurs when the circle is completed and "joins its circumference." The circle is "close" for short-lived species because their gestation period is short, and vice versa. Note above that there are many bodies but only one soul.
[5]The translation is quite literal, and the mathematical details are unimportant for the main argument of *The Republic.* The number is $(3 \times 4 \times 5)^4 = 12{,}960{,}000$. The best interpretation of this difficult passage may be found in M. A. Diès, *Le Nombre de Platon: Essai d'exégèse et d'histoire (Mémoires présentés à l'Académie des Inscriptions et Belles-Lettres),* vol. 14, Paris 1936. James Adam (*The Republic of Plato,* 2nd ed., Cambridge 1963) and others argue that this number has cosmic significance, representing the number of days in the Pythagorean "Great Year" of the universe (36,000 lunar years, of 360 days each). They also derive other significant numbers from the passage, but with little support from the text. While it seems likely that some such significance is intended, the evidence so far advanced for any consistent theory is not compelling, and it may be best (with Diès) to regard the passage as an elaborate jest by the Muses, a mathematical, poetical myth illustrating that even the ideal state is destined at some time to collapse, and reminding us of the regulations governing marriage and child-rearing presented in Book 5.

" 'This entire geometrical number is lord of superior and
inferior births, and when in ignorance of it your guardians d
bed brides with grooms out of season, their children will not
be well formed or fortuned. The best of them will be installed by their elders, and when, though unworthy, they
have succeeded in turn to their fathers' power, they will as
guardians be the first to begin to neglect us, holding first
poetry, then gymnastics in lower esteem than they ought,
and so your young will grow Museless. Thence will issue
rulers unequal to guarding and scrutinizing Hesiod's[6] races e
and yours: gold, silver, bronze, and iron. When iron mixes 547
with silver, bronze with gold, they will deliver inequality and
disjointed imbalance, which whenever and wherever engendered, always breed hatred and war. That, you must say, is
Faction's lineage, wherever she may be born.' "

"We'll also say it's a very good answer," he said.

"It must be," I said, "—they're Muses."

"What do the Muses say after that?" b

"That after Faction was born two groups of guardians
began pulling apart, the ones polluted with iron and bronze
toward making money and possessing land and houses and
silver and gold, while the others, of silver and gold, being
not impoverished but rich in their natures, tried to draw
their souls back to excellence and the ancient arrangement.
And so from opposing each other by violence they compromised in the middle and distributed houses and land as
private possessions; and those they formerly guarded as free c
friends and providers they then enslaved as lackeys and
serfs, giving themselves over to warfare and to guarding
against them."

"It seems to me that that's where the change begins."

"Won't this regime be somewhere in the middle between aristocracy and oligarchy?" I asked.

"Certainly."

"Thus it will change, but how will it be governed? Being
in the middle, won't timarchy—rule by honor—imitate the d
former regime in some things, oligarchy in others, and have
some features of its own?"

"Correct."

"Won't it imitate aristocracy in honoring its rulers and

[6]Hesiod had divided men historically into races named after these four metals in *Works and Days* 109–201.

exempting its defender class from farming, crafts, and other
ways of making money, in maintaining public messes and in
practicing gymnastics and the contest of war?"

"Yes."

e "Won't it also have many distinctive features, such as being afraid to take wise men into public offices—because in
this regime such men are no longer simple and intense but
mixed—inclining instead to spirited men who are simpler
and by nature more suited to war than to peace, honoring
548 military stratagems and tricks, and spending all its time on
war?"

"Yes."

"Men like that," I said, "will desire possessions, as in an
oligarchy. They'll fiercely honor silver and gold and squirrel
it away in treasuries of their own, making their homes into
enclosures, private nests where they can spend lavishly on
b women and whomever else they may wish. They'll be sparing of their own money because they honor it and don't
possess it openly, but squander other people's money because they desire. Such men will sneak their pleasures and
run away from the law like boys from their father, having
been educated not by persuasion but by force because they
c neglect the true Muse of philosophy and discussion and
honor gymnastics higher than poetry."

"You're describing a completely mixed regime of good and evil," said Glaucon.

"It is mixed," I said. "But one feature stands out sharply because the spirited part prevails: love of honor and victory."

"Very sharply," he said.

"That's how timocracy comes about and what it would be
d like—drawn in outline, not in detail, because all we need is
a sketch to see the most just and unjust man. It would be a
hopeless task to describe every regime and disposition without leaving anything out."

"You're right," said Glaucon.

"Now how about the man who corresponds to it? How did he come about and what would he be like?"

"I think his love of victory would make him a lot like Glaucon here," said Adeimantus.

e "Perhaps in that way," I said. "But it seems to me he'd
have other traits that wouldn't correspond."

"Like what?"

"He must be rather self-willed and unmusical, though still
fond of the Muses; fond also of listening, but in no way a
speaker. Such a man will be harsh toward slaves and not 549
disdain them like a well-educated person, but he'll be gentle
toward free men, subservient to rulers, and fond of rule and
honor. He'll expect to rule not from speech or anything like
that, but from warlike deeds and the things of war, and he'll
love gymnastics and hunting."

"That's the timocratic disposition, all right."

"And won't he despise money while young, but welcome
it more and more as he grows older, because he partakes of b
the avaricious nature and no longer devotes himself purely
to excellence after the best guardian has deserted him?"

"What guardian is that?" Adeimantus asked.

"The power of reasoned, educated speech," I said, "the sole preserver of excellence for its possessor all through life."

"Well put," he said.

"Such is the timocratic youth, similar to his city. He comes c
about something like this: Sometimes he's the young son of
a good father who lives in a poorly governed city and shuns
offices, honors, lawsuits, and all such meddling, who pur-
posely lets himself be bested so as not to have trouble—"

"But how does the timocratic man come about?"

"When he hears his mother first complaining that her
husband isn't one of the rulers and that the other women
slight her for this; then, when she sees that he has little d
interest in money or in brawling and fighting in courts or the
assembly, that he's always occupied with his own thoughts
and neither particularly honors nor dishonors her, she
grows resentful and tells the boy that his father is unmanly
and too easygoing, and harps on all the other things women
love to say about men like that." e

"Yes," said Adeimantus, "—nasty things, like themselves."

"And you know that seemingly well-intentioned servants
also take the sons aside sometimes and talk to them secretly,
and if the father doesn't prosecute someone who owes him
money or has done him some other injustice, they tell the
boy to punish all such men when he grows up and to be more
of a man than his father. When he goes out he sees and hears 550

more of the same: that men in the city who tend their own business are called foolish and held in low esteem while busybodies are honored and admired. When the young man has seen and heard all that, and also heard his father's words and seen his pursuits close up and against those of the oth-
b ers, he's pulled in both directions: his father waters and grows his soul's rational part, the others its desiring and spirited parts. And since he didn't have the nature of a bad man but kept bad company, he was pulled from both sides and came out in the middle as a compromise: he turned the rule of his soul over to its victory-loving, middle, spirited part and became a highminded lover of honor."

"It seems you've completely described the origin of the honor-loving, timocratic man."

c "Then we have our second regime and man," I said. "Shouldn't we next, like Aeschylus, 'Set another man against another town'[7] —or rather follow our plan and put the city first?"

"Certainly."

"I think the next would be oligarchy, the rule of the few."

"What kind of constitution do you mean by that?"

"One based on property assessment, where the rich rule
d and the poor have no part in government."

"I understand," said Adeimantus.

"Shouldn't we first discuss how oligarchy develops from timarchy?—but really, how it develops should be clear to a blind man."

"How?"

"That treasury full of gold that each of them had—that's what destroys timocracy. First, they discover things to spend their money on and pervert the laws accordingly, since they
e and their women disobey them. Next, I think, they each watched and competed with the others and made the majority like themselves."

"Most likely," he said.

"From there they progress deeper into moneymaking, and the more they honor that, the less they honor excellence. Doesn't excellence pull against wealth as though they lay in the scales of a balance and always weighed in opposite directions?"

[7]A paraphrase of *Seven against Thebes* 451.

"Exactly," said Adeimantus.

"Then as wealth and the wealthy are honored in a city, excellence and the excellent are dishonored." 551

"Clearly."

"And whatever is honored will be practiced; whatever is dishonored will be ignored."

"True."

"So finally they become money-loving businessmen instead of lovers of victory and honor. They admire the rich man and put him in office, but dishonor the poor."

"Of course."

"Then they make a law assigning a sum of money as the limit of an oligarchic regime, larger for an extreme oli- b
garchy, smaller for a moderate one, disbarring everyone from office whose property falls below the assigned evaluation. They accomplish this either by force of arms or by terror without resorting to arms. Isn't that so?"

"Yes," he said.

"That, more or less, is how the oligarchic rule of the few is established."

"Yes, but what is oligarchy's character, and what are those faults we said it had?"[8] c

"The first is the limit that defines it. Think what would happen if they made navigators by property assessment and rejected the poor but better qualified man."

"They'd sail a pretty poor voyage."

"The same for any kind of rule?"

"I think so."

"Except a city's? Or is it also true of a city?"

"All the more; that's the greatest, most difficult rule."

"So that's one serious fault of oligarchy." d

"It seems to be."

"What about having to be two cities instead of one—one of the rich and one of the poor—inhabiting the same place and constantly plotting against each other?"

"That's just as bad, by Zeus."

"And we'll hardly admire them for being unable to fight a war, no doubt, because they must either arm the mob and fear it more than the enemy, or not arm it and prove in battle e
that they literally are oligarchs—rulers of only a few—espe-

[8]The reference is to "numerous evils," 544c, p. 202.

cially since they'll resist paying war taxes because they're fond of money."

"No, that's not a beautiful feature."

"What about that meddling we've been denouncing so
552 long? Does it seem right that in an oligarchy the same men are farmers, businessmen, and soldiers all at the same time?"

"No," he said.

"Now see if this is the first regime to permit the worst evil of this kind."

"What?"

"Permission to sell all your property and live in the city without belonging to any of its classes, so that you're neither a businessman nor a craftsman, neither an infantryman nor a cavalryman, but simply a poor and helpless pauper."

b "Yes, it's the first," he said. "Oligarchies don't prohibit that. Otherwise their citizens wouldn't be either penniless or filthy rich."

"Right. Now consider this: When that impoverished oligarch was rich and spending his money, did he benefit his city in any of the ways we just said? Or did he seem to be a ruler while really being neither a ruler nor a servant of the city, but a squanderer of whatever resources were available?"

c "Right. He seemed to be a ruler, but was only a squanderer."

"Then can we say that as a drone is hatched in a cell to be a plague to the hive, so a drone like this is born in a home to be a plague to his city?"

"We certainly can, Socrates."

"And didn't god make all winged drones stingless, Adeimantus, but the two-footed ones some stingless and some with dreadful stings? In old age the stingless ones turn into
d beggars, the stinged ones into what we call criminals."

"True," he said.

"So wherever you see beggars you'll also find thieves, pickpockets, temple robbers, and practitioners of every shady craft lurking around."

"Obviously."

"Well? Don't you see beggars in oligarchic cities?"

"Nearly everyone is a beggar except the few rulers."

"Then shouldn't we suppose there's also a swarm of those e
stinged criminals around, whom the rulers deliberately restrain by force?"

"Indeed."

"Won't we say they're hatched by noneducation, bad upbringing, and the constitution of the regime?"

"Yes."

"Such would be the oligarchic city, with rulers determined 553
by property assessment and with the evils we've described,
perhaps even worse. Shall we consider the regime complete
and go on to examine the man who resembles it—how he
arises and what he's like?"

"Certainly."

"I think the oligarchic man would most likely develop
from our timocratic man like this: The timocratic man has
a son who first emulates him and follows in his footsteps,
then sees him suddenly run aground on the city as though b
on a reef and spill out both himself and his possessions. He
may have been a general or held some other high office until
lying informers took him to court and had him executed,
disfranchised, or exiled, and he lost all his property."

"Very likely," he said.

"After the son has seen and suffered all that, my friend,
and lost his possessions, I think he'll be terrified and instantly push his honor-loving spirited part off on its head c
from the throne of his soul. Humbled by poverty, he devotes
himself to making money, greedily earning and saving until
he accumulates wealth. Don't you think a man like that will
install his money-loving desiring part on his vacant throne
and invest it with tiara, link collar, and scimitar, like the
Great King of Persia?"

"Yes."

"And I think he'll enslave his rational and spirited parts d
and seat them right and left at its feet, allowing the rational
part to calculate and examine nothing but how to make more
money, the spirited part to admire and honor nothing but
wealth and the wealthy, and to love no honor but that connected with the possession of money and whatever contrib-
utes to it."

"Nothing else could change an honor-loving youth into a
money-loving one so surely and quick."

e “Then isn't this the oligarchic man?” I asked.

“At least he develops from the man who resembles the regime that oligarchy came from,” he said.

“Then let's see if he's similar, Adeimantus.”

554 “All right.”

“Wouldn't he resemble it in prizing money above everything?”

“Certainly.”

“Of course he'll be a frugal drudge who gratifies only his necessary desires, refuses to make expenditures for anything else, and enslaves his other desires as useless. Since he's the filthy type that tries to make a profit from everything, a
b hoarder admired by the horde—or wouldn't a man like that resemble oligarchy?”

“I think so—both the city and the man honor money above everything.”

“I doubt if he'll have thought much about education.”

“I don't think so. Otherwise he wouldn't have appointed a blind[9] leader for his chorus and honor him above everything.”

“Good,” I said. “Now can we say that because of his lack of education dronelike desires are hatched in him—some of
c them beggars, others criminals—which he restrains by force because of his concern for other things?”

“Absolutely.”

“Do you know where to look for the criminal ones?”

“Where?”

“Put him in charge of orphans, or in some other position that gives him an opportunity to commit injustice.”

“True.”

“Doesn't this show that in his other dealings which earn him a reputation for seeming just, such a man has something
d decent in him that restrains other, evil desires—not by persuading them that it's not for the best or by taming them with reason, but by compulsion and terror, because he trembles for his other property?”

“It certainly does.”

“Give men like that a chance to spend other people's money, my friend, and in most of them, by Zeus, you'll find desires related to the drone. Such a man would be at civil

[9]The Greeks pictured Wealth as blind.

war with himself; not one, but somehow double, with his
desires mastering desires, generally the better the worse." e

"True."

"Therefore I think he'll have more charm than many, but the true excellence of the integrated, harmonious soul will elude him."

"I think so."

"And a miser would surely make a poor competitor for
winning personal victory or honor in any of his city's noble
competitions—he refuses to spend money for glory in con- 555
tests like that because he's afraid to arouse his spendthrift
desires and summon them as allies to help him win honor.
So he fights oligarchically, deploying only a few of his forces,
usually loses, and stays rich."

"He certainly does."

"Can we still doubt that we've matched the stingy, moneymaking man with the oligarchic city by similarity?" b

"No," he said.

"Next, it seems, we must examine democracy—how rule of the people comes about and what it's like—so we can recognize the democratic man's character and set him up for judgment along with the others."

"At least that will be consistent."

"Doesn't oligarchy somehow change to democracy because of insatiable greed for what it established as the good: the need to get as rich as possible?"

"How?"

"Since the rulers rule by possessing wealth, I imagine c
they're reluctant to prohibit self-indulgent young men from
squandering and losing their property; they buy it up or lend
them money against it in order to increase even more in
wealth and honor. Doesn't this show that a city can't honor
wealth and still have enough temperance in her citizens? It d
must neglect the one or the other."

"Very clearly."

"So when an oligarchy neglects temperance and encourages self-indulgence, it sometimes forces uncommon men into poverty."

"Absolutely."

"—Who sit in the city armed with stings and weapons, I suppose, in debt, disfranchised, or both, filled with hate and

plotting against the ones who took their property and
e against the others too, in love with revolution."

"True."

"But the moneymakers, stooped and pretending not to
see them, sting any unresisting victim that remains and in-
ject him with money, whose offspring, many times increased,
556 they withdraw as 'interest' and swell the city's beggarly
drone."

"They'll hardly shrink it."

"And when this evil bursts into flame they refuse to put it out by prohibiting people from disposing of their property or by stopping it with a different law."

"What law?"

"The second-best one for forcing citizens to be concerned
for excellence: There'd be less shameless moneymaking in
b the city and fewer evils such as we've described if they decreed that most voluntary contracts be made at the con-
tractor's own risk."

"Much less," he said.

"But as things are, the rulers put their subjects in the
position we described. As for themselves and their families
—don't they spoil their children and make them unfit for
either physical or mental labor and too soft to hold up
c against pleasures, pains, and loafers, while they themselves
neglect everything but making money and care no more
about excellence than do the poor?"

"Indeed."

"In this state of affairs, whenever rulers and ruled come
alongside and observe each other in the streets or at a communal gathering—at public spectacles or out on campaigns
as fellow soldiers and sailors, or especially in the actual
d combat—there the rich can no longer despise the poor:
when a tough, sun-baked pauper finds himself next to a
shadow-bleached rich man hung with superfluous fat and
sees him panting in helpless confusion, don't you suppose
he'll think that such men are rich because of his own cowardice and say to his friends when they get by themselves, 'The
e gentlemen are ours—they're nothing'?"

"I know he will," he said.

"And just as a sick body needs only a tiny push from without to make it collapse, and sometimes falls into strife even without an external impulse, so a city in this condition

falls sick and fights with itself on the slightest pretext: externally, when one faction calls in allies from an oligarchic city or the other from a democracy, and sometimes even without
an external cause. And I think democracy arises when the 557
poor conquer, kill off some of their enemies and exile the rest, and then give everyone an equal share in government and in offices, which they determine mostly by lot."[10]

"Yes, that's how democracy is instituted, whether in battle or because the others slip away out of terror."

"Next we must see how they live, Adeimantus, and what
their regime is like. Obviously the man who resembles that b
will turn out to be the democratic one."

"Obviously."

"Aren't they above all free? The city is bursting with liberty and freedom of speech, and permits everyone to do whatever he wants."

"So they say, certainly."

"And where this is permitted, each citizen will arrange his own life privately, however he pleases."

"Clearly."

"So this regime, I think, will produce a multifarious vari- c
ety of people. Like a variegated cloak splashed with every color, democracy is embellished with every personality and may appear the most gorgeous; and many, gaping like women and children at its colors, perhaps will judge it the most beautiful."

"They certainly will."

"And, you know, it's just the place to go shopping for a d
regime."

"How come?"

"Because it's permissive and has every kind, so that anyone who wants to construct a city, as we just did, ought to shop in a democracy as in a regime bazaar, select the style he likes, and found his city accordingly."

"At least I don't think he'd be embarrassed for models." e

"And its total lack of compulsion," I said, "so that even if competent you don't have to rule, or be ruled if you don't feel like it, or fight when the rest are at war or keep peace when they do if you don't want to, nor yet, if some law

[10]All officials at Athens were chosen by lot, except the generals, who were elected.

prohibits you from holding office or being a juror—why, you
558 can do both if it comes into your head—isn't that way of life
divinely sweet in the short run?"

"In the short run, perhaps," he said.

"And isn't it exquisite how mild some of them are when
convicted? Or haven't you noticed how in a democracy criminals condemned to death or to exile remain at large and
haunt the streets like spirits, as though people would see
right through them and not pay any attention?"

"Yes, many," he said.

b "How about its indulgence and total lack of pettiness, its
lofty contempt for the pretentious nonsense we discussed
earlier when we were founding our city and said that no one,
unless he has a transcendent nature, will ever become a
good man without having played in and practiced beautiful
pursuits from childhood—how magnificently they trample
all that underfoot and don't care what pursuits a man has
gone through to get into politics—they'll honor him if only
c he says he's a friend of the people."

"Oh yes, it's a noble regime."

"These," I said, "and other kindred traits characterize
democracy, a delightful, anarchic, colorful regime, it seems,
that dispenses 'equality' equally to equals and unequals
alike."

"Yes, that's all common knowledge."

"Next observe what the corresponding man is like. As
with the regime, let's first examine how he comes about.
Isn't it something like this?—that stingy oligarch has a son
d and raises him, I suppose, in his own habits. Therefore,
since the son too restrains by force those pleasures in himself that are not moneymaking but spendthrift, which are
called unnecessary—"

"Obviously," he said.

"—Maybe we should first define necessary and unnecessary desires so we don't talk in the dark, Adeimantus."

"Yes, we should."

"Well, can't we justly call desires that we're unable to
e divert necessary, and also ones that benefit us if they're
satisfied? Isn't it necessary for our nature to strive for both
of these kinds?"

"Absolutely."

559 "So we'll be right in calling them necessary."

"Right."

"What about desires a person can get rid of by disciplining himself from childhood, some of which, moreover, do him no good, while others actually harm him? Can't we rightly call all those unnecessary?"

"Of course."

"Now let's give an example of each so we can grasp them as types. Wouldn't we class as necessary the desire for bread
and other food and for eating to the point of well-being and b
health?"

"I think so."

"Isn't the desire for bread necessary in both ways—it's beneficial and without it we die?"

"Yes."

"And for other foods if it somehow promotes well-being?"

"Certainly."

"But desire that goes beyond that and craves entirely different kinds of food harms the body and impairs the soul for knowledge and temperance, though most people can get rid of it by training and restraining it from childhood.
Shouldn't this desire be termed unnecessary?" c

"Absolutely."

"Shall we call such desires spendthrift, the others productive because they're useful for production?"

"Yes."

"The same with desire for sex and other pleasures?"

"Of course."

"And didn't we just call one man a drone because he's full of those unnecessary pleasures and desires and is ruled by
them, just as the man ruled by the necessary ones is oli- d
garchic and stingy?"

"Certainly."

"Now let's go back and tell how the democratic man comes from the oligarchic. I think it's usually like this."

"How?"

"When a young man raised in the stingy, uneducated way we just described gets a taste of drone's honey[11] and associates with cunning, fiery creatures who can provide multi-

[11]I.e. unnecessary, spendthrift pleasures. The "fiery creatures," below, are the stinging drones, filled with criminal desires.

farious, colorful pleasures that go in every direction, there,
e you may assume, begins the change in him from an oligarchic to a democratic regime."

"An absolute necessity," he said.

"And just as the city changed when outside allies helped one of its parties, like with like, doesn't our youth change when a class of similar, related desires enters from outside to help his democratic faction?"

"Absolutely."

"If his father or some other relations now call up a counteralliance to aid his oligarchic faction by admonishing and
560 berating him, then, I think, strife and counterstrife arise in him and plunge him into civil war with himself. Sometimes, I imagine, the democratic party retreated from the oligarchic, some desires were wiped out and others exiled, and a kind of shame was engendered in the young man's soul and brought him back to order."

"That does happen."

"But owing to his father's ignorance of childrearing, rela-
b tives of those exiled desires were again secretly nurtured and grew to be numerous and strong."

"There is that tendency."

"—And dragged him back to the same old companions, copulated furtively, and bred a new mob of desires. Finally, I suppose, they seized the citadel of the young man's soul, seeing it abandoned by learning, beautiful pursuits, and true argument, the best guardians and sentinels in the minds of
c god-beloved men. Boastful arguments and lying opinions charged up and occupied the territory in their place."

"Undoubtedly."

"So back he moves to the Lotus eaters[12] and lives with them openly, and should reinforcements arrive from his family for his soul's thrifty part, those boastful arguments slam his palace gates on them and refuse to let them pass or
d to receive ambassador arguments from older citizens; they subdue him in battle, denounce his shame as foolishness and

[12]The "drones" again. The lotus was a drug (perhaps opium) that produced a sensual stupor and made men forget the world around them. The reference is to Odysseus's visit to the Lotus eaters in *Odyssey* 9.82–104. The "citadel," "palace," or "fortress" of the soul is intelligence, the rational part.

push it out in shameful exile, define temperance as cowardice and banish it with foul abuse, and persuade him that
moderation and reasonable spending are slavish peasant
virtues which, with the help of a mob of useless desires, they
drive beyond the borders of his soul."

"Absolutely."

"And when they've emptied their victim of all that and
purified his soul for initiation into their Great Mysteries,[13] e
they bring back insolence, anarchy, extravagance, and
shamelessness, crowned and radiant amidst their attendant
choir, and adulate them with fair-sounding names, calling
insolence 'good breeding,' anarchy 'freedom,' extravagance
'generosity,' and shamelessness 'courage.' Isn't that some- 561
how the way, Adeimantus, that a young man raised among
necessary desires changes into one who grants liberty and
license to his useless, unnecessary pleasures?"

"Yes," he said, "—you've made it rather vivid."

"After that, I think, he spends as much time, money, and
effort on his unnecessary pleasures as on his necessary ones.
If he's lucky and not too frenzied—and also as he grows
older his excessive agitation may pass—if he recalls some of b
the exiles and doesn't surrender all of himself to the invad-
ers, then he grants a kind of 'equality' to his pleasures and
submits the rule of himself to whichever one turns up—as
if chosen by lot—until he's sated, then to another, and so on:
he dishonors none but treats them all as equals. And he
refuses to accept a true argument and allow it to pass into
the fortress of his soul—if told that some pleasures come
from good and beautiful desires, others from ones that are c
base, and that those should be pursued and honored, the
others chastened and enslaved, he shakes his head and says
they're all alike and should all be honored equally."

"That's just what a man in such a state would do."

"So," I said, "he lives from day to day, gratifying whatever
desire happens to turn up—now drinking to the sound of
flutes, now wasting away and drinking only water; now exer- d
cising, now loafing around indifferent to everything; and
sometimes pretending to dabble in philosophy. Often he
gets involved in politics and jumps up and says and does

[13]A reference to the Eleusinian mystery religion, into which members were initiated by secret rites.

whatever comes into his head. If he admires some military men he drifts into that; if businessmen, into that. There's no order or necessity in his life, but he calls it blissful, free, and pleasant, and clings to it to the end."

e “A perfect description of the man who grants equal rights to everything."

"I think this is the multifarious man of many personalities, colorful and gorgeous like his city. He contains countless models of dispositions and regimes, and many men and women might envy him his life."

"Yes, he's the one."

562 “Then isn't he the one to set up against democracy as the man properly called democratic?"

"Indeed," he said.

"Then we still have the most beautiful pair to describe, Adeimantus: tyranny and the tyrant."

"We surely do."

"Come, my friend, what is tyranny's character? That it comes from democracy seems pretty clear."

"Pretty clear."

b “Much as democracy came from oligarchy?"

"How?"

"What it set up for itself as the good, the reason that oligarchy was instituted—wasn't that wealth?"

"Yes."

"And it was destroyed by its insatiable greed for that and by its neglect of everything else to make money."

"True."

"Doesn't democracy also define a good, for which it has an insatiable greed that also destroys it?"

"What?"

"Freedom," I said. "In a democracy you'll hear that free-
c dom is its most beautiful possession, which makes it the only
place for a naturally free man to live."

"One hears that slogan frequently."

"This is what I was just going to say: Doesn't insatiable greed—for freedom—and neglect of everything else transform this regime too and prepare it to need a tyrant?"

"How?"

"When a democratic city thirsty for liberty has bad wine-
d pourers for advocates and gets drunk on too much unmixed
freedom, then, unless its rulers are obliging and provide
plenty of liberty, it punishes them as 'accursed oligarchs.' "

"It certainly does."

"And if anyone obeys the rulers, people denounce him as a no-good voluntary slave; but they honor rulers who act like subjects, subjects who act like rulers, and praise them in public and private. Doesn't the itch for freedom in a democracy necessarily extend to everything?" e

"Of course."

"So the anarchic growth spreads into private homes, my friend, and finally even to the animals."

"How do you mean?"

"Fathers get in the habit of acting like children and fear their sons; sons act like fathers and neither fear nor respect their parents in order to be 'free.' Resident aliens and even foreigners make themselves equal to citizens, and vice 563
versa."

"Yes, that happens."

"So do many other little things: The teacher is terrified of his pupils and wheedles them; they hold both him and their tutors[14] in contempt. Children ape adults in everything and argue and fight with them; old people condescend to the young by affecting a cute impertinence, and mimic them in b
order not to seem crabby or authoritative."

"They surely do."

"Mob liberty culminates in a city like this, Adeimantus, when purchased slaves, male and female, are as free as their owners. Oh, I almost forgot—there's also complete freedom and equal rights in the relations between the sexes."

"Well, shouldn't we follow Aeschylus and 'say whatever c
comes to our lips'?"[15]

"Of course," I said. "That's what I'm doing. Unless you've seen it, you'd never believe the freedom that even animals subject to man enjoy in a democracy. Dogs behave like the proverbial masters—why, the very horses and mules stalk about in stately freedom and shoulder aside anyone who doesn't step out of their way, and everything else is equally bristling with freedom." d

"You're telling me my own nightmare," he said. "That often happens to me on my way out to the country."

"Add this all up and you'll find that it makes the citizen's soul too sensitive to endure any slavery; the slightest touch

[14]Slaves who took the children to and from school.
[15]From a lost play.

makes it irritated. Finally, as I imagine you know, they even disregard the laws, written and unwritten; of course they
e mustn't have any master over them."

"Yes, I know."

"It seems to me," I said, "that this is the beautiful, vigorous seed from which tyranny sprouts."

"Vigorous indeed. But what next?"

"Because of democracy's permissiveness, the same disease that killed oligarchy strikes democracy even harder and enslaves it. Excess in anything tends to produce a violent change to the opposite. That's true of weather, crops, bod-
564 ies, and not least of governments."

"Most likely," he said.

"So an excess of freedom, most likely, turns into an excess of slavery for both city and individuals."

"Very likely."

"Then," I said, "it's very likely that tyranny results from no other regime than democracy—from unmixed freedom to complete and savage slavery."

"That makes sense."

"But I don't think that was your question. You wanted to
b know what that same disease is that grows in a democracy as well as in an oligarchy and enslaves it."

"You're right."

"Well, I meant that class of lazy, spendthrift men, led by the brave, followed by the cowardly. We likened them to drones, the former with, the latter without stings."

"Rightly too."

"When these two kinds of drone appear they agitate the whole regime like bile and phlegm in the body, and a good
c doctor and lawgiver must take precautions like a wise beekeeper preferably to prevent them from hatching, or if they do, to have both them and their cells cut out of the hive."

"Absolutely, by Zeus."

"Now let's dissect democracy into its three parts, Adei-
d mantus, so we can more critically see what we're after. One, I suppose, is the class of drones. Because of democracy's permissiveness, this class grows as large here as in an oligarchy, and much fiercer."

"Why?"

"Because there they were held in dishonor and shooed away from the offices, so that they got no exercise and

couldn't grow strong. But in a democracy this is the domi-
nant class, with a few exceptions. The fiercest ones speak
and transact the business, while the others settle down
around the rostrum and buzz off anyone who tries to dissent, e
so that with few exceptions this class runs everything."

"It surely does."

"Then there's another class the mob is always secreting."

"Which one?"

"Where everyone tries to make money, the ones most orderly by nature generally make the most, I suppose."

"Most likely," he said.

"—And form a large, abundant comb from which the drones squeeze out honey."

"They could hardly squeeze it out of people who don't have very much."

"I believe this class is called the rich—the drone garden."

"That's just about what it is."

"The third class would be the people: the peaceful, self- 565
employed workers and farmers with little property. When
they cluster in the assembly they form democracy's largest,
most sovereign class."

"Yes, but they won't do that very often unless they get a share of the honey."

"They always get a share," I said. "Their leaders confiscate the property of the 'haves' to distribute to the people and then keep most of it for themselves."

"That's the share they get, all right."

"The ones they rob are thus forced to defend themselves b
by speaking in the assembly and doing whatever they can."

"Of course."

"Therefore, even if the rich don't want a revolution, the
people accuse them of being oligarchs and plotting against
the democracy. Finally, when the rich see the people trying
to wrong them, not intentionally, but out of ignorance and
deceived by the slanderers, then, whether they want to or c
not, they do become oligarchs; not intentionally, but because that drone stung them and begot this evil too."

"Absolutely."

"Which hatches into arraignments, indictments, and lawsuits on both sides."

"Certainly."

"And don't the people always have one outstanding advocate that they nurture and allow to grow big?"

"Yes."

d "So this much is clear: where a tyrant flourishes he sprouts from the root of advocacy."

"Very clear."

"What begins the change from advocate to tyrant? Isn't it when he starts doing what they do in the story about the shrine of Lycaean Zeus in Arcadia?"

"What story?"

"Whoever tastes of human flesh—of the one man chopped up with the other sacrificial victims—necessarily
e turns into a wolf. Haven't you heard the tale?"

"Yes."

"An advocate of the people with an all-too-obedient mob, who shrinks neither from shedding citizen blood nor from dragging a man to court on the usual trumped-up charges to murder him and so eradicate a human life, whose sacrilegious mouth, having tasted kindred blood, banishes and kills
566 and hints at cancellation of debts and redistribution of land —doesn't necessity inexorably decree that such a man either be destroyed by his enemies or become a tyrant and a wolf instead of a man?"

"Inexorably," he said.

"So this is the one who fights in civil war against the property holders."

"It is indeed."

"If exiled and then returned in spite of his enemies, he
b returns as a full-fledged tyrant.[16] If his enemies can't get him banished or executed by turning the city against him, they plot to assassinate him secretly."

"That tends to happen."

"When tyrants get this far they all invent the notorious 'tyrant's request:' they ask the people for bodyguards to protect the 'defender of democracy.' "

"They certainly do."

"Which the people give him, I think, because they're afraid for his safety and confident in their own."

c "Extremely."

[16]As did Pisistratus, tyrant of Athens ca. 560–527 B.C. Plato seems to have Athenian history in mind throughout this section.

"When a man with money, and therefore the reputation of being an enemy of the people, sees this, my friend, he obeys the oracle Croesus received and 'abides not, but flees to pebbly Hermus,/ and has no shame of being a coward.' "[17]

"If he stays he'll get no second chance to be ashamed."

"Because anyone caught is handed over to Death, I believe."

"Necessarily."

"The advocate obviously won't be content to rest 'great
in his greatness;'[18] felling many another he mounts the d
chariot of state as a perfected tyrant."

"He'd hardly do much else."

"Shall we now describe the happiness of the man and of the city that whelps such a creature?"

"Of course."

"In the early days won't he greet everyone he meets with
a smile, deny being a tyrant, make promises to individuals e
and to the state, cancel debts and distribute land to the people and to his associates, and pretend to be gracious and kind to everyone?"

"Necessarily," he said.

"But after destroying some of his exiled enemies and becoming reconciled with the rest so that they leave him in peace, then, I think, he constantly stirs up new wars so that the people will always need a leader."

"Most likely."

"—And grow impoverished from paying war taxes, and so 567
be forced to look after their daily needs and have less time to plot against him."

"Clearly."

"I think it also gives him an excuse to liquidate anyone suspected of resenting his rule and entertaining ideas of freedom, by betraying them to the enemy. All of these motives make it necessary that the tyrant constantly foment war."

"Necessarily."

"—Which makes the citizens hate him even more, where- b
upon some of his bravest supporters, who helped put him

[17]Herodotus quotes this oracle in his *History,* I.55.
[18]*Iliad* 16.776 (of a fallen hero).

in office and hold positions of power themselves, speak out openly to each other and to him, and rebuke him for what's going on."

"Most likely."

"Therefore if he wants his rule to continue, the tyrant is forced to eliminate them until he's left without a single person, friend or foe, that's worth a thing."

"Obviously."

"He must keep a sharp lookout for anyone brave, large-
c minded, thoughtful, or rich. So great is his happiness that it forces him, whether he wants it or not, to be their enemy and to plot until he's purged the city of them."

"A noble purge!"

"Yes," I said, "the opposite of a bodily purge. A doctor eliminates the bad and leaves the good; a tyrant does the opposite."

"It seems he has to if he wants to rule."

d "So he's trapped in a blissful necessity that commands him either to live mostly with worthless people who hate him, or die."

"Utterly blissful!"

"And the more the citizens hate him for what he's doing, the more loyal bodyguards he needs."

"Of course."

"But whom can he trust? Where can he get them from?"

"They'll swarm to him themselves if he pays well enough."

"By the dog, Adeimantus—I think you're referring to
e drones again, foreign and multifarious."

"You catch my meaning well."

"What about at home? Won't he want to—"

"What?"

"—take away the citizens' slaves, free them, and make them part of his bodyguard?"

"Certainly; they'd be the most loyal."

"What fantastic bliss you claim the tyrant has! He gets to
568 kill off his old friends and keep 'loyalists' like these."

"Yes, that's what he keeps."

"—Who admire and associate with him as new citizens, while the decent people hate and avoid him. No wonder tragedy seems so wise, and Euripides above all tragedians."

"Why?"

"Because of pithy sayings like 'tyrants grow wise by consorting with the wise,'[19] where 'the wise' clearly refers to the b
tyrant's associates."

"Yes, Euripides and the others glorify the tyrant's estate as being equal to the gods', and so forth."

"Then since they're so wise, the tragedians will pardon us and others governed like us for barring them from our regime as eulogists of tyranny."

"I'm sure the more sophisticated ones will," he said. c

"—And go around to the other cities drawing mobs and
hiring loud, beautiful, persuasive voices to convert the
regimes to tyranny or democracy, and getting paid for it to
boot, in both money and honor. Tyrants pay best, of course,
and democracy second best. The higher they climb the
mountain of government, the more their honor lags behind, d
as though out of breath and unable to follow."

"Indeed."

"But we've gotten off the path. Let's get back to that big, beautiful, colorful, ever-changing army of his: how does the tyrant support it?"

"If there's any sacred money[20] in the town, he'll obviously spend that as long as it lasts, and also the estates of his victims, so he can tax the people less."

"And when that runs out?" I asked. e

"Obviously he'll use his inheritance to support himself, his cronies, drinking companions, and mistresses."

"I see—the people who begot the tyrant get to support both him and his companions."

"Necessarily," he said, "—there's no way around it."

"Suppose the people get indignant and say that it's not
right for a father to support his grown son, but the other way
around. What if they tell him that they didn't beget him and
appoint him as their leader so that they could be slaves to 569
their own slaves when he got big, or so that they could
support him and his slaves and his other riffraff washed in
by every sea, but so that he could be their advocate and free
them from the rich and the so-called 'beautiful and good'?
Suppose they then order him and his cronies out of town,

[19]From a lost play.

[20]Public revenues were stored in temples, and called "sacred money."

like a father throwing his son and his gang of wastrels out of the house. What happens then?"

"Then, by Zeus," said Adeimantus, "the people will learn
b what they are and what kind of creature they've raised, and that the weak don't throw out the strong."

"What? he'll dare to use force against his father and hit him if he doesn't obey?"

"Yes, after taking away his weapons."

"You allege that the tyrant is a parricide and a cheerless comfort to his father in his old age. It seems that this at last is open tyranny, and that the people, in trying to escape the
c frying pan of servitude to free men, have landed in the fire of slavery to slaves—they've exchanged that cloak of excessive, ill-considered freedom for the rags of the bitterest, most oppressive bondage: thralldom to slaves."

"That's exactly what they've done," he said.

"Well, Adeimantus, will we be in harmony if we say we've adequately explained how tyranny arises from democracy and what it's like when it does?"

"Quite adequately," he said.

Book 9

571[1] "Then we still have the tyrannical man to examine," I said, "—how he changes from the democratic man, what he's like, and whether he lives in wretchedness or bliss."

"Yes, he's still left," he said.

"Do you know what I miss, Adeimantus?"

"What?"

"I don't think we've sorted out the desires well enough. Our search won't be very clear until we know how many
b there are and what they're like."

"Well, can't we do it now?"

"Of course. Here's what I'd like to see in them: Some of the unnecessary pleasures and desires strike me as lawless. They're probably born into everyone, but custom, law, and the better desires together with reason normally curb them,

so that in some people they're eliminated entirely or only a few weak ones remain, while in others they stay numerous
and strong." c

"Which do you call lawless?"

"The ones awakened in sleep," I said, "whenever the soul's tame, rational, ruling part sleeps and the wild, bestial part, sated with food or drink, shrugs off sleep and skitters out to gratify its instincts. You know that in this condition it abandons all shame and good sense and dares anything:
nothing prevents it from trying to mount its mother, it d
thinks, or anyone else—man, animal, or god—from committing foul murder or eating any food. In short, it scales the heights of unreason and shamelessness."

"I know," he said.

"But imagine a man in a state of healthy, temperate self-control: If he has attained consciousness of himself before he goes to sleep and has awakened his rational part and feasted it on beautiful reasoning and examination; if, again,
he has neither sated nor deprived his desiring part, so that e
it may slumber and not disturb the best part with its joys or
sorrows but instead leave it alone—all to itself and pure— 572
to observe, reach out for, and perceive that which it does not know in the past, the present, or even the future; and if he has also soothed his spirited part, and thus avoids going to bed with his spirit stirred up from a quarrel—so that he falls asleep with two parts at peace and the third, in which thought is engendered, stirred up—you know that in this condition a man is most apt to touch truth and not have
lawless visions appear in his dreams." b

"That seems absolutely correct," he said.

"Well, we got carried too far away with it. All we want to know is that there's a class of wild, terrible, lawless desires in each of us—even in some of us who seem the most moderate—which reveal themselves in our sleep. See if that makes sense and if you agree."

"Yes, I agree."

"Now remember what we said the democratic man is like:
Raised under a thrifty father who honored only the money- c
making desires and disregarded the unnecessary ones concerned with play and adornment, he associated with more sophisticated men full of those lawless desires we just described, and hating his father's frugality, rushed into total

insolence and their way of life, and since he had a better
d nature than his corrupters, was pulled from both sides and
came out in the middle. He therefore enjoys the pleasures
of both personalities—moderately, he thinks—leads a life
neither lawless nor slavish, and from the oligarchic man
became the democratic."

"He did; that's our opinion of him."

"Now," I said, "assume that he in turn has a young son and raises him in his own habits."

"All right."

"Assume further that the same thing happens to the son
as happened to his father: Pulled to total lawlessness—which
e his seducers call total freedom—with his father and relatives
aiding his intermediate desires, the seducers reinforcing the
others. If these cunning wizards and tyrant-makers[1] have no
other hope of possessing the youth, they now devise a sort
of Love in him and make it the advocate of those lazy desires
573 that squander all his resources, as sort of a big, winged
drone—or do you think that such a man's love amounts to
anything else?"

"No, that's what it is," he said.

"Around this drone buzz the other desires filled with incense, perfume, garlands, wine, and the loose pleasures of
low company, feed it until it grows to its absolute limit, then
arm it with the sting of yearning. Whereupon this soul's
advocate obtains Madness as its bodyguard and goes ber-
b serk, and should it catch in itself any opinions or desires
made out to be good or still capable of shame, it kills and
drives them out till it has purged itself of temperance and
filled itself with imported madness."

"That fully describes the origin of the tyrannical man."

"Isn't that why Love has long been called a tyrant?"

"Could be."

"Doesn't a man also get ideas of being a tyrant when
c drunk, my friend?"

"Yes."

"And deranged maniacs attempt and fancy themselves able to rule not only men but even gods."

"Certainly."

[1]I.e. the seducers or lawless companions, the "drones" and "Lotus eaters" of Book 8. "Love," below, is *Eros:* sensual love, or lust.

"So strictly speaking, Adeimantus, a man becomes tyrannical whenever his nature, habits, or both make him amorous, demented, or drunk."

"Absolutely."

"That, it seems, is what the man is like and how he comes about. But how does he live?"

"Tell me and we'll both know, as the wags say." d

"All right," I said. "After that, I imagine, the one in whom tyrant Love dwells as pilot of all his soul's affairs has feasts, parties, revels, mistresses, and all that sort of thing. Don't numerous dreadful desires therefore shoot up in him night and day, demanding many things?"

"Indeed."

"And quickly squander whatever revenues he may have."

"Of course."

"Which leads to loans, and reduction of his property." e

"Certainly."

"And when all that runs out, mustn't the desires squawk
and cry incessantly like baby birds, necessarily driving him
like stings, most especially Love, the captain of the bodyguard, who makes him run amuck and forces him to examine
who has what that he can steal by deceit or force?" 574

"Absolutely."

"Then he must necessarily loot from everywhere or else be seized by fearful agony."

"Necessarily."

"Therefore, just as those latecoming pleasures got the better of his old ones and robbed them, so he, as the younger, presumes to get the better of his father and mother, and after spending his share of the estate he usurps and steals his parents' share."

"What else?"

"And if they won't give in to him, won't he at first try to b
rob them by deceit, and if that doesn't work, plunder them
by force?"

"I think so," he said.

"And if the old man and woman resist and fight him, will he spare them and carefully avoid doing anything tyrannical?"

"I wouldn't have much hope for the parents of a child like that, Socrates."

"For the love of Zeus, Adeimantus, you mean that for the

c sake of a new-found, dear, unnecessary mistress or a new-
found, young, unnecessary friend, a man like that would
beat his dear old mother and father—his oldest friends,
bound to him by necessity—and enslave them to these new
ones if he brings them into the house?"

"Yes, by Zeus."

"What bliss, it seems, to have a tyrant son!"

"Of course," he said.

d "And when his parents' possessions run out, won't a man
like that, having by now collected a huge swarm of desires,
first break into someone's house or rob a pedestrian late at
night, then clean out some temple? And in all this won't his
newly-liberated opinions accompany Love as bodyguards to
help overpower his old opinions—held since childhood and
made out to be just—of what's beautiful and ugly? Before
e that, when he was still ruled as a democracy under his father
and the laws, these new opinions were enslaved and broke
out only as dreams in his sleep, but now, under the tyranny
of Love, the man is constantly in waking life what before he
occasionally became in a dream, and he shrinks from no foul
575 murder, food, or cunning deed; Love lives in him tyranically,
in total anarchy and lawlessness, and since Love holds absolute sway, he incites this man who houses him like a city to
any reckless act that can sustain both him and the confusion
that attends him—partly brought in from outside by evil
company, partly set free from within by the same habits in
Love himself. Isn't that how such a man lives?"

"Yes."

"If only a few such men arise in a city where the rest of
b the mob is temperate, they leave and become bodyguards
for some other tyrant or hire out as mercenaries if there's a
war somewhere. If not, they stay in the city and commit many
small crimes."

"Such as?"

"Oh, stealing, housebreaking, kidnapping, picking pockets, lifting clothes, and robbing temples.[2] Competent speakers may also go into bribery, perjury, and blackmail."

c "Small crimes, you mean, if such men are few."

"Well, small is small compared to large, and crimes like

[2]I.e. robbing banks, since the temples were where state monies were kept.

those can't, as they say, hold a candle to a tyrant for the wretchedness and misery of a city. But when such men and their followers grow numerous and realize their numbers, then they're the ones who couple with the people's folly and beget as tyrant the one among them with the biggest tyrant in his soul." d

"Most likely," he said. "He'd be the most tyrannical."

"All's well if the citizens willingly give in. If not, then just as he punished his mother and father before, so now he'll punish his country if he can, bring in new companions, and support his dear old fatherland (or motherland, as the Cretans call it) in slavery to these men. That would be the end of such a man's desire."

"It surely would," he said. e

"How do men like that behave in private and before they rule? Don't they associate only with flatterers ready to serve them in anything, or if they should need something themselves, grovel and brazenly cavort like relatives till they get 576
what they want and then become strangers again?"

"Absolutely."

"Therefore they live out their lives as friends to no one, but always as either masters or slaves. A tyrannical nature never tastes freedom or true friendship."

"Never."

"So we can rightly call them faithless, and also completely unjust, if our earlier agreement about the nature of justice b
was correct."

"Which it was," said Adeimantus.

"To sum up then," I said: "In waking life the worst man is as we described a dream to be. He develops from a man with a tyrannical nature who gets absolute rule, and the longer he rules, the worse a tyrant he becomes."

"Necessarily," said Glaucon, picking up the discussion.

"Won't the man shown to be the most wicked also turn out to be the most wretched? And the more tyrannical he is c
and the longer he rules, the worse his condition becomes and the longer he stays in it. That's the truth, though the many also have many opinions."

"That much is necessarily true," said Glaucon.

"Doesn't the tyrannical man resemble the tyrannical city, the democratic man the democratic city, and so on?"

"Certainly."

"Then as one city compares with another in excellence and happiness, so one man compares with another."

d "Of course."

"Then how does a tyrannical city compare in excellence with the kingship we first described, Glaucon?"

"Exact opposites," he said. "One is the best, the other the worst."

"I won't ask you which is which—that's obvious. Now do
you judge them the same way in happiness and misery? And
let's not be dazzled by looking only at the tyrant or at the
few men who surround him, but go in as we ought and
e contemplate the city as a whole, plunging in everywhere and
seeing it all before we give an opinion."

"A fair challenge," he said. "And anyone can see that nothing is more wretched than a tyranny or happier than a kingship."

"Would it also be fair if I challenged us to do the same
577 with the men, and insisted that their judge be that man[3] who
can enter in his mind another man's disposition and see
through him without being dazzled like a child by the majes-
tic facade that tyrants present to the world? What if I
thought we all should listen to him, the one able to judge,
who had shared a tyrant's roof and followed his behavior
both at home with his servants and family, where he can best
b be seen stripped of the robes and the mask of tragedy, and
again in community crises, and invited the man who had
seen all that to report how the tyrant compares with the
others in happiness and misery?"

"That would also be a fair challenge," he said.

"Shall we pretend we're already acquainted with tyrants and can judge them, so we'll have someone to answer our questions?"

"Certainly," said Glaucon.

c "All right," I said, "examine it like this: Keeping in mind
the similarity between the city and the man, observe them in
turn and tell what happens to each."

[3]This sounds like a reference to Plato himself, who visited Dionysius I, tyrant of Syracuse, in 387 B.C., about twenty-four years after this dialogue is supposed to take place. Dionysius wrote tragedies, which may be alluded to below. A reference to Plato would explain Socrates' odd words in *b,* below: "Shall we pretend we're *already* acquainted with tyrants?"

"How do you mean?"

"Well, to speak first of the city, would you call the tyrannized one free or a slave?"

"An absolute slave."

"Yet you see masters and free men in it."

"Yes, but that part is small. The whole, so to speak, and the most decent part, lives in wretched, ignominious slavery."

"Then if the man resembles the city, mustn't he have the d
same arrangement in him? His soul teems with slavery and lack of freedom, its most decent parts enslaved to a small, depraved, demented one."

"Necessarily."

"Well? would you call such a soul free or a slave?"

"A slave, certainly."

"Doesn't the enslaved, tyrannized city least of all do what it wants?"

"Yes."

"So a tyrannized soul will also least of all do what it wants, c
speaking of it as a whole. Being forever goaded and dragged, it abounds in confusion and regret."

"Naturally."

"Is a tyrannical city necessarily rich or impoverished?"

"Impoverished."

"So a tyrannical soul is necessarily always needy and in- 578
satiable."

"True."

"And don't both the city and the man swarm with fears?"

"Necessarily."

"Do you think you could find a city more filled with weeping, wailing, lamentation, and grief?"

"No."

"Then do you think you could find a man more filled with grief than that tyrant maddened by desires and lusts?"

"I don't know where."

"So looking at all that and much more, I think, you judged b
this to be the most wretched city and—"

"Wasn't I right?"

"Absolutely. And what do you say about the tyrannical man when you look at the same things in him?"

"That he's by far the most wretched."

"Then you're no longer right, Glaucon."

"Why not?"

"Because he's not yet the one."

"Who then?"

"One who'll probably strike you as even more wretched."

"Who?"

c "A tyrannical man who doesn't live a private life, but meets with the added misfortune of becoming a tyrant."

"From what we've said I infer that you're right."

"Yes, but such things shouldn't be guessed; they should be carefully examined in discussions like these. We're exploring the most important issue, you know: the good and the bad life."

"I know," he said.

"Now see if this makes sense. I think we should examine
d the man by imagining a situation like this: Take any rich
private citizen who owns many slaves. He resembles a tyrant
in ruling over many. The only difference is in the number."

"Correct."

"Do you know that men like that aren't afraid of their servants?"

"What should they be afraid of?"

"Nothing. But do you know why?"

"Yes. The whole city defends each individual."

e "Good," I said. "Now what if some god took one man who owned fifty or more slaves, lifted him, his wife, and his children out of the city, and set him down in a wilderness with his possessions and servants in a place where there were no free men to help him—do you think he'd be afraid that his servants might kill him and his family?"

"No, he'd be utterly terrified."

579 "Wouldn't he be forced to fawn on some of his slaves, make promises, free them against his will, and make himself a flatterer of his own servants?"

"Either that or be killed," he said.

"Suppose the god settles neighbors all around him who won't tolerate anyone presuming to be another man's master; anyone they catch doing that they punish with the ultimate penalty."

b "Then he'll be sunk in even deeper misery, hemmed in on all sides by nothing but enemies."

"Isn't this the prison that cages the tyrant, whose nature swarms with the multifarious fears and passions we described? He alone in the city is forbidden to travel abroad

to see the games and sights that free men love to see, avid as his soul is to see them. He skulks in his house and lives mostly the life of a woman, jealous of his fellow citizens
whenever one of them takes a trip and sees something c
worthwhile."

"Absolutely," he said.

"Such, then, is the harvest of evils reaped by the man governed badly within, the tyrannical man you just pronounced the most wretched; who, however, lives not as a private citizen, but is compelled by some chance to be a tyrant and try to rule others when he can't rule himself, like some incontinent invalid who isn't permitted to live privately but is forced to spend his life fighting and competing d
with others."

"Your simile is true and exact, Socrates."

"Then, dear Glaucon, isn't this utter wretchedness, and the life of a ruling tyrant even harder than the one you judged the hardest?"

"Absolutely."

"So the truth is this, whatever people may think: A real tyrant is really a slave who must fawn on the basest people
with the most abject and servile flattery. He never satisfies e
his desires, and to one who knows how to observe a soul in its entirety he appears truly a pauper utterly deprived, overrun with fears all his life and convulsed with pains and spastic twitches, if he resembles the condition of the city he rules. Does he?"

"Completely."

"Besides that, let's give him those traits we mentioned 580
before: Of necessity he must be, and through his rule become even more, envious, faithless, unjust, friendless, impious, a nursemaid and host to absolute evil, and from all that the most unfortunate of men who makes his fellows the same."

"No sensible man would dispute that, Socrates."

"Then this is the final decision. Like a judge in the theater[4] reveal your opinion: Which of our five competitors b

[4]Greek dramatists competed in the theater for first, second, and third prize. A herald announced the judges' decision to the audience. There is a pun on "Ariston's," below, which means "the best man's."

wins the first prize for happiness, which the second, and so
on—the kingly man, the timocratic, the oligarchic, the
democratic, or the tyrannical?"

"That's an easy decision. Judging them like plays for excellence and happiness, I rank them in the order in which they appeared."

"Shall we hire a herald, or shall I myself proclaim that
Ariston's son has declared the winner in happiness to be the
c best and most just man—the kingly man who is also king
over himself—and the loser to be the worst and most unjust
man—the tyrannical man who is the greatest tyrant over
himself and his city?"

"Your proclamation will do, Socrates."

"Shall I add, 'Whether or not they're seen for what they are by all gods and men'?"

"Yes, add that too."

"Well, that's one demonstration, Glaucon. See if this will
d do for the second. Since the individual soul is divided like
the city into three classes, I think it admits of another proof:
It seems to me there are three kinds of pleasures, desires,
and rule, one for each part of the soul."

"How do you mean?"

"One was the part with which a man learns, another the
part in which he feels spirit, and the third had so many forms
e that we couldn't give it a specific name. We named it the
'desiring part' after its largest component and because the
desires for food, drink, sex, and so forth are so intense; and
also the 'money-loving part' because money especially satis-
581 fies such desires."

"Yes, and that was right," he said.

"So if we say that it loves and gets its pleasure from profit, will that sum it up and indicate that we're referring to this part of the soul? Can we rightly call it the money-loving or profit-loving part?"

"I think so."

"Don't we say that the spirited part as a whole always
pursues victory, mastery, and repute?"

b "Certainly."

"So we'll be on key in calling it the victory-loving or honor-loving part."

"Exactly on key."

"And anyone can see that the part we learn with is always

bent on knowing the truth and the nature of everything, and that of the three it cares the least about money and reputation."

"By far."

"So 'wisdom-loving' and 'fond of learning' would appropriately designate that part."

"Why not?"

"And doesn't one of these parts rule in some people's
souls, another in others', whichever one it may be?" c

"Yes."

"That's why we divide men into three primary classes: lovers of wisdom, victory, and profit."

"You're right."

"—For which there exist three kinds of pleasures, one for each class."

"Of course."

"Now you know if you go around to each of these three
types of men and ask them which of their lives is the most
pleasant, each will commend his own. The moneymaker will
call the pleasures of honor and learning worthless compared d
to profit, unless he can make some money from them."

"True," he said.

"What about the lover of honor? Won't he consider monetary pleasure rather vulgar, intellectual pleasure, except so far as learning brings honor, to be merely smoke and rubbish?"

"Exactly."

"And what of the philosopher's opinion of the other pleasures compared to knowing about the truth and to the enjoy- e
ment he gets from learning? Shouldn't we suppose he'll
consider them a far cry from true pleasure and call them
merely necessary because he'd have no use for them if they
weren't absolutely necessary?"

"We should be certain he will."

"But if they dispute which class lives the best and most
beautiful life and which has the most pleasure and least pain,
how can we know who's telling the truth?" 582

"You've got me, Socrates."

"Look at it like this: What must we judge with to judge anything well? Isn't it experience, knowledge, and argument? Can you find a better standard than those?"

"I don't know where."

"Now look: Which of these three men has the most experience in all of these pleasures? Do you think the profit-lover who tries to learn the nature of absolute truth will have more
b experience in the pleasure of knowledge than the philosopher has in the pleasure of profit?"

"Much less," he said. "The philosopher must necessarily taste both of the other pleasures from childhood, but there's no necessity for the profit-lover to taste the sweet pleasure of learning the nature of what *is,* which wouldn't be easy for him to do even if he were eager to do it."

"So the philosopher has much more experience in both of
c these pleasures than the profit-lover. Does he have less experience in the pleasure of honor than the honor-lover has in the pleasure of knowing?"

"Honor attends all three if they reach their goals," he said. "The rich man, no less than the brave or the wise, is honored by many, so that all three are experienced in the pleasure of honor. None but the philosopher, however, can taste how sweet is the pleasure of contemplating what *is.*"

d "Then as to experience," I said, "the philosopher is the best judge of the three."

"By far."

"And only he combines knowledge with experience."

"Of course."

"And the tool they must judge with belongs not to the lover of profit or honor, but to the lover of wisdom."

"What tool?"

"Didn't we say they must judge by argument?"

"Yes."

"—Which is pre-eminently the philosopher's tool."

"Indeed."

"If profit were the best standard of judgment, then the
e truest things would be the ones the profit-lover praises and blames."

"Necessarily," he said.

"If honor, victory, and courage, then the ones that the lover of honor and victory praises and blames."

"Obviously."

"But since it's experience, knowledge, and argument?"

"Then the truest things are necessarily the ones that the lover of wisdom and argument praises," he said.

583 "So of these three pleasures wouldn't the most pleasant

be the one of that part of the soul by which we learn, and the most pleasant life his in whom that part rules?"

"What else? At least that's the way of life that the intelligent, qualified judge recommends."

"Which life and pleasure does he rank second?"

"Clearly the military and honor-loving. He's closer to that than to the moneymaking life."

"Then the profit-loving life is last, it seems."

"Certainly."

"Well, Glaucon, the just man has defeated the unjust man b
twice in a row. As the third, dedicated Olympically to Savior and Olympian Zeus, observe that only the intelligent man's pleasure is absolutely true and pure; the others resemble shadow drawings, as I think I've heard a wise man say. And this will be the greatest, most decisive fall."

"By far.—But what do you mean?"

"I'll find out by searching, if you answer." c

"Ask," he said.

"All right. Don't we call pain the opposite of pleasure?"

"Completely."

"And say there's a state that is neither?"

"Indeed."

"—Which lies between them as a kind of peace of soul in regard to both. Isn't that so?"

"Yes."

"Do you recall what people say when they're sick?"

"What?"

"That nothing is really more pleasant than being healthy,
but they hadn't noticed until they got sick." d

"I remember."

"You've also heard people in severe pain say that nothing is more pleasant than an end to suffering."

"Yes."

"I think there are many situations in which you've heard people in pain praise not joy, but peace and the absence of pain as the highest pleasure."

"Yes, peace then probably becomes a positive pleasure."

"That would make peace painful when someone ceases e
from pleasure."

"Perhaps," he said.

"Then peace, which we just said was between the two, will at times be both pleasure and pain."

"So it seems."

"Can what's neither become both?"

"I don't think so."

"When pleasure or pain occur in the soul, aren't they both a kind of movement?"

"Yes."

584 "And didn't the absence of both just now appear to be peace, between the two?"

"Yes, it did."

"Then how can it be right to regard absence of suffering as pleasure or absence of joy as agony?"

"It can't."

"Therefore," I said, "peace appears to be but is not pleasure when set beside pain, pain when set beside pleasure. There's nothing solid about these apparitions compared to true pleasure—they merely beguile us."

"So the argument seems to indicate."

b "Well, look at pleasures that don't come from pain then, so you don't think in this case that pleasure is cessation of pain and pain cessation of pleasure."

"Which case? What pleasures?"

"There are many," I said, "but you'll see it best in the pleasures of smell. They occur suddenly with terrific intensity and without prior suffering, and they cease without leaving pain."

"True."

c "So let's not believe that pure pleasure is the elimination of pain, or pain the elimination of pleasure."

"No."

"But still," I said, "most of the so-called pleasures that enter the soul through the body, and the strongest of them, belong to this class: the elimination of pains."

"True."

"Don't forepleasures and forepains in anticipation of expected pleasures and pains work the same way?"

"Yes."

d "Do you know their nature and what they most resemble?"

"What?"

"Do you believe there's an above, a below, and a middle in nature?"

"Certainly."

"Wouldn't a man being brought from below toward the middle think he was going above? And if he stood in the middle and looked down at where he had come from, would he believe he was anywhere but above, if he had never seen the true above?"

"I don't think he could believe anything else, by Zeus."

"If brought back down again, wouldn't he think—rightly e
—that he was moving toward the below?"

"Of course."

"And he believes all this because he has no experience of the truly existing above, below, and middle?"

"Obviously," said Glaucon.

"Then does it surprise you that men with no experience of truth have sick opinions about other things too, so that, as regards pleasure, pain, and what lies between them, when
brought to pain they consider it real and truly suffer, and 585
when carried from pain toward the in-between, they firmly believe they're approaching pleasure and fulfillment? They're deceived, and like men who contrast black with gray because they've never seen white, they contrast pain with painlessness because they have no experience of pleasure."

"No, by Zeus," he said, "I'd be much more surprised if that weren't so."

"Now look at it this way: Aren't hunger, thirst, and so b
forth depleted states of the body?"

"Yes."

"And ignorance and lack of intelligence an empty state of the soul?"

"Exactly."

"And whoever partakes of nourishment or intelligence gets filled?"

"Of course."

"Which is truer: to be filled with what has more or less being?"

"More, obviously."

"Then which class do you think partakes of more pure being—the class of things like bread, drink, meat, and food in general, or the class of true opinion, knowledge, intelligence and, in short, of complete excellence? Judge like this: c
Which more fully *is*—something that partakes of the always alike, immortal, and true, is that way itself, and appears in

things like that, or something that partakes of and appears in the never alike and the mortal, and is that way itself?"

"What partakes of the always alike is far superior."

"Then does the essence of the always *un*like participate in being any more than in knowledge?"[5]

"No."

"In truth, then?"

"No."

"And if less in truth, then less in being."

"Necessarily."

d "So the classes that care for the body must as a whole
participate in truth and being less than the classes that care
for the soul."

"Much less."

"And the body itself less than the soul, right?"

"Right."

"Doesn't something that more fully *is* and that gets filled with what more fully *is* get more truly filled than something that less *is* and that gets filled with what less *is?*"

"Of course."

"So if it's pleasant to be filled with the naturally suited,
then something that gets more and more truly filled with
e what *is* causes a deeper and truer joy in true pleasure,
whereas a thing that partakes less of what *is* fills one less
truly and reliably and partakes of a less true and trustworthy
pleasure."

"Absolutely necessary," he said.

586 "Then people inexperienced in knowledge and excellence, who attend feasts and so on, are swept down, it seems,
and then back to the middle again, and spend all their lives
wandering back and forth; they never climb out to look up
and be lifted to the true above and be truly filled with what
truly *is,* or taste pure, reliable pleasure. Like cattle they
always look down, stooped to the earth and their tables,
grazing, feeding, and copulating, kicking and butting each
b other out of greed for these delights with iron horns and
hooves, killing each other in their insatiable lust, because
they're trying to fill an unreal, leaky thing in themselves with
something that *is not.*"

[5]Both the argument and the text are uncertain. All manuscripts read "of the always *a*like" here, which makes no sense.

"Socrates," said Glaucon, "that sounds like an oracle on
the life of the many."

"Aren't they therefore condemned to traffic with pleasures mixed with pains, the shadow-drawn phantoms of true
pleasure, which take their colors from being situated next to c
the pains, so that they appear intense, beget insane lusts in
thoughtless people, and become fought over, as Stesichorus
says the heroes at Troy fought over a phantom of Helen out
of ignorance of the truth?"[6]

"It must be something like that," he said.

"Isn't it much the same with the spirited part? Whoever
satisfies his love of honor by envy, his love of victory by
violence, or his irritability by venting his anger is pursuing d
their satisfaction without reason or mind."

"That must also be true."

"Well, can we confidently assert that if the desires of the
victory-and profit-loving parts follow knowledge and reason
and with them pursue and attain pleasures sanctioned by the
intelligent part, these desires will, so far as such things can
attain true pleasures, attain true pleasures, because they
follow the truth; and their own proper pleasures, if that e
which is best for a thing is also most properly its own?"

"They certainly will be their own."

"So when the whole soul follows the wisdom-loving part
and is free from civil war, all its parts will be just and tend
their own business, and each will enjoy its own pleasures, the
best and truest possible." 587

"Absolutely."

"But when one of the other parts dominates, it will never
find its own pleasure, and will force the others to pursue
pleasures that are alien and untrue."

"True."

"And won't the parts farthest from philosophy and reason
cause that the most?"

"By far."

"Wouldn't what's farthest from reason also be the farthest
from law and order?"

[6]Stesichorus was a sixth-century lyric poet who composed a version of the Helen story in which the real Helen was in Egypt while the heroes fought at Troy over a phantom the gods had made of her. Euripides' *Helen* is based on this version.

"Obviously."

"And weren't the erotic, tyrannical desires shown to be
b the farthest away; the orderly, kingly ones the closest?"

"Yes."

"Then, I think, the tyrant will be the farthest from true, kindred pleasures, the king the closest."

"Necessarily."

"So the tyrant will live the most unpleasant life, the king the most pleasant."

"An absolute necessity," said Glaucon.

"Do you know how much more unpleasant?"

"I will if you tell me."

"Well, Glaucon, it seems there are three pleasures, one
c legitimate and two bastard, and that by shunning law and reason the tyrant oversteps the bounds of even the two bastard ones and lives with slavish bodyguard pleasures, which makes it hard to say how much lower he is, except perhaps like this."

"How?"

"The tyrant was probably thrice[7] removed from the oligarch, with the democrat in the middle."

"Yes."

"Then if what we said before was true, doesn't he also live with a phantom of pleasure three times further away from true pleasure?"

"Yes."

"The oligarch was also thrice removed from the king, if we
d may regard the aristocrat and the king as identical."

"True."

"So the tyrant," I said, "must stand thrice three times removed from true pleasure."

"Apparently."

"The phantom of a tyrant's pleasure must then be a plane number,[8] measured on its length."

"Positively."

"—Which raised to its second and then to its third power, will clearly give us the distance."

[7]I.e. "twice-removed." The Greeks counted both the first and the last number of a series.

[8]Nine is a plane number because it is the square of 3 (and a square is a plane figure). Socrates next cubes this to get the third dimension. The exercise is whimsical, as in 546, p. 204.

"Well, clear to a mathematician."

"Conversely, if one reckons how far the king is separated
from the tyrant in true pleasure, one discovers by multiplica- e
tion that his life is seven hundred and twenty-nine times
more pleasant; the tyrant's life more grievous by the same
distance."

"A monstrous calculation you've dumped on the two men,
the just and the unjust, of the difference between them in 588
pleasure and pain!"

"But a true and pertinent one, if days and nights and months and years pertain to them."

"Which they do."

"If the good, just man beats the bad, unjust man by that much in pleasure, he must beat him by a staggering amount in the grace, beauty, and excellence of his life."

"Staggering indeed, by Zeus."

"Now that we've gotten this far," I said, "let's go back to b
that statement made at the beginning, which brought us
here: that it pays for a man to be perfectly unjust if he
appears to be just. Isn't that what someone said?"

"Yes."

"Then since we've agreed what power justice and injustice each have, let's have a discussion with him."

"How?"

"By molding in words an image of the soul, so that the one who said that will realize what he was saying."

"What kind of image?" c

"Oh, something like those natures the myths tell us were born in ancient times—the Chimaera, Scylla, Cerberus, and others in which many different shapes were supposed to have grown into one."

"So they tell us," he said.

"Then mold one figure of a colorful, many-headed beast with heads of wild and tame animals growing in a circle all around it; one that can change and grow all of them out of itself."

"That's a job for a skilled artist. Still, words mold easier d
than wax or clay, so consider it done."

"And another of a lion, and one of a man. Make the first by far the biggest, the second second largest."

"That's easier, and already done."

"Now join the three together so that they somehow grow into one."

"All right."

"Next mold the image of one, the man, around them all,
so that to someone who can't see what's inside but looks
e only at the container it appears to be a single animal, man."

"I have."

"Then shall we inform the gentleman that when he says
it pays for this man to be unjust, he's saying that it profits
him to feast his multifarious beast and his lion and make
589 them grow strong, but to starve and enfeeble the man in him
so that he gets dragged wherever the animals lead him, and
instead of making them friends and used to each other, to
let them bite and fight and eat each other?"

"That's just what he's saying by praising injustice."

"The one who says justice pays, however, would be saying
that he should practice and say whatever will give the most
b mastery to his inner man, who should care for the many-
headed beast like a farmer, raising and domesticating its
tame heads and preventing the wild ones from growing,
making the lion's nature his partner and ally, and so raise
them both to be friends to each other and to him.

"That's exactly what he means by praising justice."

"So in every way the commender of justice is telling the
c truth, the other a lie. Whether we examine pleasure, reputation, or profit, we find that the man who praises justice
speaks truly, the one who disparages it disparages sickly and
knows nothing of what he disparages."

"I don't think he does at all."

"Then let's gently persuade him—his error wasn't intended—by asking him a question: 'Shouldn't we say that
the traditions of the beautiful and the ugly have come about
like this: Beautiful things are those that make our bestial
d parts subservient to the human—or rather, perhaps, to the
divine—part of our nature, while ugly ones are those that
enslave the tame to the wild?' Won't he agree?"

"If he takes my advice."

" 'On this argument then, can it pay for a man to take
money unjustly if that means making his best part a slave to
e the worst? If it wouldn't profit a man to sell his son or his
daughter into slavery—to wild and evil men at that—even if
he got a fortune for it, then if he has no pity on himself and
enslaves the most godlike thing in him to the most godless

and polluted, isn't he a wretch who gets bribed for gold into
a destruction more horrible than Euriphyle's, who sold her 590
husband's life for a necklace?' "

"Much more horrible," said Glaucon, "—I'll answer you for him, Socrates."

"Don't you think that this is why self-indulgence has long been criticized, because it turns loose that horrible, great and multiformed monster too much?"

"Obviously."

"And don't we criticize willfulness and irascibility when
they expand and intensify the snake and lion part all out of b
proportion; luxury and softness when they engender cowardice there and make it limp and lax?"

"Of course."

"And flattery and slavishness when they subdue this same part—the spirited—to the unruly beast, expose it to insult for the sake of money and the beast's insatiable appetite, and inure the lion to act from childhood like an ape?"

"Exactly," he said. c

"And why does servile mechanical labor bring reproach? Doesn't that happen only when the best part of a person is by nature too weak to rule the creatures in him and serves them instead, and can learn nothing except how to fawn on them?"

"Most likely."

"In order that both he and the best man may be ruled by
a similar thing, we say he should be a slave to that best man
who has a divine ruler in him—not to the detriment of the d
slave, as Thrasymachus thought about subjects,[9] but because everyone is better off being ruled by the godlike and intelligent; preferably if he has it inside, but if not, it should be imposed on him from without so that we may all be friends and as nearly alike as possible, all steered by the same thing."

"Yes, and we're right," he said.

"Law, the ally of everyone in the city, clearly intends the e
same thing, as does the rule of children, which forbids us to
let them be free until we've instituted a regime in them as
in a city. We serve their best part with a similar part in us, 591

[9]Thrasymachus had said in Book 1 that subjects must obey rulers to the rulers' advantage and to the subjects' own detriment.

install a like guardian and ruler in them, and only then set them free."

"Clearly."

"Then how, by what argument, Glaucon, can we say that it pays for a man to be unjust or self-indulgent or to do something shameful to get more money or power if by doing so he makes himself worse?"

"We can't," he said.

"And how can it pay to commit injustice without getting
b caught and being punished? Doesn't getting away with it
make a man even worse? Whereas if a man gets caught and punished, his beastlike part is taken in and tamed, his tame part is set free, and his whole soul acquires justice and temperance and knowledge. Therefore his soul recovers its best nature and attains a state more honorable than the state the body attains when it acquires health and strength and beauty, by as much as the soul is more honorable than the body."

"Absolutely."

c "Then won't a sensible man spend his life directing all his
efforts to this end, and first honor any studies that will make his soul like that, and disregard the rest?"

"Clearly."

"Next, refuse to entrust the care of his body to irrational animal pleasure and live immersed in that, and even ignore his health and despise physical strength and beauty except
d as they may contribute to temperance, making it ever mani-
fest that he tunes his body's concord only for the sake of harmony in his soul?"

"Absolutely, if he's going to be a true musician."

"Won't he look for the same order and harmony in his possessions and refuse to let the glorification of the many dazzle him into piling up an unlimited mass of wealth attended by its limitless evils?"

"I think so," he said.

e "He'll look beyond that," I said, "to the regime within,
guard against its being disturbed by either abundance or lack of possessions, and steer his course as straight as he can between depleting his property and adding to it."

"Exactly," said Glaucon.

592 "The same with honors. He'll freely partake and taste of

any he thinks will improve him, but shun all honors, public or private, that might dissolve his existing state."

"If that's his concern he won't be willing to go into politics."

"He will, by the dog," I said, "—in his own proper city, though perhaps not in the land of his birth, unless some divine chance should occur."

"I understand—you mean in the city we've been founding
in words; I don't think it exists on the earth." b

"But perhaps it's laid up as a model in heaven for anyone to look at who wishes to found himself. It makes no difference whether it exists or ever will exist here. He'll practice the politics only of it and of no other."

"Most likely," said Glaucon.

Book 10

"And while many things about our city suggest that we 595
founded it absolutely right, I say so chiefly with poetry[1] in mind."

"How so?" he asked.

"Admitting none that's imitative," I replied. "Now that we've sorted out all the classes in the soul, it seems even more obvious to me that we must forbid imitative poetry
altogether." b

"Why?"

"Just between us—you won't denounce me to the tragedians and the other imitative poets—all poetry like that seems to poison the mind of the audience unless they have an antidote in knowing what it's like."

"What do you mean?"

"I must speak," I said, "—though a certain reverence and

[1]Here "poetry" *(poiesis)* rather than "music" as earlier. The word literally means "something made;" a poet is a "maker," and "make" also means "compose." The following analogies between poets ("makers") and craftsmen ("furniture makers," etc.) are therefore closer in Greek than in English.

love that I've had for him since childhood would prevent me
c from speaking of Homer. He, it seems, was the first teacher and leader of all these lovely tragic poets. Still, we mustn't honor a man above the truth, so, as I said, I must speak."

"Absolutely," he said.

"Listen then; or rather, answer."

"Ask."

"Can you tell me what imitation in general is? I don't think I understand very well myself what it's supposed to be."

"And I should, I suppose?"

"It wouldn't be strange if you did: dim eyes often see
596 things before sharp ones."

"True, but with you here I'm not so eager to say how things look to me. You look instead."

"Then let's begin our examination in our usual way. We normally posit one unique form for each group of many things to which we apply the same name. Do you understand?"

"Yes."

"Then take any group you'd like. Aren't beds and tables,
b for instance, many?"

"Of course."

"But there are only two shapes[2] for them all, I suppose: one of bed and one of table."

"Yes."

"And don't we say that furniture makers look at the shapes when one of them makes the beds, another the tables we use, and so on for the others? No craftsman, I imagine, makes the shape itself—how could he?"

"He couldn't."

"What would you call a craftsman who can make anything
c that any other workman can make?"

"An amazingly clever fellow."

"Wait till you hear the rest: This workman can not only make all kinds of furniture, but everything that grows in the ground, all living creatures including himself, heaven and earth and the gods, and everything in heaven and in Hades under the ground."

d "What a genius!"

"You don't believe it? You doubt that such a craftsman

[2]A synonym for "form" above. Cf. footnote 13, p. 144.

exists, that in one way he makes[3] all these things, though in another way not? Or do you see that you too can make them all after a fashion?"

"What fashion?"

"Nothing hard—you could quickly fashion them in many ways, but the quickest would be to take a mirror and turn it
around in every direction. You'll quickly make the sun, the e
earth, stars, furniture, plants, animals, yourself—everything we just said."

"Yes—make them appear, not truly be."

"Excellent," I said. "You've come to the argument's rescue just in time, because I think a painter is that kind of a craftsman, don't you?"

"Certainly."

"I suspect you'll deny that his works are real. Yet in a way a painter makes a bed, doesn't he?"

"Yes, again an apparent one."

"What about the bedmaker? Didn't you just say he makes 507
not the form, which we say *is* the bed, but a particular bed?"

"Yes."

"But if he doesn't make what *is,* he doesn't make what's real, merely something like it. If someone says the work of a bedmaker or any other workman perfectly *is* and is real, I'll bet he's not telling the truth."

"It wouldn't seem so to someone who spent his time in discussions like these," he said.

"So we won't be surprised if this bed is rather faint compared to truth."

"Not at all." b

"Shall we investigate from our examples what this imitator is?"

"If you like," he replied.

"We have these three beds then," I said. "One exists in nature, and I think we'll say it was fashioned by a god. Or was it someone else?"

"I doubt it."

"And one by a carpenter, the third by a painter, right?"

"Right."

"The painter, the carpenter, and the god: these three are in charge of three forms[4] of bed."

[3]"Make" also means "compose" (a poem).
[4]Here in the sense of "classes" or "kinds."

"Indeed."

c "Now the god, either because he wished it so or because some necessity stood over him to fashion no more than one bed in nature, made only that one, which *is* the bed itself. He did not and will not bring forth two or more of them."

"Why not?"

"Because even if he made only two, one would again appear, whose form those other two would take, and that one would be the bed that *is,* not the other two."

"Right."

d "I think the god knew this, and wishing to be the true maker[5] of the truly existing bed rather than the particular maker of some particular bed, he brought forth the one bed itself in nature."

"Most likely."

"Shall we call him the bed's 'naturalizer' or something?"

"That would be good, because he has made it and everything that is by nature."

"And the carpenter its craftsman?"

"Yes."

"Is the painter also a craftsman and maker of the bed?"

"No."

"What then?"

e "I think we could reasonably call him an imitator of what the others make as craftsmen."

"Aha! You call the one that produces the third product away from nature an imitator."

"Certainly," he said.

"Then the tragedian too, if he's an imitator, must by nature be the third away from the king and truth, and all other imitators likewise."

"Evidently."

"So we're agreed on the imitator. Now do you think a
598 painter tries to imitate each thing itself in nature, or the works of craftsmen?"

"The works of craftsmen."

"As they *are* or *appear?* Define that too."

"What do you mean?"

"This: Does a bed or anything else change when you look

[5]I.e. "poet."

at it straight on and then from the side or some other angle?
Or does it appear different but stay the same?"
"Yes, it appears different but stays the same."
"Which of these aspects does painting adhere to—reality b
as it *is* or appearance as it appears? Does it imitate truth or
an apparition?"
"An apparition."
"Then imitation lies far from the truth and can make all
things because it captures only a tiny bit of each one, and
that but a phantom. We say a painter, for instance, can paint
us a carpenter, a shoemaker, or any other craftsman without
claiming knowledge of any of their crafts. Still, a good c
painter might paint a carpenter and deceive children and
simpletons into thinking it real, if he shows it to them from
a distance."
"Of course."
"I think this should be our attitude toward all such imitators, my friend: Whenever someone tells us he has met a
man with knowledge of all crafts and of everything that any
individual knows, and no one has more detailed knowledge d
of anything than he, we should inform the speaker that he
must be a rather simple person who met an imitation wizard
and got deceived into thinking him omniscient because he
himself couldn't distinguish between knowledge, ignorance,
and imitation."
"True."
"Then," I said, "we must next examine tragedy and
Homer, its leader. Some people say that the poets know all
crafts and everything human concerning excellence and evil, e
and all things divine, because to compose well a good poet
must know what he's writing about. Therefore we must decide whether they're telling the truth and good poets really
do know what they seem to say so well, or whether these
people ran into imitators and got deceived, and so can't see
that poets' works are thrice removed from reality and there- 599
fore easy to make—even for a man ignorant of the truth—
because they're not real, but apparitions."
"We surely must," he said.
"If a man could make the thing to be imitated as well as
its semblance, do you think he'd seriously allow himself to
craft phantoms and cite that as his life's best possession?" b
"Not at all."

"I think someone who truly understood the things that he imitated would much rather apply himself to the things than to their copies, try to leave behind many beautiful works as memorials of himself, and prefer to be the one eulogized rather than the eulogizer."

"I agree: both the honor and the usefulness are greater."

"Then let's let the other crafts go and not demand an
c account of them from Homer or any other poet, asking how
many people any poet, ancient or modern, if he knew medicine and didn't just imitate medical language, is supposed to have cured, like Asclepius, or how many students he left behind him as doctors, as Asclepius did his descendants. Homer attempts to speak of the greatest, most beautiful things—war, generalship, the governing of cities, and the
d education of man. It would therefore be fair to question him
and say: 'If, dear Homer, you're not the third from truth concerning excellence, an imitator, which we defined as a craftsman of phantoms, but only the second, and you knew what pursuits make men better in public and private, then tell us what city was ever governed better because of you, as Sparta because of Lycurgus and many other cities, large and
e small, because of many other men. What city acknowledges
you as its lawgiver and benefactor, as Italy and Sicily acknowledge Charondas and we Solon?' Will he be able to name one?"

"I don't think so," said Glaucon. "Not even the Homerists claim that."

600 "Well, was there some war in Homer's day reputedly
fought well under his leadership or counsel?"

"No."

"Did he invent some ingenious contrivance for the crafts or something, such as people attribute to practical wise men like Thales of Miletus and Anacharsis of Scythia?"[6]

"No, nothing like that."

"Maybe something in private life then. Do they say that Homer was a leader in education during his lifetime, whose
b pupils cherished his companionship and handed down a

[6]Thales was the first philosopher of the Milesian school, which speculated in natural science. He predicted the solar eclipse of 585 B.C. Anacharsis (ca. 600 B.C.) was an early geometer, supposed to have been able to calculate the distance of ships at sea.

Homeric way of life, the way Pythagoras's disciples cherished him for a discipline that his followers even today call the 'Pythagorean Way,' which makes them somehow stand out from everyone else?"

"No, Socrates. Otherwise his companion Creophylus would seem even sillier for his education than for his name,[7] if what they say about Homer is true. They say he was much neglected in his day, while he lived." c

"So they say, Glaucon. But if Homer knew, and didn't just imitate, how to educate and improve people, don't you think he'd have gotten many companions to honor and love him? When Protagoras of Abdira, Prodicus of Ceos,[8] and countless other teachers can meet with their contemporaries on a private basis and convince them that they'll never be able to d
manage their homes or their cities unless they have experts like themselves to direct their education, and when their students love them so intensely for this wisdom that they practically carry them around on their shoulders, would the people of Homer's time have let him and Hesiod run around as minstrels if the two of them really had been able to promote excellence? Why, people would have clung to them tighter than gold; they'd have insisted that they live with them; and if they couldn't get them to stay, they'd have e
followed them around as their pupils until they got a decent education."

"That seems absolutely true, Socrates."

"Then shall we say that all poetic imitators from Homer on down imitate phantoms of excellence and of everything else they create, but never touch truth, like that painter who we just said will make a seeming shoemaker for people as 601
ignorant of cobbling as he, who judge only by colors and figures?"

"Certainly."

"In the same way, I think we'll say that the poet too gives the colors of various crafts in words and phrases without knowing anything but imitation, so that to others like him who judge only by words, his words will, when delivered in harmony, rhythm, and meter, seem spoken exceedingly well,

[7]Creophylus means "Beefborn." A legendary, perhaps fictitious character, about whom little is known.

[8]Two of the most popular sophists of Socrates' time.

whether they deal with shoemaking, generalship, or any-
b thing else. Such things have by nature some powerful en-
chantment, because if you strip a poem of its musical colors
and speak the words by themselves, you know what it will
sound like. You've heard it, I think."[9]

"Yes."

"Aren't they like young, unbeautiful faces after the bloom of youth has departed?"

"Exactly."

"Now," I said, "look at it like this: The imitator, or phantommaker, understands nothing of reality, but only of ap-
c pearance. Is that what we say?"

"Yes."

"Let's look at this thoroughly, not leave it half-said."

"Speak."

"Can a painter paint reins and a bridle?"

"Yes."

"But a shoemaker and blacksmith will make them."

"Indeed."

"Does the painter claim to know what they must be like? Isn't it true that not even the makers, the cobbler and the smith, pretend to have that knowledge, and that the only one who claims to have it is the one who knows how to use them: the rider?"

"Yes."

"Won't we say that this is true of everything?"

"What?"

d "Three skills exist for each thing: one uses, one makes,
and one imitates."

"Yes."

"Don't the excellence, rightness, and beauty of any artifact, creature, or act depend solely on the *use* for which it has been grown or made?"

"Yes."

"Then it necessarily follows that the user of each has the
most experience in it and must inform the maker how it
works well or badly in use. The flute-player, for instance,
e informs the flutemaker which flutes work well in playing and
prescribes how they must be made, and the maker serves
him."

[9]Socrates himself demonstrated this with the opening of the *Iliad*, in Book 3, 393d–394a, p. 63.

"Of course."

"So the one knows and reports about good and bad flutes; the other believes him and makes them."

"Yes."

"Therefore the maker of any artifact gets right belief about its beauty and baseness by associating with and being forced to listen to its user, who has knowledge." 602

"Certainly."

"Does the imitator get knowledge of the rightness and beauty of the things he draws by using them, or right opinion by being forced to associate with the knower, who prescribes how they must be drawn?"

"Neither."

"So he has neither knowledge nor right opinion about the beauty or baseness of the things that he imitates."

"It doesn't seem so."

"What charming wisdom the poetic imitator has about the things he creates!"

"Not very," he said.

"But still he will imitate, knowing nothing of how anything b
may be useful or bad. Most likely he'll imitate whatever seems beautiful to the ignorant mob."

"What else?"

"Then, it appears, we agree fairly well: The imitator knows nothing worth mentioning about what he imitates; imitation is nothing serious, but a kind of play; and those who latch onto tragical poetry in iambs and dactyls are the most imitative of all."

"Of course."

"By Zeus!" I exclaimed, "doesn't this imitation deal with c
something three times removed from the truth?"

"Yes."

"Then to what part of a man does it direct its power?"

"What do you mean?"

"This: when we see the same thing from near or afar it doesn't appear the same size."

"No."

"And the same things look bent or straight when viewed in or out of water, concave or convex as our sight wanders in regard to their colors—every kind of confusion like this
clearly inheres in our souls. Painting is right up with witch- d
craft in attacking this weakness in our nature, as are conjuring and similar tricks."

"True."

"Weren't measuring, weighing, and counting invented as charming helpers for this, so that it's not the apparently larger, smaller, heavier, and more that rules in us, but that which calculates, measures, and weighs?"

"Of course."

e "But that's the task of the soul's calculating, rational part."

"Exactly."

"And the things it has measured and reports as equal, or as larger or smaller than each other, often appear to it to be the contrary, the same things at the same time."

"Yes."

"Didn't we declare it impossible for the same thing to hold contrary opinions about the same things at the same time?"

"And rightly."

603 "So the part of the soul that conjectures contrary to measurements can't be the same as the part that agrees with them."

"Certainly not."

"Certainly the part that relies on measurement and calculation must be the best."

"Certainly."

"And the part that contradicts them must be a trivial one."

"Necessarily."

"This is the agreement I wanted when I said that painting and imitation in general accomplishes its own work, which
b lies far from the truth, by consorting with something in us that lies far from intelligence, like a friendly prostitute up to no good."

"Absolutely," he said.

"So imitation is trivia that couples with trivia to reproduce trivia."

"Very likely."

"Only imitation for sight, or also for hearing, which we call poetry?"

"That too, most likely."

"Let's not just believe an analogy drawn from painting,
c but go on to the part of the mind that poetic imitation consorts with and see if it's serious or trivial."

"Yes, that's what we should do."

"Let's put it like this: Poetic imitation imitates people in action performing enforced or voluntary acts, who think they've done well or badly from the acts themselves, and who feel joy or grief through it all. It didn't go beyond that, did it?"

"No."

"Does a person keep a constant state of mind through all
this, or as sight plunged him into strife with himself and gave d
him contrary opinions about the same things at the same time, does he also contend and fight with himself in his acts? —Now I remember: we needn't agree on this, because in the discussion above[10] we already agreed that our soul teems with thousands of such simultaneous contradictions."

"Right," he said.

"Right indeed," I replied. "But I think we now must go
through what we left out then." e

"What?"

"I believe we said[11] that when a good man loses a son or anything else that he values, he'll bear the misfortune more lightly than others."

"Certainly."

"But now we must ask whether he feels no sorrow whatever, or whether that's impossible and he somehow moderates himself toward his pain."

"That would be nearer the truth."

"Now tell me: Do you think he'll fight and resist his pain 604
more when observed by his equals, or when he's alone by himself in solitude?"

"Much more when observed."

"In seclusion I think he'd dare to say things he'd be ashamed to have others hear and to do things he'd prefer not to have seen."

"Exactly," he said.

"Reason and law encourage resistance, while the emotion
itself drags him back to the pain." b

"True."

"But when a man is pulled in opposite ways over the same thing at the same time, we say he must have two things in him."

"Of course."

[10]The reference is to 439b, ff., p. 106, ff.
[11]The reference is to 387e, p. 57.

"One ready to obey the law wherever it leads."

"How do you mean?"

"I suppose the law declares it best to keep calm in adver-
sity and not grieve, because the good and the bad of such
things is uncertain, taking them hard doesn't improve the
c situation, nothing human is worthy of serious attention anyway, and sorrow hinders the thing that should come to our
aid in misfortune as quickly as possible."

"What thing?"

"Deliberation," I said, "over what's happened, and arranging one's affairs to the way things have fallen like dice,
however reason dictates as best; not wasting your time bawl-
ing like a child, staggered by the blow and hugging the spot
d that was hit, but habituating your soul to turn quickly to
righting and healing what's fallen and sick, eliminating
lamentation with healing."

"That's surely the way to behave in misfortune."

"The best part, we say, willingly follows this reasoning."

"Clearly."

"Then shall we call the part that drags us back to the memory of the suffering and to the laments it can't get enough of the irrational part, Cowardice's indolent friend?"

"We certainly should."

e "This, the grieving part, permits much imitation and embellishment, whereas the intelligent, calm disposition, always very similar to itself, is hard both to imitate and to
understand when imitated, especially at a festival by multifarious folk gathered in the theater. It imitates a condition
foreign to them."

"Absolutely."

605 "Then our imitative poet, if he wants repute with the
many, clearly won't work with this part of the soul, which his
wisdom wasn't fashioned to please, but with the grieving,
colorful disposition, so easy to imitate."

"Clearly."

"Now we'll be justified in seizing the poet and setting him
up as a counterpart to the painter. Like him, he produces
b trivia compared to the truth and trafficks with a trivial rather
than with the best part of the soul. Thus in justice we may
now bar him from our city, if it's to have good laws, because
by arousing, feeding, and strengthening that part he destroys the soul's rational part, as when one destroys men of

refinement in a city and puts the rabble in charge. In the
same way, we'll say, the imitative poet installs an evil regime
in each individual soul, gratifying an irrational thing in it
that distinguishes neither larger nor smaller but thinks the c
same things now large and now small; he's a phantommaker
of phantoms who stands far from the truth."

"Certainly."

"But we still haven't brought the most serious charge against imitation: its appalling ability to deform even decent people, except for a very few."

"It must be appalling if it does that."

"Listen and see. When the best of us listen to Homer or
some other tragic poet imitate a grief-stricken hero deliver-
ing a tirade filled with laments or singing a dirge, perhaps, d
while he beats his breast, you know we thrill with delight; we
surrender ourselves to the mood, sympathize with his sufferings, and seriously praise as the best poet the one that can
do this the most."

"I know."

"But when we have some personal grief, you notice we
plume ourselves on the opposite—on our ability to keep
calm and endure, as though this were the behavior of a man e
and the other, which we praised in the poetry, of a woman."

"I've noticed," he said.

"Isn't it a marvelous endorsement that when we see a man who's unworthy of us doing something we'd be ashamed of, we praise and enjoy it rather than gag?"

"By Zeus, it doesn't make sense."

"It does if you consider that the part the poet satisfies and 606
delights is the one we restrain by force in personal misfortune and starve of the tears, lamentations, and fulfillment it
naturally craves. Our nature's best part, insufficiently educated by reason and habit, relaxes its guard over this dirging
part because the sufferings it sees belong to another and it b
considers it no shame to itself to pity and praise another man
alleged to be good when he vents his untimely grief; in fact,
the listener regards the pleasure as a profit he'd be loathe
to give up out of contempt for the entire poem. I think it is
given to few to calculate that vicarious enjoyment is necessarily transferred to ourselves, and that pity, fed strong on
the sufferings of others, will be hard to restrain in our own."

"True," he said. c

"Isn't it the same with laughter? Whenever you listen to jokes, on stage or in conversation, that you yourself would be ashamed to tell and delight in them instead of detesting them as base, you're doing the same as in the piteous spectacles. You release a part in you that wants to joke, which you normally restrain by reason for fear of being thought a buffoon; and this, after growing vigorous here, often sweeps you into inadvertently playing the fool in your private affairs."

"Exactly," he said.

d "The same with sex, anger, and all the desires, pleasures,
and pains in the soul, which we say accompany us in every
activity: poetic imitation causes us to be like them. It waters
and feeds what ought to be starved, and sets up as rulers
what ought to be ruled, if we're to become better and happier rather than poorer and more miserable."

"I can't dispute that," he said.

e "Then Glaucon," I said, "whenever you run into men who
eulogize Homer as the educator of Greece, who say that he
is worth taking up and studying for the administration and
refinement of human affairs, and that every man ought to
607 model his life on this poet, you must love and embrace them
for being the best men they can possibly be, agree that
Homer is the most poetic of poets and the first of tragedians,
and know that except for hymns to the gods and eulogies for
good men no poetry may enter our city. If you accept the
honeyed Muse in epic and song, pain and pleasure will reign
in your city in place of law and those principles accepted by
the community as best."

"Most true," he said.

b "Let that, then, stand as our defense after reviewing Poetry's cause: we acted reasonably in banishing her from our
city, being such as she is—reason dictated our course. And
let's also remind her—lest she accuse us of being harsh and
uncouth—that an ancient feud persists between philosophy
and poetry. Expressions[12] that call Philosophy 'great in the
idle chatter of fools' and 'a yapping bitch who snaps at her
c master,' and philosophers 'pointy-headed riffraff' who 'after
subtle agonizing conclude—that they're broke,' and countless others like them all attest to that ancient quarrel. Never-

[12]Quotations from lost poems or comedies.

theless be it said that should imitative poetry directed to
pleasure be able to give reasons for her existence in a well-
regulated city, we'd gladly take her back from her exile,
acknowledging that we too are enchanted by her. But to
betray the truth as we see it would be impious. —Doesn't she
enchant you too, my friend, especially when you hear her d
through Homer's mouth?"

"Very much," he said.

"Shouldn't she in justice return if she can make a defense in lyric or some other verse form?"

"Certainly."

"We'll also give her advocates—not poets, but poetry lovers—a chance to defend her in prose and show that she's not
only pleasing, but useful to regimes and to human life. And
we'll listen favorably, because we'll undoubtedly profit if e
she's shown to be useful as well as pleasant."

"How could we help but profit from that?"

"But if not, my companion, then just as lovers renounce
even by force a love that they no longer think beneficial, so
we, because our beautiful regimes have raised us to love this
kind of poetry, will favor her defense and hope she may be 608
proved good and true; but until she is, we'll chant this argument to ourselves whenever we hear her, as a charm to ward
off her spell and keep us from falling back into that childish
love we shared with the many, treating poetry not seriously
as touching the truth, but cautiously lest it destroy the b
regime within us, believing what we've said about poetry."

"I agree entirely," he said.

"Great is the contest, dear Glaucon—greater than people imagine: the struggle to become a good man or bad, and neither money nor honor, not power and not even poetry must entice us away from justice and the rest of excellence."

"I agree from what we've gone through. Anyone would, I think."

"Though we still haven't gone through the greatest re- c
wards of excellence, and the prizes that await the victor."

"They must surely be huge if they surpass what we've already said."

"What can be great in a little time? Yet our whole life from childhood to old age is probably only a little time compared with the whole."

"Nothing at all," he said.

"Do you think an immortal thing should be seriously con-
d cerned with this little time and not with the whole?"

"No, but what do you mean?"

"Haven't you noticed that our soul is immortal and doesn't perish?"

He looked at me in surprise: "No, by Zeus, I haven't. Can you argue that?"

"If I'm not mistaken," I said. "So can you, I think—it's nothing difficult."

"Maybe not," he said, "but I'd like to hear you explain this undifficult thing."

"You will," I said: "Do you say there's a good and an evil?"

"Yes."

e "Do you share my idea of them?"

"What is it?"

"Evil is that which corrupts and destroys; good is that which helps and preserves."

"Yes," he said.

"Well, do you think each thing has a good and an evil, as
609 the eyes inflammation and the whole body disease, grain blight, wood rot, bronze and iron corrosion and, as I said, almost everything some natural evil and sickness?"

"Yes."

"And when its evil strikes a thing, it debases it and finally destroys and disintegrates it."

"Of course."

"And each thing is destroyed by its natural evil or vice: if
b that doesn't do it, nothing will. Surely the good will never destroy anything, nor that which is neither."

"How could it?"

"Then if we can discover some existing thing by nature so constituted as to have an evil that corrupts but does not dissolve or destroy it, can't we be certain that nothing will ever destroy it?"

"Very likely," he said.

"Well, isn't there something that corrupts the soul?"

"Certainly—everything we just went through: injustice,
c intemperance, cowardice, and ignorance."

"Can any of them destroy and disintegrate it? —And don't be misled into thinking that an unjust, thoughtless man caught committing a crime is destroyed by injustice, the vice

of the soul. Do it like this: As the body's vice, disease, wastes and destroys it until it's not even a body, so everything else we just mentioned ceases to exist when its own evil settles d
in it and corrupts it. Isn't that so?"

"Yes."

"Now examine the soul the same way. When injustice and its other evils settle in it, do they wither and corrupt it until they've separated it from the body and dragged it down to death?"

"No, not that far."

"And it's illogical to think that another thing's vice will destroy something if its own does not."

"Indeed."

"Notice, Glaucon, that we don't think that an evil which e
belongs to food, whether staleness, rot, or anything else, can destroy the body. If the food's viciousness engenders the body's depravity in it, then we'll say that it was the body's own evil—disease—caused by the food, that destroyed it. Food is distinct from the body, and we'll never expect its vice 610
—an alien evil—to corrupt the body unless it engenders the body's own natural evil in it."

"Right," he said.

"By the same reasoning then, unless the body's vice engenders the soul's vice in it, we'll never expect the soul to be destroyed by an alien evil in place of its own, one thing by another thing's evil."

"That makes sense," he said.

"Then let's either refute this argument as unsound, or for as long as it stands refuse to admit that the soul can be b
destroyed by fever or by any disease, by murder or even by chopping the body to bits, unless someone can prove that these bodily sufferings make the soul less just or pious. Let's refuse to accept that the soul or anything else is destroyed c
by an alien evil if it doesn't have its own proper evil in it."

"Surely no one will ever be able to prove that death makes a dying man's soul less just."

"But if, to avoid having to admit that souls are immortal, someone should dare to tackle our argument and say that a dying man does turn base and unjust, then if he's telling the truth, we'd expect injustice to be fatal to its possessor, like a disease, and by its own nature to be the killer that kills off d
its victims—those who catch it worse more quickly; the oth-

ers more slowly—so that unjust men would not, as now, need others to kill them for their injustice by imposing justice on them."

"By Zeus," he said, "if injustice were fatal it wouldn't be
the terrifying thing that it is; death would deliver its possessor from evil. But I think it'll prove to be the exact opposite:
e it kills others if it can, and gives its possessor an extreme,
even sleepless vitality. Injustice, it seems, has pitched her
tent far from fatality."

"Well put," I replied. "And since the soul's own vice doesn't suffice to kill or destroy it, an evil intent on something else's destruction hardly will do so, or destroy anything else but its victim."

"Not very likely," he said.

"Then since no evil, its own or anything else's, destroys
611 it, the soul must necessarily always exist. And if it always
exists, it must be immortal."

"It must be," he said.

"So be it then," I said. "And if it is so, notice that it's the same souls that will always exist. They could hardly decrease if none are destroyed, nor again increase: if anything immortal increased, you know it would take its increase from the mortal and everything would end up being immortal."

"True."

"So let's not believe that—the argument won't permit it
b —nor again that in its truest nature the soul possesses great
variety, dissimilarity, and self-contradiction."

"How do you mean?"

"It would be hard for a thing to be eternal if it were composed of several parts, as we presented the soul a while back, and didn't have the finest composition."

"Apparently," he said.

"That the soul is immortal, this and our other arguments
would compel us to believe. But to learn the soul's true
c nature you must observe it not as we did, disfigured by its
partnership with the body and other evils, but as it is when
pure; you must examine it thoroughly by reason, and then
you'll find it a far more beautiful thing and more distinctly
discern justice and injustice and all we went through. What
we said was true for it in its present condition: like men
d seeing Glaucus, the sea god, and finding it hard to make out
his ancient nature because the waves have worn and

pounded away some of his body's original parts and completely disfigured him, while other things—rocks and shells and seaweed—have grown on to him, so that he looks more like a monster than what by nature he was, so we observe the soul encrusted by thousands of evils. Instead, Glaucon, we should look over there."

"Where?"

"To its philosophy, and note what the soul clings to and e
what company it seeks, being akin to the divine, immortal,
and ever-existing, and what again it would be if all of it leapt
after that and the surge lifted it clean out of the sea that
tumbles it now, scraped of its shells and barnacles—these
wild, rocklike and earthy growths that encrust it now because 612
it feasts upon earth in these so-called happy feasts. Then you
could see our soul's true nature, exactly what it is and how,
whether multiple or single in form. For now, though, I think
we've pretty well described its forms and sufferings in this
life."

"Absolutely," he said.

"Well," I said, "haven't we acquitted Justice of the
charges against her without praising rewards and reputa- b
tions, as you accused Homer and Hesiod of doing, and discovered justice itself to be the best thing for the soul itself, something it should practice whether or not it has Gyges' ring and even Hades' cap?"[13]

"We certainly have," he said.

"Would anyone object now, Glaucon, if we returned, in all
their variety and profusion, the rewards that justice and the
rest of excellence bring the soul from gods and men, both c
during a man's lifetime and after he dies?"

"Absolutely not."

"Will you two give back what you borrowed earlier in the discussion?"

"What was that?"

"You asked that the just man seem unjust and the unjust
man just, even if it is impossible for them to escape the
notice of gods and men. I lent you that for the argument's
sake, so we could judge justice itself against injustice itself.
Don't you remember?" d

[13]For Gyges' ring, see 359d–360a, p. 33. Hades' cap also made its wearer invisible.

"I'd be unjust if I didn't," he said.

"Well, now that they've been judged I'm asking you for Justice's sake to give her back the reputation she enjoys among gods and men, and to agree that this *is* her reputation, so that she may collect the prizes she wins from the *seeming* and gives to her possessors, since we've already shown the goods that come from the *being,* which she actually presents to her true possessors and doesn't just deceive them with."

e "That's a fair request," he said.

"Then will you grant that the gods will know what each of our two men, the just and the unjust, is really like?"

"Yes."

"If so, they'll love the one and hate the other, as we said at the start."[14]

"True."

"Won't we also agree that the one the gods love will
613 receive the very best of everything they give, except for necessary evils incurred by sins in a former life?"

"Of course."

"Therefore when a just man suffers poverty, illness, or any other seeming evil, we must assume it will turn out best for him either in this life or after he dies. The gods will never neglect someone willing and eager to be just, who by pursuing excellence tries to be as much like them as a human
b being can be."

"A man like that isn't likely to be neglected by his like."

"Mustn't we have the opposite opinion of the unjust man?"

"Completely," he said.

"Such, then, are the victory prizes the gods bestow on the just man."

"At least in my opinion," he said.

"What does he get from men? Shouldn't we put it like this?—Your clever scoundrels fare like runners who run well going down the track, but not so well coming back up. They break away smartly but finish in contemptible shape, their
c ears drooping on their shoulders, and trot off uncrowned. The true runners keep on till the finish and win both the prizes and the crown. Don't most things turn out like that for

[14]The reference is to 352b, p. 28.

just men?—toward the end of each activity and transaction
and of life itself they win reputation and prizes from their
fellow men."

"They surely do."

"Then may I say of them what you said about unjust
men?[15] When older they'll rule in their cities (assuming they d
want to), marry into the families of their choice, and match
their daughters with whomever they wish. Everything you
said about the unjust I'll say about the just. As for the unjust,
though they may get away with it while young, at the end of
the race most will be caught, townsmen and strangers alike
will revile and abuse them, and you can imagine me saying e
that they get whipped and everything else you rightly
termed uncouth. Will you permit me to say all that?"

"Of course, since it's just."

"Such are the prizes, rewards, and gifts bestowed on the
just man by gods and men while he lives, besides the goods 614
provided by justice itself."

"They certainly are beautiful and stable."

"Yet nothing at all compared in size and amount to those
that await each man when he's dead. We must tell those too,
so that each may get his due of the words the argument owes
him."

"Tell them," he said. "There aren't many things I'd rather b
hear."

"The story I shall tell," I said, "isn't some yarn spun out
to Alcinous, but the tale of a valorous man, Er, son of Ar-
menius, of the race of Everyman.[16] He was once killed in
battle and on the tenth day they took up the bodies, his still
fresh though the others were decaying, and brought them
home to be buried. On the twelfth day he lay on his funeral
pyre, came back to life, and told what he had seen over there.
When his soul had left him, he said, it went with many others
and came to a mysterious place where two chasms lay side c
by side in the earth, and two others split the heavens directly
above those. Between them sat judges who judged the souls
and commanded the just to go to the right and up through

[15]The reference is to 361e–362b, pp. 34–35.

[16]I.e. "Pamphylia." Er is an invented character from an imaginary land. "Yarn to Alcinous" refers to Odysseus's account of his wanderings, related to Alcinous in the *Odyssey,* Books 9–12.

heaven, hanging a sign with their judgment in front of each
one, and the unjust to go to the left and down, putting a sign
d on their backs telling what each had done. When Er stepped
up, he said they commanded him to hear and observe everything well, for he was to be a messenger to men of the things
over there.

"And there, by those two chasms in heaven and earth, he
saw the judged souls departing, and by the two others, others arriving: those coming up out of the earth from the one
were parched and full of dust, but those coming down out
e of heaven from the other were pure. They all seemed returned from a long journey: they joyfully went off to the
meadow and made camp as though for a fair, old friends
greeted each other, and each group asked the other how
they had fared. The ones from below recalled with sorrow
615 and weeping all they had suffered and seen in their underground journey—a journey of a thousand years—while the
ones back from heaven described its delights and the incredible beauty of the things they had seen.

"It would take a long time, Glaucon, to recount all that
they said. The gist of it, however, was this: Each had paid in
turn the penalty for every crime against another, ten times
over for each; that is, once every hundred years, taking that
b as the length of human life to make the requital tenfold, so
that those responsible for many deaths, who had betrayed
cities or armies and reduced them to slavery, or had been
partners to any other iniquity might suffer tenfold torment
for each, whereas any who had done good deeds for others
and had been pious and just would receive recompense in
c the same proportion. What he said about the ones who had
died at birth or had lived only a short time isn't worth recol-
lecting. But he described still greater requitals for piety or
impiety toward gods or parents, as well as for homicide.

"He said, for instance, that he was present when one soul
asked another where Ardiaeus the Great was. This Ardiaeus
had been tyrant in a city in Everyland just a thousand years
d before, had murdered his old father and elder brother and
had committed many other impious crimes, it was said. 'He
hasn't come,' said the other, 'nor shall he ever. That was one
of the horrible things that we saw. When we were close to
the mouth and about to emerge after all that suffering, we
suddenly saw him and some others—nearly all tyrants,

though a few had been big private criminals. They thought e
that at last they were about to step out, but whenever one
of those incurably evil souls, or one not yet sufficiently punished, tried to go up through the mouth it bellowed and
wouldn't accept him. Then,' he said, 'savage men stationed
there, fiery to see, heard it, seized most of them and led them
away, but Ardiaeus and a few others they bound hand, foot, 616
and neck, threw down and skinned, shredded by dragging
through thorns alongside the path, and then indicated to
every soul that came up their reasons for hauling them off
and hurling them down into Tartarus.' Then, he said, terror
had seized them, exceeding all the multifarious terrors they
had suffered before, lest the voice sound when they come
up, and great was their joy when the mouth was silent for
them.

"Such, he said, were the judgments and punishments, as
well as the rewards, antiphonal to them. And when they had b
been on the meadow seven days they must get up and march
on the eighth, arriving after four more from where they
beheld a straight light, like a pillar, stretched from above
through all of heaven and earth, most like the rainbow, but
purer and brighter. This they reached in a day's journey,
where at the light's center they saw extended from heaven c
the tips of its bonds—for this light holds all heaven together,
binding its entire circumference like the understraps of a
warship—and stretched from the tips the spindle of Necessity,[17] through which turn all of heaven's revolutions. The
shaft and hook of the spindle were of adamant, its whorl an
alloy of adamant and other materials.

"The whorl's nature was something like this: In shape it d
resembled a whorl here, but from what he said we must
imagine it as one great, hollowed-out whorl with a similar
smaller one nestled inside, like cups stacked together, and
a third and a fourth inside that, and then four more. There
were eight all together, one snug in the other, with their rims
facing upward as circles to form the unbroken top of a single e
whorl around the shaft, which was driven through the center
of the eighth. The first and outermost whorl had the thickest
rim, the sixth the next thickest, the fourth the third thickest,

[17]The cosmological details of this passage are discussed in the Appendix, p. 279.

the eighth the fourth thickest, the seventh the fifth thickest,
the fifth the sixth thickest, the third the seventh thickest, and
the second the thinnest. The rim of the largest was spangled,
617 of the seventh the brightest, the eighth took its color from
the glow of the seventh, the second and fifth were alike and
more yellow than those, the third was the whitest, the fourth
reddish, and the sixth was the second in whiteness.

"The entire spindle, he said, revolved together, but within
this overall movement the seven inner circles gently turned
contrary to the whole. Of these seven the eighth turned the
fastest, while the seventh, sixth, and fifth moved next fastest
b and kept the same pace. Third in speed, as it appeared to
them, was the fourth, which turned retrograde to the others,
fourth fastest was the third, and fifth fastest the second. It
all turned on the knees of Necessity. On top of each rim,
carried around by its motion, stood a Siren who sang one
constant note, all eight of which blended into a single harmony. Equidistant around the spindle, seated white-robed
c in thrones with holy bands on their heads, sat the three
Moirae,[18] Necessity's daughters, Lachesis, Clotho, and
Atropos, and sang to the Sirens' harmony: Lachesis of the
past, Clotho of the present, and Atropos of the future. At
regular intervals Clotho would touch the spindle's outer
circumference with her right hand to help spin it, and
Atropos did the same to the inner ones with her left. Lachesis touched each in turn with alternate hands.

d "When they arrived, he said, they had to go straight up to
Lachesis. A speaker first stood them in order, then took lots
and patterns of lives from Lachesis' knees, mounted a high
rostrum, and spoke: 'The word of Necessity's maiden
daughter Lachesis: "Souls of a day, here begins a new round
of mortal life leading to death. Guiding deities shall not
e draw lots for you; you will choose them. Let him that draws
first be first to choose the life he shall of necessity lead.
Excellence has no master; as you honor or dishonor her, so
shall you receive more of her or less. Guilt to the chooser;
god has no guilt." '

"With that he threw down the lots and each picked up the
one nearest him, except Er, who was forbidden to do so. The
618 lots showed the order in which they would choose. Next he

[18]The Parcae, or Fates.

set the patterns of lives before them on the ground, many
more than the souls. They were of every description: of all
animals and every sort of person. There were tyrants among
them, some to survive, others to be destroyed in mid-career
or to end in poverty, exile, and begging. There were lives of
illustrious men, to be renowned for physical beauty and
strength and athletic ability, or for their families and their b
ancestors' virtues; others of unrenowned men, and similar
lives of women. The quality of soul was not given, because
of the necessity for it to change to conform to the life that
it chose. But all the other characteristics were there, mingled
with each other, with wealth and poverty, sickness and
health, and with their intermediate conditions.

"Here, dear Glaucon, it seems, lies the supreme hazard
for man, and for this reason each of us must carefully ignore c
all other studies and become an avid seeker and student of
this: to learn, if he can, who can give him the knowledge and
power to distinguish a good life from a bad and to choose
always and everywhere the best from out of the possible. He
must weigh all the things we have said, separately and in
combination, to see how they contribute to the excellence of
life, learn what good and what evil beauty can do when d
joined with poverty or wealth and with any given state of the
soul, and what all the other native and acquired attributes of
the soul—high and low birth, private life and public office,
strength and weakness, ease and difficulty of learning—can
do when blended together, so that by weighing all this and
looking at the nature of the soul he may be able to choose
for himself a better or worse life, calling one that will make e
his soul less just worse, more just better, and let everything
else go, because we've seen that this is the best choice for
him both while living and dead. He must go down to Hades 619
with this iron conviction, so that even there wealth and similar evils will not dazzle him and make him fall into tyranny
or other business where he commits incurable crimes that
will bring him even greater suffering, but know instead how
always to choose the mean from such lives and to avoid the
extremes on either side, both in this life, so far as is possible,
and for all future time. Thus will a man be the happiest. b

"Then, said the messenger from over there, the speaker
continued: 'Even the last to approach will find, if he chooses
with intelligence, a tolerable life lying here, not at all evil, for

one that lives intensely. Let not the first choose carelessly, nor the last give up hope.'

"With that, he said, the one who had drawn first lot went right up and took the life of the greatest tyrant. He chose out of greed and stupidity, without weighing everything well or
c noticing that it decreed among other evils that he eat his own children. When he examined it at his leisure he beat his breast and lamented his choice. He didn't heed the speaker's warning, but blamed his luck and the gods and everything but himself. He was one who had come down from heaven, and he had spent his former life in an ordered regime where he partook of excellence by habit without philosophy. Per-
d haps most of those trapped by such lives were back from heaven, where they had grown unpracticed in toil. But few that had come from the earth made an impulsive choice, because they had suffered and seen others suffer. For this reason, and also because of the luck of the draw, most of the souls exchanged good and evil. If, therefore, a person practices sound philosophy whenever he comes to this life, and
e if his lot doesn't fall with the last, he should, from this report we've received, not only be happy here, but find the journey from here to there and back again to be smooth and heavenly rather than earthy and rough.

"He said it was worth seeing how the various souls chose
620 their lives—a pitiful, funny, astonishing sight. Most chose according to the habits of their former lives. He saw a soul that had once been Orpheus choose the life of a swan, not wishing to be conceived and born of a woman because he hated the entire sex for having put him to death. He saw the soul of Thamyras[19] choose the life of a nightingale, a swan exchanged its life for a man's, and other musical creatures
b did likewise. The twentieth soul chose the life of a lion. This

[19] A singer blinded for boasting that he could rival the Muses (*Iliad.* 2.595–600). Ajax, below, was the hero at Troy, who went insane and committed suicide after the Greek generals awarded the armor of the dead Achilles to Odysseus rather than to him (Sophocles' *Ajax*). Atalanta was a beautiful huntress who would only marry the man who could beat her in a foot race; the losers were killed. Epeius was a skilled carpenter at Troy, who built the Trojan horse. Thersites was an ugly Greek soldier at Troy. In *Iliad* 2.211–277, he insults his general, Agamemnon, gets beaten and laughed at.

had been Telamonian Ajax, and it shunned becoming a man
because it remembered the judgment over the arms of
Achilles. Next came the soul of Agamemnon, which also
hated the human race for what it had suffered, and exchanged its life for an eagle's. Near the middle drew the soul
of Atalanta, and when she saw the honors of an athletic man
she couldn't resist taking them. After that he saw the soul of
Epeius, son of Panopeus, go into the nature of a talented c
lady, and way back with the last the soul of the buffoon
Thersites, who put on an ape. As luck would have it, the soul
of Odysseus had drawn the very last lot, and because the
memory of its previous struggles had cured its ambition, it
walked around for a long time looking for the life of a peaceful, uninvolved man. It finally found one, lying there neglected by everyone else, happily took it, and said it would d
have made the same choice if it had drawn the first lot. And
the animals likewise turned into men and into other animals,
the unjust into wild ones, the just into tame, and every sort
of mixture took place.

"After all the souls had chosen their lives, they went up
to Lachesis in the order in which they had drawn. To each
she presented the deity it had selected, to be guardian of its
life and to fulfill what was chosen. The deity first led the soul e
up to Clotho, under her hand and the whirl of the spindle,
to ratify the destiny chosen. After touching that, each was
brought to Atropos' spinning to make destiny's web irre-
versible, then without turning around they passed under the
throne of Necessity and out.

"When all had emerged, they marched through terrible, 621
stifling heat to the Plain of Lethe,[20] barren of plants and
trees. In the evening they camped near the River of Indiffer-
ence, whose waters no pail can hold. Each had to drink a
measure of water; some lost their heads and drank more.
They forgot everything when they had drunk. In the middle b
of the night, as they slept, there was thunder and earthquake
and all were suddenly swept up in different directions to
birth, leaping upward like stars. But Er had been forbidden
to drink of the water. How he returned to his body he didn't
remember; he suddenly looked up and found himself on the
funeral pyre.

[20]Lethe means "Forgetfulness."

"Thus, Glaucon, the tale was preserved and did not pass
c away. And if we listen to it, it may preserve us and we shall cross the River of Lethe without defiling our souls. And if we believe what I say, convinced that the soul is immortal and strong to endure all good and all evil, we shall ever hold to the upward path and practice justice with knowledge in all that we do, to the end that, while lingering here, we may be friends with ourselves and the gods, and when, like victo-
d rious athletes collecting their spoils, we have won the prize for justice both here and in the thousand-year journey we have gone through, we shall fare well."

Appendix: The Spindle of Necessity

(book 10, 616b–617c)

The interpretations of this passage are so numerous that adding another will scarcely disturb their mass. Like the others, this one relies heavily on speculation and conjecture. The passage opens like this:

> . . . they beheld a straight light, like a pillar, stretched from above through all of heaven and earth, most like the rainbow, but purer and brighter. This they reached in a day's journey, where at the light's center they saw extended from heaven the tips of its bonds —for this light holds all heaven together, binding its entire circumference like the understraps of a warship —and stretched from the tips the spindle of Necessity, through which turn all of heaven's revolutions.

The description consists of two main parts, the light and the spindle. The spindle seems clearly intended to represent the physical universe. The light and the circumference of heaven which it binds together give the impression of being vastly larger than the spindle and the earth from where the souls are observing. Aside from the earth and the spindle, no material features are attributed to this arrangement, only incorporeal or figurative ones: "light," "circumference," "bonds," "heaven." We are not even told its shape; we must infer that it forms a sphere from the mention of "circumference" and "revolutions,"[1] and from our knowledge that for Plato the sphere was "the most perfect figure" (*Timaeus* 33b) and the only thinkable shape for the cosmos. This huge, immaterial structure must therefore be the intelligible world, which the souls, now pure and rid of their bodies, can "see." If so, we are moving in the realm of true astronomy as described in 529c–d; the realm of "motions, in true number and in all true figures, of speed that *is* and slowness that *is,* etc." The light too must then be intelligible rather than sensible: it is truth, the emanation of the good, as visible light is the emanation of the sun (cf. 508b, ff.).

This light is "straight . . . like a pillar," and "most like the rainbow." The second simile does not refer to the rainbow's shape (it would then contradict the first), but to the quality of its light, as the following words, "purer and brighter," suggest.

The universe, then, is conceived as a sphere with the shaft of light extended through its center. At the center of this column of light, and therefore at the exact center of the sphere, are found the earth and the spindle (how two things can occupy the same place is not clear; perhaps they do so mythically, or the earth may be slightly displaced). The spindle is suspended from the tips of heaven's bonds. These bonds are perhaps best taken as radii extending toward the center from the intelligible bodies (or motions) revolving in heaven, with the fixed stars (or their intelligible motions) at the outermost circumference. The radii meet and end at the center, and are pictured as having "tips," which support the spindle. We would say that such radii are invisible and imaginary; Plato would agree that they are invisable, being intelligible, but "real." And in the intelligible realm they would be visible to "the eye of the soul." All heavenly revolutions circle the center, and therefore their radii "turn through the spindle." The radii are bonds in the sense that they bind all the heavenly motions together; if the radii collapsed, the whole structure would collapse. The light too (= truth), we are told, binds heaven together, in the sense that it makes the whole intelligible and rational, and therefore "real." It

[1]Perhaps also from the words "from above." The center of a sphere is "the truly existing below" (584e), from which everything is "up."

is unclear what the simile "like the understraps of a warship" refers to (since we don't know exactly what these understraps were), but it is possible that the simile was not meant to be pressed. The details of the Sirens and of Necessity and her daughters (617b–c) are taken from mythology and are probably not intended to fit physically into the representation of the universe. They are eternally valid, but do not occupy space, as it were; they exist on a different plane of reality.

The spindle is a divine model of the physical universe, or perhaps it *is* the physical universe, viewed intelligibly by the "eyes of the souls." It appears to be much smaller than the sphere that encloses it, as the sensible world is smaller than the intelligible. Some, perhaps all, of the features of the intelligible cosmos, such as the orbits of the stars and the planets, are reproduced on a smaller scale here, just as the perfect realities of the intelligible world are faintly and imperfectly copied in the sensible world. The spindle, though divine and presumably intelligible, nevertheless is more material than the sphere that contains it; we are no longer solely in the realm of pure astronomy and perfect motions. Its shaft is of adamant, the hardest material, representing truth under the aspect of Necessity; like Necessity, adamant cannot be bent or changed. The whorls of the spindle consist "of adamant and other [necessarily less perfect] materials."

These whorls (616d, ff.) represent the orbits of the fixed stars and of the planets of the physical world, in this order (following Adam): In the first (outermost) rim, the fixed stars. In the second, Saturn. In the third, Jupiter. In the fourth, Mars. In the fifth, Mercury. In the sixth, Venus. In the seventh, the sun. In the eighth, the moon. The widths of the rims probably represent the distances between the orbits.

Plato's ordering of the heavenly bodies has, as Adam points out, nothing to do with fact or probability, but is purely mathematical, based on numerical combinations that all yield the number 9. The following scheme is Cook Wilson's, quoted in Adam.

1. Arrangement expressed by order of width of rim. Put the numbers of the whorls in the order of their rim width and connect the numbers that add up to 9. The arrangement is

symmetrical, centered between 4 and 5 in the straight number series:

whorl number:	1 2 3 4 5 6 7 8
order of width of rim:	1 8 7 3 6 2 5 4

2. Colors. The numbers of the whorls in the order in which Plato mentions them in describing their colors:

1 7 8 2 5 3 4 6

3. Speed:

1 8	7 (move at 6 same 5 speed)	4 3 2
=9	=18 (2 X 9)	=9

The Sirens' singing (617b) is the "music of the spheres." Since there are eight Sirens and therefore eight notes, their harmony spans a full octave.

For further details the reader may consult Adam's notes. A brief bibliography may be found in Rees's introduction to *The Republic of Plato* by James Adam (2nd ed., Cambridge 1963) vol. I, pp. li-lii.

bibliography

Books about Plato and the *Republic* are legion, and only a few can be listed here. For a full bibliography the reader may consult Guthrie's *History* (listed below). The beginner may want to start by reading a general article on Plato, such as "Plato and the Academy" in *A History of Greek Literature* by Albin Lesky (New York, 1966), pp. 505–547, or "Plato" by Gilbert Ryle in *The Encyclopedia of Philosophy,* edited by Paul Edwards (New York, 1967), Vol. VI, pp. 314–333. Many of the books listed below have chapters devoted to the historical background of Plato's times; for a fuller treatment see *Plato and his Contemporaries: A Study in Fourth-Century Life and Thought* by G. C. Field (London, 1930).

Study Aids to the *Republic*

Cliff's Notes on the Republic (Lincoln, Nebraska, 1963), and *Monarch Notes to Plato's Republic and Selected Dialogues* (New York, 1965).

Aids for "cramming." They provide historical information, summaries and explanations, and may be used as substitutes for reading the text (*Cliff's* warns against this). The summaries should be good for review, but probably no better than the "Synoptic Table of Contents" above. The explanations are superficial and tend to trivialize Plato's ideas. As a substitute for the text either set *might* get a student through an exam, but with a strange conception of the *Republic.*

General Studies of Socrates and Plato

Bambrough, Renford, ed., *New Essays on Plato and Aristotle* (London, 1965).

Cornford, Francis M., *Before and After Socrates* (Cambridge, 1932).

A brief history of Greek philosophy with Socrates as the pivotal figure. Covers the pre-Socratics, Socrates, Plato, and Aristotle.

Cushman, Robert E., *Therapeia: Plato's Conception of Philosophy* (Chapel Hill, 1958).

A study of Plato's philosophy as it concerns man's salvation in his social and political life.

Friedländer, Paul, *Plato,* Vol. I, *An Introduction* (2nd ed., Princeton, 1969).

A detailed study of Plato's life and works. Treats the influence of Socrates on Plato, the importance of irony, myth, and of writing itself in Plato's writings, and compares Plato's philosophy with modern philosophers (Heidegger and Jaspers). Views Plato in several roles, as physicist, geographer, jurist, city planner, etc.

Grube, G. M. A., *Plato's Thought* (London, 1935).

An exposition of Plato's thought by topic: Theory of Ideas, Art, Education, Statecraft, etc. Helpful for beginners as well as for advanced students.

Guthrie, W. K. C., *A History of Greek Philosophy,* Vol. IV, *Plato, The Earlier Period,* Vol. V, *The Later Plato and the Academy* (Cambridge, 1975).

Volume IV of this monumental study deals with Plato's earlier life and works (*Republic,* pp. 434–560). Detailed analysis of Plato's arguments and full presentation of the divergent views of modern scholars on each problem. Extensive bibliography.

Jaeger, Werner, *Paedeia: The Ideals of Greek Culture,* Vol. II, *In Search of the Divine Centre* (Oxford, 1943).

The intent of this three-volume study is "to explain the social structure and function of Greek ideals of culture against their historical background" (II, x). Volume II deals with Socrates and the early Plato. The *Republic* is subjected to a lengthy analysis (pp. 198–370) from the point of view of its theories of education and culture.

Koyré, Alexandre, *Discovering Plato* (New York, 1945).
A short, lucid introduction to Plato. Concentrates on the *Meno, Protagoras, Theaetetus,* and *Republic.* Emphasizes the importance of the dialogue form and the connection between theory and action, politics and philosophy in Plato's works.

Sallis, John, *Being and Logos: The Way of Platonic Dialogue* (Pittsburgh, 1975).
A detailed interpretation of several Platonic dialogues, including the *Republic* (pp. 312–455).

Shorey, Paul, *What Plato Said* (Chicago, 1933).
A résumé of Plato's writings dialogue by dialogue (*Republic,* pp. 208–58), intended to establish Plato's ideas and avoid abstract analysis and misleading interpretations. Lengthy chapters on Plato's life and on his writings in general (pp. 1–73).

Taylor, A. E., *Plato, The Man and his Work* (London, 1926).
A detailed exposition of Plato's life and work, dealing with each dialogue in turn. The author's intent is to restate and analyse what Plato says rather than to force a modern interpretation on his works.

———, *Plato* (London, 1922; Ann Arbor Paperback reprint, *The Mind of Plato,* 1960).
A short introduction to Plato's life and work, arranged by topic rather than by dialogue.

Vlastos, Gregory, ed., *The Philosophy of Socrates* (Doubleday Anchor Books, 1971).
A collection of critical essays dealing with the life, philosophy, and historical identity of Socrates as he is presented primarily in the writings of Plato, but also in those of Xenophon, Aristophanes, and Aristotle.

Wild, John, *Plato's Theory of Man* (Harvard, 1946).
The disintegration of modern man and society examined in the light of Plato's philosophy.

Studies on Specific Aspects of Plato's Thought

Allen, R. E., ed., *Studies in Plato's Metaphysics* (London, 1965).
A collection of essays on the topic indicated.

Barker, Ernest, *Greek Political Theory* (London, 1947).
Extensive discussion of Plato's political views, including those of the *Republic.*

———, *The Political Thought of Plato and Aristotle* (Paperback reprint, New York, 1959).
Chapters III and IV (pp. 81–183) deal with the *Republic.*

Barrow, Robin, *Plato and Education* (London, 1976).
An elementary exposition of Plato's thought. The emphasis is on Plato's educational ideas and on the *Republic,* but most of Plato's major ideas are touched upon. Contains a brief account of the historical and philosophical background of Plato's work.

Havelock, Eric A., *Preface to Plato* (Oxford, 1963).
Plato's views of art and poetry examined in the light of the role played by poetry in traditional Greek society.

Solmsen, Friedrich, *Plato's Theology* (Ithaca, N.Y., 1942).

Vlastos, Gregory, ed., *Plato,* Vol. I, *Metaphysics and Epistemology,* Vol. II, *Ethics, Politics, and Philosophy of Art and Religion* (Doubleday Anchor Books, 1971).
Collections of critical essays on the topics indicated.

Plato: Pro and Con

In recent years a heated controversy has developed over Plato's politics. One side, which numbers among its adherents such eminent figures as Bertrand Russell and Karl Popper, has denounced Plato as a fascist and an apologist for totalitarianism, while the other side has accused Plato's detractors of misrepresenting him.

Bambrough, Renford, ed., *Plato, Popper and Politics* (New York, 1967).
A good introduction to the controversy. A collection of

articles illustrating the various views represented in the debate.

Levinson, Ronald B., *In Defense of Plato* (Harvard, 1953).
A detailed reply to the attacks of Popper and other detractors of Plato. Extensive bibliography.

Popper, Karl R., *The Open Society and its Enemies,* Vol. I, *The Spell of Plato* (5th ed., London, 1966).
A spirited defense of the free, "open" society against its alleged enemies, the supporters of historicism and totalitarianism, with Plato at their head. Presents Plato as the originator of the modern antidemocratic tradition and as a betrayer of the Socratic spirit of free inquiry.

Wild, John, *Plato's Modern Enemies and the Theory of Natural Law* (Chicago, 1953).
Argues that the charges against Plato rest upon a misunderstanding of his moral philosophy and of the conception of natural law.

Winspear, A. D., *The Genesis of Plato's Thought* (New York, 1940).
A Marxist criticism of Plato's state (especially that of the *Republic*) as an idealization of the ruling class in a slave society.

Specific Studies of the *Republic*

Adam, James, *The Republic of Plato* (Cambridge, 2 vols., 1926 and 1929. 2nd ed., revised by D. A. Rees, 1963).
Greek text with English commentary. A standard work, intended for the reader of Greek, but the introduction and some of the notes are useful to the general reader.

Cross, R. C., and Woozley, A. D., *Plato's Republic: A Philosophical Commentary* (London, 1964).
A detailed commentary, with special emphasis on logic and politics. The authors' intent is to illustrate some of the major issues of philosophy by means of the *Republic* rather than to discuss every problem that arises in the work.

Else, Gerald F., *The Structure and Date of Book 10 of Plato's Republic* (Heidelberg, 1972).

Murphy, N. R., *The Interpretation of Plato's Republic* (Oxford, 1951).

A paraphrase of the main arguments, intended to bring out what Plato really says rather than what he is sometimes supposed to have said; also a criticism of some of his doctrines. Extensive discussion of the meaning of crucial words in Plato's vocabulary.

Nettleship, Richard Lewis, *Lectures on The Republic of Plato* (London, 1898).

An old but still useful commentary on the Republic, which emphasizes the significance of each argument of Plato's text for his overall philosophy more than its significance apart from his philosophy. Special stress on Plato's views of education.

———, *The Theory of Education in Plato's Republic* (Oxford, 1935).

Sesonske, Alexander, ed., *Plato's Republic: Interpretation and Criticism* (Belmont, California, 1966).

A collection of critical essays dealing with various aspects of the *Republic.*